RUKMINI DEVI ARUNDALE
(1904-1986)

A Visionary Architect of
Indian Culture and the Performing Arts

Rukmini Devi Arundale (1904-1986)

A Visionary Architect of Indian Culture and the Performing Arts

Edited by
DR. AVANTHI MEDURI

MOTILAL BANARSIDASS PUBLISHERS
PRIVATE LIMITED • DELHI

First Edition: Delhi, 2005

ISBN: 81-208-2740-6

MOTILAL BANARSIDASS
41 U.A. Bungalow Road, Jawahar Nagar, Delhi 110 007
8 Mahalaxmi Chamber, 22 Bhulabhai Desai Road, Mumbai 400 026
120 Royapettah High Road, Mylapore, Chennai 600 004
236, 9th Main III Block, Jayanagar, Bangalore 560 011
Sanas Plaza, 1302 Baji Rao Road, Pune 411 002
8 Camac Street, Kolkata 700 017
Ashok Rajpath, Patna 800 004
Chowk, Varanasi 221 001

Printed in India
BY JAINENDRA PRAKASH JAIN AT SHRI JAINENDRA PRESS,
A-45 NARAINA, PHASE-I, NEW DELHI 110 028
AND PUBLISHED BY NARENDRA PRAKASH JAIN FOR
MOTILAL BANARSIDASS PUBLISHERS PRIVATE LIMITED,
BUNGALOW ROAD, DELHI 110 007

CONTENTS

LIST OF FIGURES

PREFACE AND ACKNOWLEDGEMENTS

It was after completing my doctoral dissertation in 1996, and during my teaching appointment in the Department of Performance Studies, at Northwestern University that I was inspired to re-examine the cultural, aesthetic, and intellectual legacy of the legendary Rukmini Devi Arundale. I was motivated because much of the critical and academic scholarship pertaining to Rukmini Devi in the US had reductively described her within the denominational category of a 'nationalist' and more specifically as an 'upper-class Brahmin woman.' American scholars called attention to Rukmini Devi's class and caste background in order to question the elitist politics of the dance revival, and argued that it was Rukmini Devi, the privileged cosmopolitan who had appropriated the *Sadir* dance from traditional practitioners known as *devadasis,* during the period of Indian nationalism in the 1930s.

It is true that Rukmini Devi envisioned an elite, classical and neo-classical aesthetic for Bharatanatyam. But her aesthetic work, in my opinion, needs to be examined not just from within the political context of Indian nationalism in which Rukmini Devi worked, but also from within the transnational worldview of the Theosophical Society. It is well-known that Rukmini Devi was an integral part of the Society and worked on behalf of its transnational vision through her long and distinguished career between 1920-1986. She founded five institutions, including the famous *Kalakshetra* centre, and all five centres were patronized by the Society in the formative years of the national revival of Indian culture and the performing arts between 1930-1950.

To properly evaluate Rukmini Devi's legacy, we would have to begin by seeing her as more than a dancer/choreographer and take into account her multifaceted work as an institution builder and educationlist. We need to do more because Rukmini Devi worked locally on behalf of Indian nationlism and globally on behalf of the transnational worldview of the Society, without favouring one over the other.

Since scholars across the intellectual spectrum are all worrying the questions of globalization today, I thought we might begin our interrogation of globalization in the field of the performing arts by re-examining the unique manner in which Rukmini Devi negotiated the global and local flows of modernity as early as the 1920s. I submitted a postdoctoral research proposal to the Ford Foundation in India proposing to develop a new, contemporary and transnational research initiative for the study of Indian performing arts by using Rukmini Devi as a case study. After receiving the Ford fellowship in 2000, I returned to India and collaborated with S. Sathyamoorthy, who had served as the Joint Secretary, Department of Culture, Government of India. Together we founded the Centre for Contemporary Culture, New Delhi, and launched what we conceived to be a new, public arts movement to enable contemporary and transnational studies of Indian culture and the performing arts.

The Rukmini Devi Photo-Archive

Upon my return, I decided to visit Rukmini Devi's *Kalakshetra* to see if her photo - archive, missing since her demise in 1986, had been returned. I made an appointment to meet with the Director and enquired about the photo - archive. The Director looked embarrassed, brushed off the tears gathering in his eyes, and said there was nothing, nothing to show. I reminded him that Rukmini Devi had maintained a Publication and Photography Department as early as 1940s and had sponsored black and white photography in India. Yes, Yes, he said. But her photographs, they were all taken away, taken away after her demise. I asked him why it was not reclaimed. They were taken away, taken away, he said. The Director then told us that the archive had been preserved, but it was in the care and custody of Shri C.T. Nachiappan, who had been in charge of the Publication and Photography Department since the 1940s.

My mind went back to the time when I was doing doctoral research in *Kalakshetra* between 1990-1992. Rukmini Devi had passed on the *Kalakshetra* was still coping with her loss. I had long conversations with her trusted colleagues who were alive then, and enquired after the missing photo - archive. I specially recall one very long conversation with late Shri Sankara Menon, who was then the Principal of

Kalaskshetra. I asked him why no single person from inside *Kalakshetra* rebutted the international perception of Rukmini Devi as an 'elitist woman' and appropriator of Bharatanatyam. Shri Sankara Menon smiled and said that Rukmini Devi is her own defense and that time had already vindicated her vision. I could not tell then whether this was Shri Sankara Menon's prophesy, or if it was his projected hope for *Kalakshetra.*

Returning to the photographs, Mr. Sathyamoorthy and I met with Shri Nachiappan who readily agreed to show us the black and white photo archive, encompassing the years from 1935, when Rukmini Devi gave her debut performance in the Diamond Jubliee Celebration of the Theosophical Society, until her demise in 1986. Fully cognizant of its historic value, Shri Nachiappan urged us to sponsor a Rukmini Devi photo - exhibition in New Delhi. As I peeled the bubble wrap off the more than 300 photographs that Shri Nachiappan dispatched to New Delhi, and displayed them randomly in the different rooms of my house, my eyes were opened. I could actually 'see' with my naked eye the contemporary and transnational aesthetic that Rukmini Devi had envisioned for Bharatanatyam in the 1930s.

While *Kalakshetra* staff and alumni who had studied there before 1986 may have had occasion to pore over the marvelous photographic records, international scholars, myself included, who had researched Rukmini Devi's legacy posthumously, worked without the benefit of this visual record. To have the opportunity to curate an exhibit from the archive and restore to view a scholarly resource that had been unavailable for long was very exciting.

When I finally saw the archive in New Delhi, fifteen years after the passing of Rukmini Devi, the question that troubled me was this: would the international scholarship on Rukmini Devi have been shaped differently had scholars been able to actually see the many photos of this historic archive? This research question pressed upon my imagination and brought to the fore larger issues around temporality, timing, ethics, accountability, death and silence that scholars pay too little attention to in dance scholarship. I also worried the question of the limit point in which all scholarship is composed, what it excludes, why, and to enable what intellectual goals?

Rukmini Devi Travelling Exhibition

As I sorted out the photographs, they seemed to group themselves into five clusters, which I then conceptualized as the five different stages in which Rukmini Devi developed her multifaceted vision for Bharatanatyam and Indian performing arts. I described the five stages as follows: Experimental Phase (1920-1933), the Solo Dance Phase (1933-1943), the Dance Drama Phase (1943-1987), the Making of *Kalakshetra* as a New Urban Institution (1936-1986). The five sections were the historical frames in which I displayed the first Rukmini Devi photo exhibition entitled "Representing Rukmini Devi" in New Delhi, March 2001. The exhibition also featured the first national seminar on Rukmini Devi, and drew attention to the contemporary and multifaceted aesthetic that she had envisioned for *Bharatanatyam* and Indian performing arts.

To inscribe Rukmini Devi's archive in the transnational and diasporic history of which it was part, I conceptualized the photo - archive as a travelling exhibition that would re-conceptualize a 'local' archive in global terms by following the path of her influence. The exhibition was presented in Kolkata, Kuala Lumpur, Singapore, Colombo, London, Tokyo, and Melbourne, all cities in which students and graduates of *Kalakshetra* established and maintained flourishing schools. I reasoned that it was timely in Rukmini Devi's Birth Centenary year to propose a global and diasporic framework to discuss Rukmini Devi's cultural and artistic work.

In London, we organized an international conference on South Asian Dance in collaboration with the Society of Dance Research Scholars, and the AHRB Cross-Cultural Centre for Music and Dance, University of Surrey. In Australia, the exhibition was presented in collaboration with the Asian Languages and Societies, and the Sidney Meyer Asia Society, University of Melbourne. It was hosted by the Drama, Theatre and Performing Arts Center, Monash University. All the institutions that we approached seeking sponsorship for the travelling exhibition responded enthusiastically because her vision, as prophesied by Sankara Menon, had indeed been vindicated by time. Chinese and Japanese scholars spoke on Rukmini Devi's legacy in Singapore and Japan, underscoring again that her vision had transcended national boundaries.

As the exhibition travelled, I learned that Rukmini Devi was a multifacted woman who exceeded all the academic categories in which we have hitherto discussed her work. In the global and Asian Diasporic world, she is not perceived as an upper-caste nationalist or appropriator but is actually revered as a cosmopolitan woman who contemporized and globalized the history of Indian performing arts. As in her own lifetime, there was no single view of her history or contribution. Some describe her as an iconoclastic dancer, visionary institution builder, educationalist, elite woman privileged to travel the world when she was barely twenty years of age, and empowered to work for global causes in Europe, Australia, England, and America. Others perceived her as uncompromising traditionalist, quintessential South Indian Brahman girl, champion of animal rights, woman parliamentarian, crafts revivalist, social reformer, cultural educator, and national icon. The different viewpoints, expressed by authors who read papers in different conferences venues where the exhibition was featured, have been gathered in this volume not merely to celebrate Rukmini Devi's achievements in the year of her Birth Centenary, but also to re-examine her legacy within the larger intellectual framework of globalization, and thus to facilitate new, interdisciplinary and transnational research on Indian culture and the performing arts.

A research and public culture initiative such as the one outlined, above would not have been possible without the support and cooperation of numerous well wishers and friends. Thanks are due firstly to S. Sathyamoorthy, the executive Director of the Centre for Contemporary Culture, whom I have known for many years, for his untiring enthusiasm and support for the Rukmini Devi project, and for carrying the exhibition on his shoulders, an account of which he provides in this volume. It was indeed his perseverance that made us realize the many auxiliary projects connected to the travelling exhibition, including the creation of an award in the name and memory of Rukmini Devi. Through much of last year, Sathyamoorthy endeavoured diligently to create a Rukmini Devi Chair for interdisciplinary studies of culture and performance. This is an objective that the Centre for Contemporary Culture hopes to realize in the near future. In this context, I want to thank Dr. L.M. Singhvi, the President of the Centre, for his invaluable support and advice, and the Trustees for enabling the publishing of this book.

Thanks also to the many contributors who have penned essays in this volume. Most of them have known Rukmini Devi intimately over a period of many years and have helped her realize her vision. Their perspectives are invaluable because they witnessed what Rukmini

Devi was struggling to realize as vision in her own time, and the unique manner in which she overcame and buckled under the strain of holding together the many institutions that she had founded. I am particularly grateful to Mr. C.T. Nachiappan for loaning us the photo-archive, to dance critics Gowri Ramnarayan and Anandhi Ramchandran, and to distinguished alumnae of Kalakshetra, inlcluding Prof. C.V. Chandrasekhar, Sarada Hoffman, the late Krishanaveni Lakshmanan, Jayalakshmi Eshwar, Shanta Dhananjayan, and many others closely associated with Rukmini Devi's *Kalakshetra.* All extended their support and made this book a reality. I want also to thank international scholars for putting aside their critical reservations and argeeing to re-examine Rukmini Devi's legacy and reclaim her positively in international dance studies be it in this US and /or the UK.

Thanks also to Kathy Foley and Patty Gallagher at the University of California, Santa Cruz, with whom I collaborated and developed an intercultural performance script titled "*Shattering The Silence*: *The Three Women of the Theosophical Society.*" The piece positions Rukmini Devi within the global discourses of the Theosophical Society and describes her as the one who carried the torch for the feminist legacy of the Theosophical Society in India. As a sequel to this work, Kathy Foley invited me to teach two courses on the globalization of Bharatanatyam, with a focus on Rukmini Devi, in the Department of Theatre Arts at Santa Cruz. I thus had the opportunity to collaborate with theatre and dance students in the Department , and developed a short script entitled *Birth of Bharatanatyam,* which was staged in the Second Stage Theatre at UCSC in June 2004. To complement this research, I wrote another performance script entitled "*Birds of the Banyan Tree,*" which described her work as global Indian and how she struggled to keep the global flame alive in her life and work in India. The play was staged as part of the Birth Centenary Celebrations in New Delhi, Bangalore and Chennai in March 2004.

In the four years that it has taken for the book to be published, and through the time of the Rukmini Devi travelling exhibition, my parents and brothers have lived with this work, always generously, and sometimes without knowing it. I owe a deep debt to them. Thanks also to Professor Jeffrey Spear, a long time colleague, who served as outside member on my dissertation committee. Our friendship goes back many years and through this time, regardless of whether I was in

India or the US, we discussed the 'work' and evolved related projects including joint publications. I am also grateful to Jim Wiltgen, Anil Lal , and Margaret Drewal for warmly supporting my ideas and always asking the next question. Thanks also to Arundhati Neuman for her warm hospitality in Los Angeles, and engaged conversations on dance, music, and musicians.

After living in India through the period of my postdoctoral fellowship, I was appointed as a Reader in the Dance Studies Program at the University of Roehampton, London, and the convener of the new, interdisciplinary MA in South Asian Dance Studies there. What makes this MA unique is that is this program, the global histories of Ballet and Bharatanatyam are taught comparatively and put in dialogical conversation with each other. This is precisely what Rukmini Devi endeavoured to do as early as the 1930s, more than seventy years before our time.

— **Dr. Avanthi Meduri**

ABOUT THE CONTRIBUTORS

RADHA BURNIER is the international President of the Theosophical Society in India, and the first student of *Kalakshetra.*

PROFESSOR C. V. CHANDRASEKHAR retired as the Dean and Head of the Department of Dance at Maharaja Sayaji Rao University, Baroda. Distinguished alumni of *Kalakshetra,* Prof. Chandrasekhar is well-known as a choreographer, musician, scholar, and teacher of *Bharatanatyam.* Performing for the last five decades, he is one of India's premier dancers today, and has received numerous awards. He has travelled widely, and performed in most countries in Europe, the United States, and in Southeast Asia. The *Centre for Contemporary Culture,* New Delhi, awarded Chandrasekhar, the Second Rukmini Devi Medal for Excellence in the Arts in 2002.

DR. UTTARA ASHA COORLAWALA received her Ph.D. from New York University. She has been teaching Dance technique, and theoretical courses at Long Island University, Barnard College (Columbia University)and Princeton University. As a dancer-choreographer, Coorlawala pioneered what is now a growing trend on the Indian dance scene towards innovation.

V. R. DEVIKA is a freelance art critic, writer and arts organizer. She studied *Bharatanatyam* from the Dhananjayans, is a keen researcher, presenter and promoter of folk arts. She has received grants and awards from the Government of India, Department of Culture and *Sangeet Natak Akademi* to pursue research in folk arts. She also received the Charles Wallace award from the United Kingdom, Woman of Substance award from the Rotary Club, Woman's Day honor from Jaycees, and the *Kala Seva Bharati* award from *Bharat Kalachar* for her contribution to folk arts and education. She serves as a consultant on numerous foundations, including *Aseema, Dakshinachitra* heritage center, and the *International Dance Council.*

V.P.Dhananjayan received his diploma and post graduate diploma in *Kathakali* and *Bharatanatyam* with distinction from Rukmini Devi's *Kalakshetra.* He founded *Bharatakalanjali,* a renowned dance institution in Chennai, along with his wife Shanta Dhananjayan, also an alumni of *Kalakshetra.* Shri Dhananjayan has received numerous awards including the *Kalaimamani, Sangeet Natak Akademi, Kerala State Sangeeta Nataka Academy* award, and the *Nrityachoodamani.* Dhananjayan has travelled widely and spread the message of Indian art and culture throughout the world. He is also the founder director of an art integrated educational center known as Bhaaskara, located in Kerala.

Shanta Dhananjayan is a well-known teacher and choreographer. She married Sri. V.P.Dhananjayan in the year 1966, and helped him establish *Bharatakalanjali,* a unique institution for the study of dance and music. She has received many awards, including the *Kalaimamani, Nrityachoodamani,* and *Sangeet Natak Akademi* awards. She is also co-founder of *Bhaaskara.*

Maneka Gandhi is a former Cabinet Minister, Government of India and is well-known for her work in Animal Welfare. She served on numerous committees associated with Animal Welfare including, *People For Animals, The Sanjay Gandhi Memorial Animal Care Centre, Society for the Prevention of Cruelty to Animals,* and *Beauty-Without-Cruelty.* She has authored over twenty books on plants, environment, vegetarianism, and animals and has been felicitated with numerous awards, including the *Prani Mitra* and *Lord Erskine* Award.

Sarada Hoffman's association with *Kalakshetra* began from the very first day that Rukmini Devi founded the institution in the year 1936. She commenced her dance training in 1939, and served *Kalakshetra* as teacher until her retirement in the 1990s. As head of the Dance Department in *Kalakshetra* for over forty- five years, Sarada has trained hundreds of students who studied in *Kalakshetra.* She was honoured with many distinctions including *The Sankarabharanam Trust* (1991), the *Sangeet Natak Akademi* Award (1996), and *The Narada Ghana Sabha* Award (2001). The *Centre for Contemporary Culture,* New Delhi, awarded the First Rukmini Devi Medal for Excellence in the Arts to Smt. Sarada Hoffman in 2001.

Dr. Sunil Kothari is a renowned dance scholar, historian and critic. He is the author of several definitive works on classical Indian dance forms including *Bharatanatyam, Odissi, Kathak, Kuchipudi* and others. His edited works include a *Photo Biography of Uday Shankar, Rasa Volume 1, Damaru,* and the latest book *New Directions in Indian Dance.* He served as professor and Chair of the Department of Dance, Rabindra Bharati University, Kolkata between 1980-1995. Dr. Kothari has received the *Padma Shri* award from the Govternment of India and the *Sangeet Natak Akademi* Award for overall contribution in the field of dance. He is currently curating a photo-exhibition on the life and times of Rukmini Devi Arundale for *Kalakshetra,* Chennai.

Dr. S. Chinny Krishna is the Managing Director, Aspick Engineering Pvt. Ltd. He is also Chairman of the Blue Cross of India, Vice Chairman Animal Welfare Board, Editor of the Blue Cross Newsletter and the Honorary Secretary of the World Coalition Against Vivisection. He has won several awards for promoting Animal Welfare.

Krishnaveni Lakshmanan joined *Kalakshetra* in 1947, lived and worked in the centre for over thirty years. A Government of India Scholarship holder from 1960 to 1963, Smt. Krishnaveni has served as the Principal of *Kalakshetra* between 1998-2000. For her contributions in the field of dance, Krishnaveni received the *Nrityachoodamani Award* in 1976, *UNESCO Medal* in 1984, *Sangeet Natak Akademi* Award in 1986, *Arunkalai Selvei* in 1993. Smt. Krishnaveni has travelled widely, and has performed in numerous dance festivals across the world. The *Centre for Contemporary Culture,* New Delhi awarded the Third Rukmini Devi Medal for Excellence in the Arts to Krishnaveni Lakshmanan in 2003.

Dr. N. Mahalingam is the Founder-Chairman of the Sakthi Group of Companies and is President of the Indian Vegetarian Congress. He has patronized numerous educational and charitable institutions. He has a strong belief in 'Universal Brotherhood' through the Worship of *Jyothi.*

Dr. Avanthi Meduri is a scholar, actress, *Kuchipudi* and *Bharatanatyam* dancer, playwright and professor of Dance and Performance Studies. She holds a Ph.D. in Performance Studies from New York University and works in the field of dance education and performance. She scripted and acted in a post-colonial play entitled *God Has Changed His Name,* which was an adaptation of her doctoral thesis featuring *devadasis* (temple-dancers)in South India. The bilingual play was presented in twenty-four cities across India. Recently, Meduri authored and perfomed in a play dealing with the life and global vision of Rukmini Devi. Entitled *Birds of the Banyan Tree,* the play was staged in New Delhi, Bangalore and Chennai. Meduri's book on Rukmini Devi, including the play, is forthcoming. She is a Ford Scholar and the Academic and Artistic Director of the *Centre for Contemporary Culture,* New Delhi.

DR. R. NAGASWAMY received an MA in Sanskrit, Ph.D. in Arts, and Archaeology from the Archaeological Survey of India, New Delhi. He was appointed the First Director of Archaeology in the Tamilnadu State Department where he served till his retirement in 1988. He was the Expert Witness in the now famous London Nataraja case in the London High court, which he won. Author of many publications, he is the leading world authority on Chola bronzes, and has led many world tours. He was closely associated with Rukmini Devi since 1970, and served as a Member of the Executive Committee of *Kalakshetra* and as the President of the U.V. Swaminatha Aiyer Library while Rukmini Devi continued as *Adhyaksha.* A prolific writer, Dr. Nagaswamy has given lectures in leading universities and museums across the world.

DR. JANET O'SHEA has studied and performed *Bharatanatyam* for the last fifteen years. She holds a Ph.D. in Dance History and Theory from the University of California, Riverside and an M.A. in Tamil from the University of California at Berkeley. She is a Lecturer in Dance Studies at the University of Surrey.

VENA RAMPHAL is a dance maker and performer based in Britain. She is currently doing her Ph.D. on Philosophy and Dance at SOAS, University of London. Vena's dance work explores embodied selfhood, emotion, transformation and human connection through live performance and dance film/video. Her training background is in *Bharatanatyam* and the contemporary *karana* technique, learnt under Dr Padma Subrahmanyam.

DR. GOWRI RAMNARAYAN is the Special Correspondent to *The Hindu,* and writes on music, theatre, cinema and literature. Author of *Past Forward,* tracing the childhood of six legendary Indian artistes, she has translated two Marathi plays of Vijay Tendulkar including *Kanyadaan* and *A Friend's Story* published by Oxford University Press. She has also translated Tamil short stories by Kalki R.Krishnamurti, published by Penguin. A trained musician, she has been a vocal accompanist to Smt. M.S. Subbulakshmi, a legendary singer from

Chennai. She has served as a member of the Critics' Jury at international film festivals in London, Venice, Valladolid, and Oslo.

S. SATHYAMOORTHY is the Honorary Executive Director of the *Centre for Contemporary Culture*, New Delhi. As Joint Secretary in the Department of Culture, Government of India, he has had occasion to oversee and interact with cultural personalities and institutions. He was a member of the Governing Board of *Kalakshetra*. He is presently serving as Deputy Comptroller and Auditor General of India.

MRINALINI SARABHAI is a well-known dancer of the *Pandanallur* tradition having learnt *Bharatanatyam* from Shri Meenakshi Sundram Pillai, Rukmini Devi's guru. She is a choreographer noted for innovative work in dance. She is also the Founder Director of *Darpana School of Arts*, Ahmedabad.

DR. KAPILA VATSYAYAN is an internationally renowned scholar of the performing arts of India. Formerly, the Academic Director of the *Indira Gandhi National Centre for the Arts*, she has won many awards and honors including the *Padma Shri*, *Srimanta Sankaradeva Award*, *Campbell Award*, and Honorary D.Litt. from Benaras Hindu University and Rabindra Bharati. Proficient in *Bharatanatyam*, *Kathak*, *Manipuri* and *Odissi*, she has trained with the greatest Gurus of Indian dance, including Shri Achhan Maharaj and Guru Amobi Singh and has travelled with three generations of dancers.

LEELA VENKATARAMAN's career as a writer for dance began as a Dance Critic for the *National Herald* in 1980. She has since served as the Dance Critic for the Delhi edition of *The Hindu* and has been with the daily for over fifteen years. Her *Friday Review* column is a treat art lovers in Delhi do not miss, and the column has 'earned the reputation for being the most incisive commentary on the dance scene in the capital.' Venkataraman has travelled widely in India and abroad, has participated in numerous international seminars and conferences across the world. Her publications include *Bharatanatyam Step by Step*, and *A Dancing Phenomenon—Birju Maharaj*.

LAKSHMI VISWANATHAN is a prominent personality in the modern renaissance of *Bharatanatyam*. She represents the Thanjavur, evocative and musical style of dance, as inherited from Kanjivaram Ellappa. A keen researcher, Lakshmi has received fellowships from the Government of India, and published *Bharatanatyam the Tamil Heritage*, and innumerable monographs on dance and music in various journals and in *The Hindu*. She choreographed a landmark production "The Banyan Tree," in 1995, tracing the history of *Bharatanatyam*, and paying tribute to Rukmini Devi. She is currently researching the *Ramayana* in performance under a *Sangeet Natak Akademi* senior fellowship programme. Her biography on Smt. M.S. Subbulakshmi, the legendary singer from Madras was released in December 2003.

PART - I

CHAPTER 1

INTRODUCTION: A CRITICAL OVERVIEW

Avanthi Meduri

Rukmini Devi Arundale (1904-1986) was a towering, multi-faceted personality who left her impress in the multiple domains of Indian culture and the arts. Because Rukmini Devi worked for many causes, including the revival of theatre arts, crafts and literatures of South India, animal welfare, and art education, people perceived her differently. Some saw her primarily as a Theosophist, the wife of the Englishman George Sydney Arundale, third President of the Theosophical Society and an advocate for global causes. Others perceived her as a local figure, a true Indian, a creative artist, who lived next door in Chennai and revived the crafts, literature, dance, drama, music, painting and folk arts of South India. Still others perceived her as a national icon, a parliamentarian, humanist, philanthropist, institution builder, and animal welfarist.

If Theosophists honoured Rukmini Devi as leader of the All India and World Federation of Young Theosophists and as one who carried on the work of Theosophist Annie Besant in India, the Indian state proclaimed her as a great Indian after the declaration of Indian Independence in 1947. The Government of India nominated Rukmini Devi to lead cultural delegations to foreign countries, and to chair national committees established for the incorporation of art and culture into higher education. The state also honoured her with numerous national awards including the *Padma Bhushan* and the *Sangeet Natak Akademi* in the 1950s.[1] In 1952, Rukmini Devi was nominated to serve as a legislative member in the upper house of the Indian Parliament. She completed two terms in Parliament, moved a bill for the Prevention of Cruelty to Animals, and received the *Prani Mitra,* or Animal Lover Award in 1968.

The Royal Society for the Prevention of Cruelty to Animals, London, also awarded Rukmini Devi with the Queen Victoria Silver Medal in 1958, and the Council of the World Federation for the Protection of Animals, the Hague, added her name to their Roll of Honor in 1959. Wayne State University awarded her an honorary Doctorate in Humanities, and the County and City of Los Angeles bestowed her with Scrolls of Honor in the 1960s. She was also proposed as a candidate to the office of the President of India. But she declined to contest the elections by reaffirming her commitment to work on behalf of art and culture.

Since Rukmini Devi left her imprint in the global world of Theosophy, the theatre arts, and the public culture domain of Indian nationalism, the essays in this volume discuss the many fields in which she worked as an arts educator, institution builder, producer of dance-dramas, animal welfarist, Theosophist, and teacher. Yet it is Rukmini Devi's abundant legacy, which challenges us today because there is no single discursive category that can truly encompass her multifaceted work and vision. Take as example the aesthetic vision that she envisioned for *Bharatanatyam* which, in fact, exceeds prevailing disciplinary categories of dance, drama, theatre, folk arts in which we describe Indian performing arts today.[2]

It is well known that Rukmini Devi developed her pioneering aesthetic for *Bharatanatyam* by selectively drawing on multiple sources of inspiration including dance, music, drama, stagecraft, and theatre arts.[3] She combined the multiple streams[4] and envisioned a three-pronged contemporary, traditional and classical aesthetic for *Bhartanatyam* on the occasion of her debut performance in 1935. She articulated her vision improvizationally and by associating the dance with the guiding tenets of the ancient dramaturgical treatise known as the *Natyasastra;* with the iconic image of *Nataraja,* the presiding deity of the dance, and the traditional *guru* or teacher all at once. Rukmini Devi used the three symbols as staging devises and techniques to envision a new temple-stage aesthetic for *Bharatanatyam.*[5]

She also incorporated her staged aesthetic into the institutional goals of the world renowned *Kalakshetra* (*kala* refers to arts and *kshetra* to a field or sanctuary)institution that she established in South India in 1936 to enable the revival of the whole complex of theatre arts. Here she evolved a new, urban pedagogy for *Bharatanatyam* modelled on the *guru-shisya* system of cultural transmission prevalent in pre-colonial India,[6] and used the icon of *Nataraja* as the institutional emblem of *Kalakshetra.* She also pioneered the practice of incorporating the study of the *Natyasastra* and Sanskrit aesthetic theory into the practical training of the dance.[7] By thus linking public performance with private training, Rukmini Devi bridged the gap between theory and performance and developed an integrated pedagogy and practice for *Bharatanatyam.*

Recently, scholars have critiqued Rukmini Devi for institutionalizing and Sanskritizing the study, research and practice of *Bharatanatyam* in *Kalakshetra.*[8] Yet it is because Rukmini Devi textualized and institutionalized the study and training of *Bharatanatyam* as early as the 1930s that we are able to trace the associative links between *Bharatanatya,* temple sculpture, and the *Natyasastra* today.

I began to understand the positive links between textualization, and institution building only after completing my doctoral thesis at New York University and when I started teaching in the Department of Performance Studies at Northwestern University. In this time, I examined the existing body of scholarship on Indian dance in the United States, and noted that much of this scholarship did not emerge from within disciplines like drama, history, sociology, or even gender studies, but from what is known as Dance Studies in the US. Even within Dance Studies, Indian dance is discussed within two major theoretical perspectives. The first is known as the 'intercultural' model of scholarship and criticism, and the second situates the study of *Bharatanatyam* within the framework of Indian nationalism.

In the first model, Rukmini Devi's work is discussed comparatively, specifically, in relation to Anna Pavlova, the great ballerina, who inspired Rukmini Devi to learn Indian dance.[9] In the second model, Rukmini Devi's work is located within what is described as the discourses of Indian nationalism and discussed specifically in relation to Indian Tradition and the legendary T. Balasaraswati, who emerged herself from the family of great *devadasi* practitioners.[10] Scholars in the US focus on T. Balasaraswati because she hailed from a distinguished family of hereditary musicians and also because she taught *Bharatanatyam* at Wesleyan University and the University of California, Los Angeles, over a period of twenty years between 1960 and 1980.[11]

I have maintained, however, that sustained aesthetic comparisons between T.Balasaraswati and Rukmini Devi are untenable because while the former was more famous for her solo performances, the latter was hailed for the dramaturgical conceptualization that she evolved for *Bharatanatyam* and specifically her evening length dance-dramas, including the *Ramayana* productions, for which she was most famous.[12] Yet none of the twenty-five magnificent dance-dramas, or ensemble creations that Rukmini Devi composed in her life-time have found their way into US classrooms, nor are they discussed in US dance scholarship.[13]

The dance-drama genre has been bracketed in US dance studies because the study of drama and dramatic literature is not considered to be part of the curriculum of dance studies but that of drama. Rukmini Devi is thus recuperated selectively as a dancer-choreographer in dance programs and departments in the US.[14] It is well known, however, that Rukmini Devi did not, at any moment in her long and distinguished career between 1930-1980, describe herself as a dancer-choreographer. She did, however, enunciate the dancer-teacher category by herself becoming a *guru* and awarding students of *Kalakshetra* their first diplomas in dance and music as early as the 1940s. Soon thereafter she enlarged colonial definitions of Indian dance by developing a dramaturgical conceptualization and projected this as the smallest and largest worldview. Because Rukmini Devi conjoined dance with drama, her interdisciplinary aesthetic presents itself as a discursive problem in US Dance studies.[15]

But what about Rukmini Devi scholarship in India? Are we able to discuss her multifaceted aesthetic encompassing Indian dramaturgy, dance, sociology, history, and musicology, within the restricted curriculum of dance studies as it exists in India today? Kapila Vatsyayan describes the future of dance studies in India by explaining that departments of dance in India are little more than venues for housing traditional masters within the university system:

> The demand of fulfilling an academic curriculum and restructuring training to conform with curricula and syllabi of other intellectual disciplines is no easy task. The result is that in normal educational system the departments of dance have not produced great performers, or for that matter great scholars. The future of dance scholarship can only be ensured if these departments become part and parcel of larger studies of the humanities in the arts or related to the departments of language and literature, sociology and anthropology and of course the visual arts. A few universities have admitted this today (1995: 5).

As a way to enlarge restrictive disciplinary frameworks in which Rukmini Devi's legacy has been recuperated both in India and abroad, the essays in this volume describe the public culture and dramaturgical aesthetic that she developed for *Bharatanatyam.* But there is much more to be done as we also need to think of Rukmini Devi's legacy historically, and by situating her vision within the intersecting local, global and pan-Asian world views in which she worked. To quote Vatsyayan again:

> The creative arts were integral to the social and cultural history of India, its philosophic and literary developments and part and parcel of religious movements; an absence of the consideration of this important facet has created an imbalance both in the study of these disciplines as also in research pertaining to the arts. Thus, there is an inadequate treatment of the arts in the books of history whether political or socio-economic or socio-cultural, socio-religious, social or cultural anthropology and little or no sense of either history or sociology or rather the cultural background in research on the performing arts (1989: 17).

In the rest of this introductory essay, I will provide a brief, historical narrative that describes what I encapsulate as the first five lives of Rukmini Devi between 1920 and 1963. I narrate this history, well known to the initiated, only to provide a 'context' for the general reader who might on the off chance pick up this volume with the desire to read the essays.

A Brief History

Rukmini Devi was born on February 29, into a traditional Brahmin family living in Madurai, Tamilnadu. Her father, Shri Nilakantha Shastri, was both a Sanskrit scholar and a Theosophist. Her mother Smt. Seshammal, on the other hand, was a traditional woman with a great love for music. Young Rukmini thus grew up in the two worlds of Theosophy and Indian tradition simultaneously. Rukmini recalls that as a child she had no exposure to any other art except music: 'I was brought up on music, and being near Tiruvaiyaru for sometime during my childhood, I got many opportunities to listen to great music" (Ramnarayan 1984a: 20).

After the sudden and unexpected demise of her father, Rukmini met Dr. George Sydney Arundale, an eminent Theosophist, educationalist and protege of Dr. Annie Besant. Dr. Arundale fell in love with the young girl barely sixteen years of age, proposed marriage, and took her to meet Dr. Annie Besant. Besant queried Rukmini and asked her if she could weather the storm that would break out if she agreed to marry a foreigner. Rukmini said that she could. The storm broke fiercer than anyone expected, and the couple had to flee Madras to register their marriage in Mumbai.

Rukmini Devi as World Mother: 1920-1933

After her marriage, Rukmini became 'daughter, pupil and helper to Dr. Besant as well as life's companion and assistant to Dr. Arundale.' She followed her husband on his world travels, was made President of the All India Federation of Young Theosophists in 1923 and of the World Federation of Young Theosophists in 1925. While the intercultural marriage enabled Rukmini Devi to travel and work in the multiple fields of culture, education, and arts, it actually enhanced her reverence for the culture and history of India.

The intercultural marriage also urged Rukmini Devi to think of India within the larger context of world culture and to recognize India's great contribution to it. In her public lectures across the world, Rukmini spoke about India's mission to world culture, and put forth her local/global message most eloquently in her speech entitled the "Message of Beauty to Civilization." As leader of the Young Theosophist movement, she inspired young recruits by asserting that to be "truly Indian one had to be truly international, exhorting them to honor the best in all civilizations and to live it in their daily lives." [16] Recognising her creative potential, and noting the 'utter absence of all that we know as personality in Rukmini," (1928:4), Dr Besant nurtured her as her own spiritual daughter and made her the leader of the World Mother Movement, conceived as a parallel movement to the World Teacher Movement, embodied by J. Krishnamurti ((1928:4).[17]

At the Theosophical Star Camp held in Ommen in 1925, Dr. Besant announced that "Rukmini of glorious past will be *Rishi Agastya*'s messenger to the women and young ones in India taking up for a large part of the work there that I have been carrying on for years. Young in body, yet she is old in wisdom and power. Child of the indomitable will is her welcome in the higher world"(1925:9-10). In 1928, Dr. Besant explained more fully what the World Mother movement would represent and asserted, "that it is well that such a movement should be led by an Indian woman, chosen for this splendid work. Wide as the World it will be. Great as the Divine Power it will be" (Besant 1928: 3-4). On one of her numerous trips abroad, Rukmini met Anna Pavlova, fell in love with ballet, and took lessons from Cleo Nordi, a member of her troupe. Rukmini explains, "that she learned ballet not with the idea of becoming a full-fledged dancer. It was just to train my body and more for the sheer joy of learning something beautiful" (Ramnarayan 1984a: 29).

While J.Krishnamurti repudiated the World Teacher movement, Devi stayed within the global worldview of the Society and continued to work in the multiple fields of culture, education and the arts. She emerged as the new Indian woman, the 'resuscitator' of all that is best in India's traditional art and culture, giving them new interpretations and dedicating herself to the "World Mother who represents the feminine side of Divinity and the Ideal Womanhood" (Ranson 1928: 485, 486). Since Theosophical Society was a transnational organization, the Society had branches in India, Europe, United States, Australia and Southeast Asia.

Rukmini Devi thus travelled widely in what I describe as the first phase of her life between 1920-1933, made a home for herself in the global world, lived between India, Europe, America and Australia, and spread India's message of beauty to the far corners of the world.

Rukmini Devi as Divine Dancer in Urban India: 1933-1950

After the demise of Dr. Annie Besant in 1933, Rukmini Devi returned to India and joined the Indian national movement for the revival of Indian culture and the arts. She began her revival work by learning *sadir,* performed by hereditary practitioners known as *devadasis* who danced in the eighteenth and nineteenth century temples and courts of South India. Rukmini Devi learned *sadir* despite strenuous opposition from her own family and the people of Madras city. The resistance was immense because the dance had been proscribed by the Anti-Nautch Social Reform movement of the 1890s and had been banned by the colonial government in 1911.[18] Respectable members of Madras society, including Devi's father, had taken public oaths not to patronize *sadir* at the turn of the century.

But Rukmini Devi overcame public resistance by articulating a new aesthetic for *sadir* in her debut performance, which she presented on the occasion of the Diamond Jubilee Celebrations of the Theosophical Society in 1935. The performance began with a few introductory remarks by Dr. Arundale, who underscored the importance of reviving *sadir* as *Bharatanatya,* the spiritual dance of India. The new name was prophetic in that it associated *sadir* with Bharat's *Natyasastra,* and with *Siva/Nataraja,* the presiding deity of the *Natyasastra.* To imprint this multidisciplinary history in the imagination of the spectator, Rukmini Devi staged the dance within three large cultural symbols of god, guru and temple stage simultaneously. Reproduced below is an eyewitness account of the historic recital:

> The stage was at first in semi-darkness: on one side the musicians, including her guru, the great Shri Meenakshi Sundram Pillai, were seated on rugs, with their picturesque instruments. From another side appeared a group of men chanting a most impressive Sanskrit invocation and dedication to Nataraja, the Divine Lord of the Dance...after a little tuning in by the violinist, singers and drummers, the music grew stronger, and against the green curtains of the background, Rukmini Devi appeared in a white and gold dress, looking like some temple carving, full of arrested movement (Ramnarayan 1984b: 22).

In her subsequent performances across the country, Rukmini Devi enlarged her inaugural aesthetic by re-conceiving the contemporary stage as a temple stage and by placing the icon of Nataraja on it. She also designed a back curtain with a temple backdrop and a front curtain with Siva's *Nandi* or vehicle painted on the screen. Devi explained that she did all this to 're-create the temple atmosphere on the urban stage and, thus, to facilitate a new kind of seeing that would enable the spiritual revival of the dance.' By staging the dance in this unique manner, Rukmini Devi transformed an ordinary stage into a temple stage, theatricalized *Sadir* and elevated it to the status of stage art or *Bharatanatya*. She then described *Bharatanatya* as the classical dance of the *Natyashastra*, and also as the traditional dance preserved by the great *gurus*, and both simultaneously.[19]

After working with the solo dance of *Bharatanatya* for nine years, Rukmini Devi enlarged the conceptual meaning of the dance by selfconsciously incorporating the *natya* or dramaturgical conceptualization into the dance. She began by reviving the *Kuravanji* dance-drama traditions, an integral part of the solo dances of *devadasis*. *Kutrala Kuravanji* was a celebrated poem composed circa 1718 by Tirikkuda Rasappa Kavirayar. Rukmini Devi transformed this much revered literary text into a musical script, and staged it as a dance-drama or ensemble production in Bombay in 1944.[20] Devi chose *Kutrala Kuravanji* because she was enamoured with its poetry and also because it was one of the premiere musical genres of eighteenth century Tamil literature, which had not been performed.[21] A minor literary genre, *Kuravanji* proliferated in Tamil learned literature in the eighteenth and nineteenth centuries. Peterson explains that since *Kutrala Kuravanji* is one of the earliest and exemplary, specimens of the genre, it has been held in high esteem and is prescribed in school and college syllabi in Tamilnadu. (1998:42)

Rukmini Devi's *Kutrala Kuravanji* was hailed as a pioneering performance because: (1) it was the first twentieth-century performance of an eighteenth century literary text; (2) it was the first time that a literary and dramatic work from the eighteenth and nineteenth century repertory of dance-dramas was presented in the *Bharatanatyam* dance style by men and women other than hereditary *devadasis*, and on the modern concert stage as opposed to traditional venues of court and temple; (3) It was the first time that *Sadir-Bharatanatyam* was self-consciously ensconced within a classical theatre typology, one that combined text, music, drama and dance.[22] Rukmini Devi contemporised the movement vocabulary used in the dance-drama by systematizing the entrances and exits, composing new music for the script, designing new costumes, and lighting the production with innovative light techniques learned from English stagecraft.[23]

In 1947, Devi enlarged her dramaturgical conceptualisation by drawing on Sanskrit texts. She adapted Kalidasa's *Kumarasambhavam,* and staged it as part of the Besant Centenary Celebrations in 1947. The celebrations enjoyed support from distinguished Indians and even Mahatma Gandhi sent his greetings on the occasion. Press and critics commended the theatrical performance and hailed the "balletizing of the *kavya* (literature) with its Himalayan background as a Himalayan feat in dance. The dance constitution of the story, flawless and artistic, with authentic dress designs...transport us to the puranic age" (Menon: 13). The dance-drama was "so striking that the Government of India invited Rukmini Devi to present the production, on the occassion of the First Republic Day Celebrations, held in New Delhi, in 1950" (Menon: 14). After showing how *sadir*, renamed as *Bharatanatyam* could be re-staged on the dance proscenium, which she redesigned as a temple stage,[24] Rukmini Devi developed the tradition of presenting dance-dramas as yearly events in her own theatre located in *Kalakshetra.*[25]

Towards the end of her life, she memorialised the temple art and drama concepts that had inspired her by constructing the *Koothambalam* temple theatre. Designed in collaboration with renowned architect Appukutan Nair, the theatre stands on the hundred acre campus of *Kalakshetra.* Rukmini Devi explained that although her theatre was conceived along the lines of the Kerala Koothambalam, it would also have a temple atmosphere. Rukmini explained that 'dance was really the art of the temple and that her temple theatre was built with that purpose in mind. It has many features of the temple, and we have adopted as much as possible all the ideals enshrined in the *Natyasastra.*'

When we try to understand Rukmini Devi's aesthetic vision, encompassing a span of over fifty years, we find that her vision moved backwards to embrace traditional pasts, adapted those pasts to serve the contemporary needs of her time, and propelled them into new futures. We also find that the two large concept metaphors of temple stage and cosmic drama return recursively in her aesthetic re-creations. The two ideas helped Rukmini Devi move from solo dance to dance-drama and structure her aesthetic vision with the grace and inevitability of predestination. Originality could be seen on the canvas, as well as conformity, contemporaniety as well as continuity with received pasts. Students of *Kalakshetra* have described Rukmini Devi variously as a 'guiding spirit' and as a 'star'. But we are only just beginning to comprehend the unique manner in which she created a 'traditional' and 'classical' aesthetic for the solo dance of *Bharatanatya,* while also evolving a larger dramaturgical and ensemble vision for the dance.

Rukmini Devi as Institution Builder: 1933-1950

One year after her debut, Rukmini Devi founded the International Academy of Arts, (later renamed as *Kalakshetra*) to enable the revival of the whole complex of south Indian arts including *Bharatanatyam, Kathakali,* dance-drama, music, painting, folk arts, crafts and literature. Besides *Kalakshetra,* Rukmini Devi established four other institutions including the Besant Memorial School renamed as Besant Theosophical High School, the Crafts and Weaving Centre, Dr. U.V. Swaminatha Aiyar Library, and the Arundale Teachers Training College.[26]

Of the five institutions, it was *Kalakshetra* that became most famous because it was in this institution that she gathered a galaxy of eminent teachers, revived the older *guru-shisya* model of cultural transmission, and developed an innovative multidisciplinary pedagogy for the arts, including the learning of Sanskrit, English and Tamil languages.[27] In the first decade of the revival, Guru Chookalingam Pillai and Shri Meenakshi Sundram Pillai taught dance; Chellapa Aiyar, mridangam; Pattamangalam Eswara Aiyar, veena; Kalidasa Nilakanta Aiyar, music; Alex Almore, drama; Rajagopal, painting and sculpture; and Arthur Chase, voice production.[28] Since the traditional and international teachers recruited in the institution were well versed in diverse fields such as dance, music, painting, weaving, Sanskrit language, dramaturgy, drama, and folk arts, Devi urged them to teach from within their fields of expertise and specialization. She thus envisioned a multidisciplinary urban institution of a kind unknown in South India in the 1940s: one in which education, crafts, music, dance, painting, and research co-existed to constitute what Kamaladevi Chattopadhyay described as a 'vision of totality' (1986: 5).

In 1942, Rukmini Devi offered *Kalakshetra* diplomas in dance, music, and painting. In 1943, Rukmini Devi received as a gift the priceless Mahamahopadhyaya, Dr. U. V. Swaminatha Aiyar's collection of Tamil manuscripts. Dr. U. V. Swaminatha Aiyar is revered as the greatest Tamil scholar of modern times because he travelled through all of South India, gathered and compiled the Tamil classics of the second century AD known collectively as the *Sangam Works.*[29] With visionary foresight, Rukmini Devi transformed this private collection into a public research library. She then began translating and publishing select works from this collection as part of the educational and publication activities of the *Kalakshetra* institution.

In 1944, Rukmini Devi affiliated *Kalakshetra* Music courses with the Madras University (Menon: 12). Ten years later, *Kalakshetra* offered short courses for foreign students, post-diploma courses in Music and Natya and part-time courses in Music *Bharatanatyam* and painting. By the 1950s, students from all over India, Tibet, Sri Lanka, Nepal, Burma, Malaysia, Singapore, and Indonesia came to study in Devi's center. International students from Europe, Australia, and America also sought out the institution. Completing their education, hundreds of *Kalakshetra* students, turned into qualified teachers, returned to their respective 'homes,' and dispersed themselves in the Indian, Asian and Western worlds to which they belonged. *Kalakshetra* students are thus scattered across the world today, teaching and performing *Kalakshetra Bharatanatyam* in schools, colleges, universities and private training academies located in South Asia, Asia, Europe, America, and Australia. In the words of Narayana

Menon, "A full flowering of the arts is only possible when Literature and Art, Philosophy and Science interact with one another. *Kalakshetra* is among the very few institutions where all such disciplines interact" (1986:94).

Rukmini Devi as Widow: 1950-1963

But the forward thrust of Devi's vision was constrained in 1950. While Rukmini Devi was claimed as a true Indian and bestowed with numerous awards, her vision was besieged by the promulgation of what came to known as the Theosophical Society's Policy of Disassociation in 1950. The Policy necessitated that Rukmini Devi move her five institutions from out of the grounds of the huge estate property of the Theosophical Society in which they had functioned in pre-independent India. These were difficult times as Dr. Arundale had passed away in 1945, and Rukmini was completely on her own. From World Mother(1920), to Divine Dancer (1935), to Institution Builder (1936), to Widow (1945), Rukmini Devi's life had moved through several stages.

Yet it was only in the post-independent phase, that Rukmini Devi actually came into her own. Undaunted by the crisis of 1950, she purchased a hundred-acre of land in the Tiruvanmayur locality, adjoining the Adyar estate of the Theosophical Society, and re-housed her five institutions in her new estate. It took Rukmini Devi thirteen years to move her centres and the cultural legacy which she had constituted in the first estate and re-house it in the second. This was the most challenging period of her life as she had to preserve the global vision that she had envisioned for the arts before the historic rupture of the 1950, and carefully transit that other vision into post-independent India. Devi was caught in a storm that we call modernization today. Only this storm was blowing simultaneously from within the Theosophical Society, across India, and from within the new Indian patronage systems that came forward to support Devi's work in the 1950.

Rukmini Devi whirled in the storm, circled herself and her institutions. She was caught between two worlds, and found herself presiding over the second transitional stage of Indian modernism. The second modernism was different from the epochal modernism that she had negotiated in the 1930s because the Indian state was now the new patron of culture, Rukmini Devi was on her own, and bereft of the protectionist patronage of the Theosophical Society.

Yet Rukmini Devi knew that she was not just an Indian nationalist but a global citizen who had worked on behalf of the transnational ideals of the Theosophical Society since the 1920s. Rukmini Devi thus split herself metaphorically: moved herself back into the past of pre-independent India, picked up everything that she had envisioned in the precincts of the Theosophical Society, gathered that other syncretic legacy and brought it piece by piece into the present of her own estate, and the future of free India. Rukmini Devi moved forward into the future of Indian modernism, albeit, with her face turned towards the Theosophical Society.

But her single overriding concern in this phase of displacement was to rehouse her five institutions in the site-specific locality of her Tiruvanmayur estate. Remembering those difficult years before her demise, Rukmini Devi marked it as a moment of rupture in her own life and the life of her institutions. She described it as a period of great stress and struggle, likened herself to Sita of the *Ramayana* and said that after the break, there were two Sitas: the real and the maya Sita as in Valmiki's *Ramayana.*[30]

Rukmini Devi in her Pan-Asian World: 1963-1986

After moving the five institutions, Rukmini Devi embarked on the fifth reconstructive phase of her life. In this time, she enlarged her *natya* vision, adapted multilingual literary texts, and re-staged them as visual spectacles. Devi adapted Valmiki's *Ramayana*, presented it as a six-part serial, and choreographed twenty-five breathtaking dance-dramas, embracing a variety of languages in the period between 1950-1986. For her dance-dramas, she drew on narrative texts from Sanskrit, Tamil, Telugu, Malayalam and other languages. She included the Kerala art of *Kathakali* among the dance styles taught at *Kalakshetra*, and used *Kathakali* and *Bhagavatamela* techniques in some portions of her dance-dramas.

Rukmini Devi also enlarged the vision of her *Kalakshetra* institution by forging new global and pan-Asian links. She created a new public culture around her dance-drama productions, featured every year in the theatre that she built within the campus of the institution. She also evolved a new arts community around *Kalakshetra* by requesting the Madras Corporation to provide roads and access to Tiruvanmayur, and conceptualised a new urban cosmopolitan arts community around *Kalakshetra*. This community known as *Kalakshetra* colony today, is part of Besant Nagar, named after Annie Besant the spiritual mother of Rukmini Devi. In all probability, Rukmini Devi created this public arts community to save the vision of her institution if it were ever to be threatened again and in the hope that the community, named after the institution, would be inspired to save the institution for itself. Rukmini Devi, as already mentioned, was also a social historian of sorts and intent on preserving history performatively.

Rukmini Devi died in 1986 after a prolonged struggle with lung cancer. But she completed the construction of the huge temple theatre known today as *Bharata Kalakshetra Theatre*, and presided over the Diamond Jubilee Celebrations of *Kalakshetra* in 1985. Any visitor to *Kalakshetra* today, will see the five institutions that she founded in pre-independent India, standing yoked together in the hundred-acre campus of her Tiruvanmayur estate. They stand as a testimony to the courage, will, and vision of a singular woman who struggled to preserve the translocal vision of her five institutions even after that history had been abrogated in 1950.

In 1993, seven years after the demise of Rukmini Devi, her multi-pronged edifice was declared as an institution of national importance by an Act of Parliament, and is now marked as a must-see site on the tourism map of South India. Visitors who go to the Tirvanmayur estate marvel at the sprawling grounds of the institution positioned against the backdrop of the roaring sea. They are fascinated by the everyday aesthetics of the institution, and awed by the *Koothambalam* temple theatre. The temple theatre stands as a jewel in the crown of the five institutions.

People gaze upon the yoked institutions and describe it variously as a cultural colossus, a cultural citadel, a cultural empire, a national institution, and a cultural heritage. Some turn their heads away and dismiss it as representing the vanity of a cosmopolitan woman privileged to travel the world and work for global causes when she was barely twenty years of age. But the large global history, the imaginative social metaphors in which the five local/global institutions were constituted in the 1930s and transplanted again to the Tiruvanmayur estate in the 1950s, is a historical story of struggle and achievement that still needs to be documented in the annals of Indian cultural and dance history.

Why Remember the Five Stages of Devi's Life?

The Rukmini Devi story that I have narrated above is well known. I have merely re-situated that story within what I have described as the first five lives of Rukmini Devi. I think it is important for us to think of Rukmini Devi's story of struggle and achievement within the five historical stages suggested above if only to grasp the intersecting global, local and pan-Asian worldviews in which Devi realized her vision.

While large histories and worldviews influenced Rukmini Devi's work and vision, it is obvious that she did not work within the ideologies of large discourses, but located herself firmly within the institutional domain of her five institutions and realized her vision within the micro worldview of her five centers.

Future studies focused on Rukmini Devi might want to discuss her institution building activities comparatively and in relation to other institutions founded, for example, by Rabindranath Tagore, in the north and Vallathol Narayana Menon, in the south. In addition Rukmini Devi's institutions can also be evaluated cross culturally, specifically in relation to key music and dance conservatories in the West.[31] Comparative sociological and ethnographic studies of cultural and educational institutions might help us trace the interconnections between global and local institutions, while also interrogating the large question of history and memory which is itself under erasure in the age of globalization.

Since urban institutions founded in the 1930s helped constitute new public culture communities and enabled the revival and dissemination of the arts, we might develop new research initiatives for the arts that focus on the sociology of cultural institutions.[32] The task of the social historian of Indian performing arts is neither to love institutions for their own sake, nor to seek emancipation from them. It is rather to see how historical pasts are still alive in translocal institutions of our time, and how those other histories are being transformed rapidly under the impact of globalization and state patronage both at once.

In conclusion, we can say that Rukmini Devi's vision was ahead of her time. She fashioned a pioneering South Asian art, culture and education movement, including the learning of literature and languages, which prevails in local and global practices of *Bharatanatyam.* Recently, there has been much criticism focused on Rukmini Devi's work. Scholars have argued that her vision was imitative, deriving from western ballet, and mimicking European models of education.[33] Without refuting these critiques, I want to suggest that it is Rukmini Devi's art and education movement, regardless of the judgment that it was imitative, that actually enables us today to re-historicize and re-conceptualize emergent 'Third World,' 'South Asian' and Indian dance forms not as "thin replicas of an experience we in the west are connoisseurs of 'always already 'but as one in which the Euro-American experience is significant but neither singular nor always the exemplary center" (Appadurai 1988:1).

Since Rukmini Devi left her impress in the multiple domains of Indian culture and the arts, the essays in this volume endeavour to capture her multifaceted legacy, preserved both in India and abroad. Authored by a wide range of Indian and international writers —including dance critics, dance scholars, dancers, dance teachers, bureaucrats, and alumni of the world-renowned *Kalakshetra* institution— the essays are grouped into three sections. S. Sathyamoorthy's essay on Rukmini Devi's travelling photo-exhibition stands alone in the first section and provides a thematic context for this volume as it was the travelling exhibition, presented around the world in the year of her Birth Centenary, that enabled the compilation of this volume.

The essays in the second section delineate specific aspects of Rukmini Devi's work as a Mother (Kapila Vatsyayan); Theosophist (Radha Burnier); Animal Welfarist (Chinny Krishna and Maneka Gandhi); Divine Dancer (R. Nagaswamy); Vegetarianist (N. Mahalingam); Educationalist (Sarada Hoffman); Institution-builder (C.V.Chandrasekhar); Aesthetic Visionary (Mrinalini Sarabhai); Guru (Krishnaveni Lakshmanan); Beacon Light (V. P. Dhananjayan); Sympathetic Teacher (Shanta Dhananjayan); and A Legend (V. R. Devika).

The essays in the third section focus on Rukmini Devi's aesthetic vision, her approach to history (Leela Venkataraman); to tradition (Lakshmi Viswanathan); to composing dance dramas (Gowri Ramnarayan, C. V. Chandrasekhar, Sunil Kothari); to 'Sanskritization' (Coorlawala, Meduri); to Classicism (O'Shea), and to Contemporary dance in the United Kingdom (Vena Ramphal). The third section brings together Indian and international scholarship on Rukmini Devi to underscore that she is not just a local but also a global figure whose work continues to be researched in dance departments all over the world. Rukmini Devi scholarship thus blurs the distinctions between there and here, building new bridges of cultural dialogue between scholars working in India and abroad.

In London alone there are over sixty flourishing dance schools teaching *Bharatanatyam*, and it is not an exaggeration to say that wherever *Bharatanatyam* is taught in the world today, there Rukmini Devi is recalled because the multifaceted classical and traditional aesthetic that she envisioned for *Bharatanatyam* prevails in the local and global practices of the dance. The essays in this volume have been assembled with an eye to the future and to enable the reader of today and tomorrow to glean some sense of Rukmini Devi's multifaceted legacy dispersed in the local and global world.

Notes

1. See *Kalakshetra Quarterly (*1986: 118-119)for a chronological listing of the awards conferred on Rukmini Devi.

2. See Maneka Gandhi and Chinny Krishna in this volume. Also see essays in Part 111, which describe the interdisciplinary vision that Rukmini Devi envisioned for Bharatanatyam.

3. See Leela Venkataraman and Meduri in this volume. Both essays describe Rukmini Devi's multi-faceted vision, albeit from different perspectives.

4. Prior to the national revival of the dance in the 1930s, the dance was known as *sadir* and performed by hereditary practitioners known as *devadasis.* See Amrit Srinivasan (1985); and Meduri (1996) for a discussion describing the Anti Nautch Social Reform movement of 1892 and its impact on *Sadir*, and the life of *devadasis.*

5. See Meduri in this volume for a discussion focussed on the staging techniques that Rukmini Devi used in her dance revival.

6. See Sarada Hoffman, C.V. Chandrasekhar, and Krishnaveni Lakshmanan in this volume. All three essays describe how important this notion of the 'guru' was to Rukmini Devi and how she used the *guru-shisya* model of cultural transmission in her *Kalakshetra* institution. Also see Meduri (1990; 1996) and Gaston (1996) for a discussion about the *Arangetram* as an urban ritual that Rukmini Devi envisioned to transit older, cultural systems into modern systems of social reproduction in the 1930s.

7. It is true that Rukmini Devi textualized *Bharatanatyam* but she also affirmed the oral traditions and embodied practices represented by traditional gurus. See S.Sarada (1985: 21). Also see C. V. Chandrasekhar in this volume.

8. See Amrit Srinivasan (1985); Mathew Allen (1997); and O'Shea (1998, 2001) for critical, elaborations on how Rukmini Devi sanskritized *Bharatanatyam.* Also see Coorlawala and Meduri in this volume.

9. See Ramnarayan's vivid account of Rukmini Devi's encounter with Anna Pavlova (1984a:28-29), and her grooming within the Theosophical Society. Joan Erdman carefully developed the intercultural model of scholarship by focusing on the work of Uday Shankar. Much of the early scholarship on Indian dance replicated and refined the intercultural model of analysis (Erdman 1987; Coorlawala 1992). This approach changed in the mid 1990s and began to focus on the study of Indian nationalism, and its impact on the revival of Indian performing arts (See Srinivasan (1985); Meduri (1996), Coorlawala (1996); and Gaston (1996). A new group of scholars began to study not just *Bharatanatyam* but also *Kathak, Odissi,* and *Manipuri.* Again, it is beyond the scope of this essay to detail that scholarship, but mention must be made of Annanya's research on *Odissi* (1996, 2004), and also Pallabhi Chakravorty's research on Kathak (1998, 2000).

10. See Pattabhi Raman and Anandhi Ramachandran (1984) for eloquent accounts of T. Balasaraswati's vision. See also Balasaraswati (1998,1991).

11. While I described the transnational traditions of *Bharatanatyam* by focusing on T. Balasaraswati and Rukmini Devi in my doctoral study (1996), I did not underscore the differences between them but maintained that they were the two polar stars of Indian performing arts

(1988, 1996). Mathew Allen (1997) and O'Shea (1998) developed my model of analysis more completely and articulated a new comparative study of the aesthetic legacies of Balasaraswati and Rukmini Devi. See Cowdery (1995) for a discussion about T. Balasaraswati's legacy in the United States.

12. Rukmini Devi contemporized the dance drama genre in many ways. See Lakshmi Viswanathan, Gowri Ramnarayan, C. V. Chandrasekhar, and Kothari for the many innovations that she realized within the dance-drama genre of performance.

13. See Gowri Ramnarayan's vivid essay about Rukmini Devi's dance-dramas in this volume.

14. See O'Shea's (1998, 2001) sustained, critical analysis of the work and vision of T. Balasaraswati and Rukmini Devi, and their different 'choreographic' approaches to dance making.

15. Yet the dim scenario that I have outlined for Indian dance research in the US is changing rapidly with the emergence of a sub-field known as cultural studies and performance studies, which has been incorporated into the larger discipline of dance studies. Scholars like O'Shea (2001) are also beginning to engage with dance-drama and opening up the field of South Asian dance studies from within. But we in India confront now the same problems faced by the US in the 1940s, when it sought to recognize dance studies as a discipline in its own right and outside physical education and health studies. While dance in India will never be perceived as part of physical education, thanks to the work of pioneers like Rukmini Devi, we still need to incorporate 'dance' into university education, not as a specialist field of study, but on par with disciplines like visual art, history, sociology and anthropology.

16. See Radha Burnier's essay in this volume.

17. In *Translocal Modernities,* (Wesleyan Univeristy Press, forthcoming), I discuss the effects of the Devi name and how the World Mother enunciation influenced Rukmini Devi's artistic and cultural work. See also Meduri (1996) and Allen(1997) for different explications on how the worldview of theosophy influenced Rukmini Devi's aesthetic vision.

18. See (Srinivasan 1985: 1873-75; Meduri 1996: 56-61) for different discussions about the World Mother movement.

19. See O'Shea's essay in this volume for a selective but interesting reinterpretation of Rukmini Devi's multifaceted aesthetic vision.

20. See Peterson (1998) for a detailed analysis of the evolution of *Kuravanji* dance drama and the many innovations that Rukmini Devi's realized within the dance-drama genre.

21. See Ramnarayan (1984c) for a detailed analysis of the unique manner in which this historical production was created.

22. See Dr. Kothari's essay on the *Kuravanji* in this volume.

23. See Gowri Ramnarayan and C.V. Chandrasekhar in this volume. Both essays describe how Rukmini Devi used 'light' in her productions.

24. See Chandrasekhar's essay on the creation of the stage in this volume and Meduri (forthcoming 2004).

25. See essays authored by Gowri Ramnarayan, Chandrasekhar, and Lakshmi Viswanathan in this volume. All three essays focus on Rukmini Devi's dance-drama.

26. See Meduri *Translocal Modernities* (Wesleyan University Press, forthcoming) for a discussion that describes the new, urban and multicultural world that Rukmini Devi developed for *Bharatanatyam.*

27. See Ramani (2003:65) for a moving account of the many distinguished teachers who taught in *Kalakshetra..*

28. See Sankara Menon's (1936:61:7) *Silver Jubliee Report on Kalakshetra.*

29. This literary corpus, belonging to the classical literature of the second century AD, was thought to be lost. But Dr. U.V. Swaminatha Iyer doggedly searched for these manuscripts, collected three thousand sixty one half leaf and paper manuscripts, provided literary commentaries, and published 91 books on different branches of literature in his own life time. He was thus hailed as *'Mahamahopadhyaya'* the unsurpassable, or the great learned man of his times.

30. There is no biography on Rukmini Devi. Shakuntla Ramani republished some interviews that Rukmini Devi gave before her demise in 1986 in which she discussed her life and struggle. See the essay entitled "Rukmini on Herself," featured in the *Rukmini Devi Birth Centenary Volume,* edited by Ramani (2003).

31. The Rukmini Devi travelling exhibition was presented in Calcutta in 2001. A seminar was featured comparing the visions of Rukmini Devi and Rabindranath Tagore, *Kalakshetra* and *Vishwa Bharati.* This represents only a beginning. More research, focussed on the study of institutions, needs to be realized in Indian dance and cultural studies.

32. See the essays of Gowri Ramnarayan and C.V Chandrasekhar in this volume, which are already pointing to these new areas of research in the performing arts.

33. See Coorlawala (1996); Allen (1997); and O'Shea (1998, 2001). The mentioned authors are also modifying their critiques in light of new data and counter critiques articulated in the local domain of Indian performing arts.

References

Appadurai, Arjun. 1988 "Why Public Culture?" *Public Culture* 1, 1: 5-10.

—1996. *Modernity at Large: Cultural Dimensions of Globalization*. Minneapolis: University of Minnesota Press.

Allen, M. H. 1997. "Rewriting the Script for South Indian Dance." *The Drama Review* 41: 63-100.

Besant, Annie. 1925. *Star Congress at Ommen*. Adyar: Theosophical Publishing House.

—1928. "The New Annunciation." Vol, 1, (1) Adyar: Theosophical Publishing House.

Chatttopadhyay, Kamaladevi. 1986. "A Vision of Totality." *Kalakshetra Quarterly* (Madras): 8 (3-4). 5-6.

Chakravorty, Pallabi. 1998. "Dance Hegemony and Nation: The Construction of Classical Indian Dance." *South Asia* 21: 107-120.

Coorlawala, Uttara A. 1992. "Ruth St Denis and India's Dance Renaissance." *Dance Chronicle* 15: 123-145.

—1996.The Birth of Bharatanatyam and the Sanskritized Body." *The Body in Dance: Modes of Inquiry: Conference Proceedings of the Congress on Research in Dance.*

Cowdery, James R. 1995. The American Students of Balasaraswati." *UCLA Journal of Dance Ethnology* 19: 50-57.

Gaston, Anne-Marie. 1996. *Bharatanatyam from Temple to Theatre*. New Delhi. Manohar

Erdman, Joan. 1987. Uday Shankar in the West." *TDR* 31, 1(T13): 164-88.

—1996. "Dance Discourses: Rethinking the history of the Oriental Dance." In *Moving Worlds: Rewriting Dance.* Edited by Gay Morris. New York: Routledge

Meduri, Avanthi. 1988. "*Bharatanatyam:* What Are You?" *Asian Theatre Journal* 5, 1:1-22.

—1990. "History as Image: Mimesis in *Bharatanatyam.*" Fifth Hong Kong International Dance Conference July 15-28: Conference Papers 11, K-Z: 107-125, Hong Kong:Hong Kong Academy of Performing Arts.

—1996. "Nation, Woman, Representation: The Sutured History of the *Devadasi* and Her Dance." Ph.D. dissertation, New York University.

—2002. "*Bharatanatyam* – What are you?" In *Dance History Reader: Moving History/Dancing Cultures*, edited by Ann Cooper Albright and Ann Dils, 103-133. Middletown, CT: Wesleyan University Press.

—2003. "Multiple Pleasures." In *Taken by Surprise: A Dance Improvization Reader*," edited by Ann Cooper Albright and David Gere, 141-150. Middletown, CT: Wesleyan University Press.

—2004a. "Knowing the Dancer: East meets West." *Victorian Literature and Culture*, Vol 32, no 2: 435-448.

—2004b. "Western Feminist Theory, Asian Indian Performance and a Notion of Agency," In *Performance: Critical Concepts in Literary and Cultural Studies*, edited by Philip Auslander, London, New York: Routledge.

—2005a. "*Bharatanatyam* as a Global Dance: Some Issues in Teaching, Practice and Research." [In Press]. *Dance Research Journal.*

—2005b. "Rukmini Devi and the Crafting of the New Aesthetic for Bharatanatyam." In *Performing Pasts: Reinventing the Arts in South India* [forthcoming] edited by Indira Peterson and Devesh Soneji, Middletown, CT: Wesleyan University Press.

—2006. *Translocal Modernities: Cultural Identity, Aesthetics and Cosmopolitanism in Bharatanatyam*, Middletown, CT: Wesleyan University Press.

Menon, Narayana. 1986. "Rukmini Devi and the Making of *Kalakshetra.*" *Kalakshetra Quarterly* (Madras): 8(3-4): 93-94.

Menon, Sankara. 1961. *Report on Kalakshetra: 1936-1961.* Adyar: Kalakshetra

O'Shea, Janet. 1998. "Traditional Indian Dance and the Making of Interpretive Communities." *Asian Theatre Journal* 15, no.1 (Spring): 45-63.

—2001. At Home in the World: Bharatanatyam's Transnational Traditions. Ph.D dissertation, University of Riverside.

Pattabhiraman, N., and Anandhi Ramachandran. 1984a. "The Whole World in Her Hands," Part 1. *Sruti* 4 (January/February): 17-31.

—1984b. "The Whole World in Her Hands," Part 2. *Sruti* 5 (March): 17-32.

Peterson, Indira Viswanathan. 1998. "The Evolution of the *Kuravanji* Dance Drama in Tamilnadu: Negotiating the Folk and the Classical in the Bharatanatyam Canon."*South Asia Research* 18, 1: 39-72.

Ranson, Josephine. 1938. *A Short History of The Theosophical Society*. Madras: The Theosophical Publishing House.

Rammarayan, Gowri. 1984a. "Rukmini Devi: A Quest for Beauty, a Profile" Part 1, *Sruti* 8 (June): 17-29.

—1984b. "Rukmini Devi: Dancer and Reformer, A Profile." *Sruti* 9 (July): 17-29.

—1984c. "Rukmini Devi: Restoration and Creation, A Profile." *Sruti* 10 (August): 26-38.

Ramani, Shakuntala 2003. *Shraddhanjali: Brief Pen Portraits of Great People who laid the Foundation of Kalakshetra.* Chennai: Kalakshetra Foundation.

Ramani, Shakuntala. 2003. *Rukmini Devi Birth Centenary Volume.* Chennai Kalakshetra Foundation.

Srinivasan, Amrit. 1983. "The Hindu Temple Dancer: Prostitute or Nun?" *Cambridge Anthropology* 8, 1: 73-99.

—1985. "Reform and Revival: The *Devadasi* and Her Dance." *Economic and Political Weekly* 20, no. 44 (November): 1869-1876.

Vatsyayan, Kapila. 1989. Dance Scholarship: The Complex Indian Situation." In *Beyond Performance: Dance Scholarship Today.* Edited by S. Au and F. Peter. Berlin: Centre of the International Theatre Institute.

—1995. "The Future of Dance Scholarship in India." *Dance Chronicle* 18: 485-90.

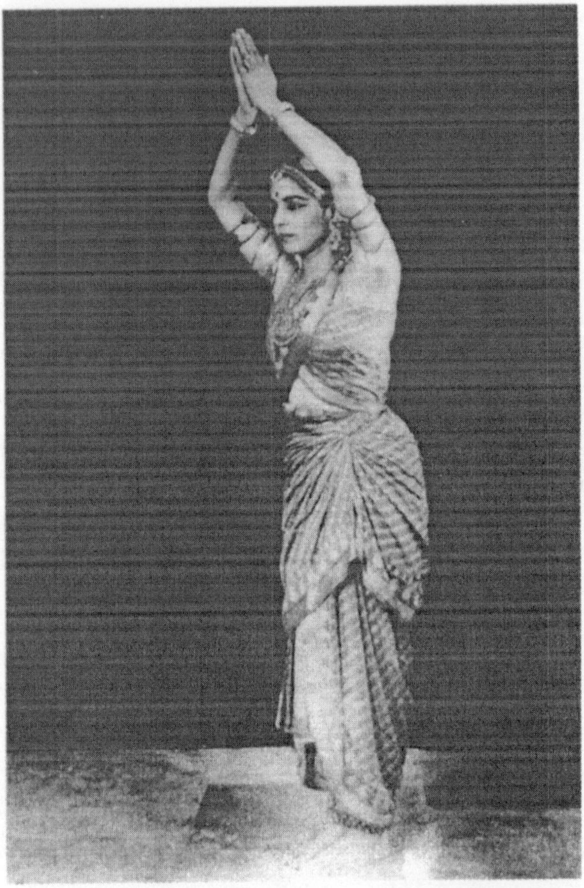

Fig. 1: Rukmini Devi: Performing the Traditional Salutation in Bharatanatyam

(Photo: C.T. Nachiappan archive)

CHAPTER 2

A DREAM RUN: THE STORY OF THE RUKMINI DEVI TRAVELLING EXHIBITION

S. Sathyamoorthy

It was a moment that seemed to have been 'Divined.' Dr. Avanthi Meduri and I went to *Kala-kshetra,* Chennai, looking for some old photographs of Rukmini Devi Arundale. Dr. Rajaram, Director of *Kala-kshetra* and his colleagues were very courteous and helpful in showing us what they possessed. In the course of the conversation, it was suggested that our efforts would bear fruit if we contacted Shri Nachiappa. While we both had heard of him, he was a hazy figure as neither of us had set eyes on him. We also did not know where he lived or how to reach him. It thus came as a surprise to us to learn that he actually lived next door to *Kala-kshetra.* Dr. Rajaram was most helpful and gave us the contact telephone numbers that we needed.

Thus, we landed in the premises of Rukmini Devi Arundale Trust. We beheld a man in his seventies, dressed in saffron clothes. He was half clad like Gandhiji but unlike him, had his bare body smeared with sacred ash (vibhuti). This was Shri Nachiappa Swamigal, heading the Koviloor Mutt. What a transformation! He had left the world of dark rooms and photography, where he had created a niche for himself, to embrace this other world of ascetics and devotion.

Half a century earlier, Shri Nachiappa was known in Madras city as an ace photographer, and a graduate from the New York Institute of Photography. He was then a celebrity, especially in the field of photography, and pioneered the development of dark room photography. His guru was Mr. Conrad Woldring, who taught drama, commercial art photography and printing in Rukmini Devi's Besant Memorial School, and he groomed his student Shri Nachiappa. Rukmini Devi, as is now well known, was astute and able to recognize the potential of photography and its importance in the domain of the performing art. The young Nachiappa approached her as Principal of the Besant School and asked to be excused from sports in order to learn the art of photography. Sensing his potential, Rukmini Devi granted him permission and dedicated the young Nachiappa to the emerging field of photography and commercial art design. Shri Nachiappan took to both like a fish to water.

Shri Nachiappa Swamigal received us with a beaming smile, and with eyes twinkling like a modern Kodak Camera. "You want a few photographs? Why don't you take the exhibition of Rukmini Devi that I have and show it in New Delhi," he said. We were speechless. Neither of us had seen these photographs, and we knew nothing at all about what it takes to put an exhibition together. We had heard that the Rukmini Devi photographic archive of Shri Nachiappan was legendary. But were we up to the task? Dr. Avanthi and I looked at each other helplessly. Rukmini Devi seemed to be calling us in her imitable manner and giving us her photographs so that we could show the world the magnificent vision she had envisioned for *Bharatanatya*, Indian culture and the performing arts. The grand lady had divined the right moment, brought in Dr Rajaram and guided us to Shri Nachiappa. The Rukmini Devi pnoto archive surfaced as if from nowhere.

Dr. Avanthi Meduri had told me earlier how Rukmini Devi had visited her in a dream—when she was writing her doctoral dissertation on the revival of *Bharatanatyam* at the Tisch School in the New York University—and urged her to tell the story of the revival from her point of view and what she had endeavored to realize in *Kala-kshetra*. This was strictly a personal experience, yet it had haunted Meduri in the 1990s. She, however, did not attach any great significance to it because she thought of it as one of the many kinds of dreams that visit students writing dissertations as they become possessed by the characters they encounter in the pages of history. But when the entire photo-archive of Rukmini Devi was handed over to us on a platter, without any design on our part, it was simply beyond rational comprehension. More importantly we wondered, what role Rukmini Devi had assigned for me in her *lila* and why she had called me into this hunt for photographs in the first place? We were to find the answers only in the future, as the pages of this essay would reveal.

So the photographs came to Delhi neatly wrapped in bubble paper and in several crates. When we opened the crates, we could not believe our eyes! The photographs were master-pieces, in black and white, and encapsulated in detail a creative moment in the history of the nationalist period! There were solo dance pictures showing how Rukmini Devi worked with light, with costume, with jewellery and with props to realize a compelling new aesthetic for the solo dance of *Bharatanatya*. The dance-drama pictures, on the other hand, described the *natya* or drama vision that she evolved for *Bharatanatyam*. We saw a generation of great dancers who had worked in *Kala-kshetra*. We saw them as they had been some thirty years ago: there was Sarada Hoffman, Krishnaveni, Subbulakshmi, Dhananjayan, Shanta, Janardhanan, Leela Samson et al playing many different roles in the dance dramas of Rukmini Devi. The photographs detailing the making of *Kala-kshetra*, informed us about the contributions of great musicians like Vasudevachar, Krishnamachar, M.D. Ramanathan, Tiger Varadachariar and others who had resided in *Kala-kshetra* and given their gifts freely to the new generation of students who learned at their feet. In one photograph we even saw Dr. Rajaram, Director of *Kala-kshetra* as a young boy in his half pants. Yet another treasure was the visitor's gallery, which included photographs of Jawaharlal Nehru, Indira Gandhi, Dalai Lama, Yehudi Menuhin, and other visiting dignitaries from all over the world including Clement Atlee, and Queen Juliana of Holland among others. We saw the history of *Kala-kshetra* institution and how it became a local/global institution all over again.

The Rukmini Devi Travelling Exhibition in New Delhi

Seeing the pictures, I became enthused about the exhibition and found myself getting involved in the administrative details of realizing its vision. I was drawn into taking care of little things such as the printing of pamphlets, invitations, hiring galleries, mobilizing people, inviting dignitaries and all of the little things that make possible the realization of public events. I confess that as a Joint Secretary in the Ministry of Culture, I had taken all these things for granted. As a bureaucrat, I was accustomed to being invited to preside over events and not used to putting things together behind the scene of public attention. I was clearly on the other side of the fence now, wearing a new hat, rolling up my sleeves, carrying measuring tapes to measure wall space, thinking about visual culture in ways I had not done before. What is more, I was actually enjoying my new role as a non-governmental administrator! Rukmini Devi had me hooked, and was now working her magic on me.

Fortunately, I found a pillar of strength in Dr. L.M. Singhvi. He readily agreed to be the President of the Centre for Contemporary Culture, New Delhi, which we conceptualized to host the exhibition. Once he agreed to shoulder the burden, I requested M/s Abid Hussain, former Ambassador to United States, Dr. Jyotinder Jain, Director, Crafts Museum, New Delhi, Dr. S.S. Biswas, Director General, National Museum, New Delhi, Dr. Tasneem Mehta, President, INTACH, Mumbai, Dr. H.K. Kaul, Information Officer, India

International Centre, New Delhi, and Dr. Avanthi Meduri, Ford Scholar, New Delhi, to form the core committee of members comprising the Society. Mr. Jitendra Nath, our capable Chartered Accountant, registered the *Centre for Contemporary Culture* as a Society.

Now we had to find a gallery. Dr. N.N. Vohra, the then Director, India International Centre was excited about the idea of presenting the Rukmini Devi photo exhibition, and offered the gallery free of charge. No doubt he realized that the archive, hitherto hidden from the public, had a tremendous potential. Equally enthused was Shri Vivek Sardana, the international expert on exhibitions. He helped design the exhibition in rich colours, keeping in mind the temple and bamboo aesthetic that was such a big part of Rukmini Devi's vision. Shri Gajwani, the ace artist designed the brochure entitled "Re-presenting Rukmini Devi Arundale (1904-1986)." The brochure had her picture and details of the show on the front and the banyan tree at the back. In between the six pages was the text of the exhibition and photographs of activities in *Kala-kshetra.* The logo for the Centre was designed by Mrs. Siddharth of M/s Creative Consultants Ltd.

Being a student of social history, Dr. Avanthi arranged the photographs within socio-historical frames. She grouped them into five clusters, representing the five stages in which Rukmini Devi had developed her multifaceted vision for *Bharatanatyam* and Indian performing arts. She described them as the Experimental Phase (1920-1933), the Solo Dance Phase (1933-1943), the Dance Drama Phase (1943-1987), the Making of *Kala-kshetra* as a New Urban Institution (1936-1986); and *Kala-kshetra* as a Global Institution (1936-1986). She did the backstage work: wrote text panels and brochures, arranged photographs, and realized the academic work behind the scene of public display.

The printing work was undertaken by Gulshan of M/s

Jumbo Printers. They were professional, artistic and supportive of our efforts. So much so, that when the publicity material was once misplaced by the Airline, they couriered a second set to Kuala Lumpur at their expense. Without the generous and timely support of several such associates, the exhibition could have floundered and not taken off in the way it did.

With goodwill from friends and well-wishers, the exhibition was assembled. Dr. Sunil Kothari and Ms. Jayalakshmi Easwar, a Delhi Dancer and Kalakshetra alumni extended themselves all through the night and helped us mount the exhibition. Dr. Karan Singh inaugurated the exhibition with an excellent speech at the India International Center, New Delhi. Happily for us the inauguration coincided with the inauguration of the Centre for Contemporary Culture, New Delhi. On this momentous occasion, the Centre for Contemporary Culture also released two books authored by the Koviloor Nachiappa Swamigal entitled *Rukmini Devi: Bharatanatyam*; and *Rukmini Devi: Dance-Drama.* These two books published by Rukmini Devi Arundale Trust, Chennai, were released by Dr. Karan Singh and Dr. L.M. Singhvi.

Dr. Avanthi Meduri conceptualized a seminar and featured it as part of the exhibition. The seminar discussed the contemporary and multifaceted vision of Rukmini Devi as an institution builder, educationalist, and aesthetician. Dr.Kapila Vatsyayan, the renowned scholar of Indian performing arts chaired the morning session, and Mr. J. Veeraraghavan, Director, Bhartiya Vidya Bhawan chaired the afternoon session. The seminar also turned out to be a lively affair with intellectuals, scholars, students and performers, participating in a spirit of collaboration. Dr. Kapila Vatsyayan, Dr. Sunil Kothari, Ms. Leela Venkataraman, Ms. Gowri Ramnarayan, Dr. Lakshmi Viswanathan, Ms. Sarada Hoffman and Dr. Avanthi Meduri presented their papers, on a variety of topics highlighting different facets of Rukmini Devi and her contributions.

All the arrangements for the seminar and the inauguration of the exhibition were undertaken by Shri Nagpal of ICES Ltd, New Delhi. His professional team, with knowledge of what needs to be done in exhibitions all over the world, lightened our burden. Prof. Arjun Appadurai, the internationally renowned scholar of culture studies from the US, was passing through, and made it a point to attend the exhibition. The "Who's Who" of Delhi were present and almost 500 people thronged to see the exhibition.

The eventful day came to an end with a dance performance by Ms. Paolomi Pandit, a student of Ms Sarada Hoffman. Appropriately, she presented a *Bharatanatyam* recital in the open air auditorium of IIC with wind and leaves keeping company which reminded us of Rukmini Devi conducting classes under the Banyan Tree in *Kala-kshetra.* The dinner that evening was graced with delegates who attended the conference and seminar, including celebrities like Geeta Chandran, Sonal Mansingh, Raja Reddy, Radha Reddy and others. Graced by Shri Nachiappa Swamigal and Subbudu, other renowned journalists and dance critics, the exhibition turned out to be a social event and became the talk of the town.

The Second Rukmini Devi Exhibition

The second Rukmini Devi exhibition was presented at the Indian Museum by Vishwa Bharati University in collaboration with Rabindra Bharati University, Kolkata and Calcutta University. Since much scholarly work remains to be done on Rukmini Devi, Dr. Avanthi suggested that the Centre for Contemporary Culture might consider instituting a Rukmini Devi Medal for Excellence in the Arts. Shri Atul Khanna, who designs the Medal for Gandhi Peace Prize, which is otherwise known as Nobel Prize of India, came forward to help us. The Rukmini Devi gold medal weighing 20 gms had Rukmini Devi's face etched on one side, and the name of the awardee, on the other. Shri Vivek Sardana designed a new set of portable panels for the exhibition at Kolkata, made of jute cloth, Manipuri mats, and *Kala-kshetra* saris providing a wonderful background to the rich variety of photographs. We were on the road and took the exhibition to Kolkata.

The Governor of West Bengal, Shri Viren Shah inaugurated the second Rukmini Devi exhibition at the Ashutosh Hall, Indian Museum, Kolkata and appreciated the effort which included a seminar which was inaugurated by Dr D.P. Chattopadhyaya, former Governor of Rajasthan. On this occasion, the first Rukmini Devi Medal for Excellence in Arts was awarded to Ms. Sarada Hoffman, one of the first students of *Kala-kshetra,* in recognition of her numerous and multifaceted services to Rukmini Devi's vision. Dr. Avanthi presented a one-woman storytelling performance entitled "Birds of the Banyan Tree," which endeavored to re-present Rukmini Devi's biographical story by situating it within a historical context.

The seminar, which followed the exhibition, discussed the aesthetic and educational visions of Rabindranath Tagore and Rukmini Devi. Professor Chintamani Kar, Dr. Ramaranjan Mukerjee, Dr. Swapan Kumar, Ms. Sarada Hoffman, Dr. Nemai Sadhan Bose, and Dr. Sitnashu Ray delivered thematic papers discussing the visions of Rukmini Devi and Rabindranath Tagore in a comparative perspective. The exhibition and seminar were much appreciated. We owe a debt of gratitude to Shri Jit Paul, the noted industrialist of Kolkata who made it possible to take the Rukmini Devi exhibition to Kolkata. The seminar was made possible by the Indian Museum and Viswa Bharati University. The scholarly article by Mr. Romani Main in the Times of India commemorating the exhibition summed up our efforts and the events in Kolkata.

On to Kuala Lumpur

After Kolkata, we began thinking of the exhibition as a travelling one and considered presenting it in Singapore and Malaysia. We were inspired to do this not just because Rukmini Devi looked to Bangkok and Bali for inspiration to create new masks and costumes for her dance-dramas, but also because scores of her students teach *Kala-kshetra Bharatanatyam* in Kuala Lumpur and Singapore. So, the next exhibition was featured in Kuala Lumpur. Courtesy Indian Airlines, we were able to transport the exhibits free of cost. Because of the kind intervention of Dr. Ramli Ibrahim, a well-known student of *Bharatanatyam* and Odissi and also an alumnus of *Kala-kshetra*, we were able to present the exhibition in the sylvan surroundings of his Sutra Theatre Academy which also features a wonderful gallery.

The Indian High Commission, co-sponsoring the exhibition made all the difference and ensured its success. Inaugurated by Dato' Seri S. Samy Vellu, the Honourable Minister for Public Works to the Government of Malaysia, and leader of the Indian community in Malaysia, the exhibition drew the attention of the press and art lovers of the city. Four dancers of *Kala-kshetra*, living in Malaysia came together to make the event memorable: Miss Shangitha Namasivayam, Apasara Ramgopal, Nadarajan Muniyandy, and Guna presented a wonderful dance recital. Girish Kumar Paniker, a well-known dancer and teacher from Singapore joined the group in Malaysia. The high point of the celebrations was the special guest performance by Prof. C.V. Chandrasekhar, who defied his years, to present special dance pieces and also a *Thillana*.

The Centre for Contemporary Culture, New Delhi conferred the second Rukmini Devi Medal for Excellence in the Arts on Professor Chandrasekhar and honoured him for spreading the vision of Rukmini Devi in North India, South Asia and the rest of the world. The event was featured as a noteworthy one. M/s Nirmala Raghavan, Rama Sankaran, Murlitharan, Leela Venkataraman, and Ooi Kok Chuen reviewed the events in leading newspapers both in Kuala Lumpur and New Delhi.

The exhibition was followed by a seminar chaired by well-known dance critic and writer, Leela Venkataraman. Girish Paniker, Professor Chandrasekhar, Ramli Ibrahim and Dr. Avanthi Meduri participated in the seminar. Students of *Kala-kshetra* also spoke about Rukmini Devi's legacy, which they carry in their memory and preserve in Malaysia.

From Kuala Lumpur, the exhibition went to Kulim in Penang and to Johore Baru, thanks to His Holiness Swami Brahmananda Saraswati of Dyana Ashram. Even in that distant town of Kulim in Penang there was a *Bharatanatyam* teacher in Smt. Sujata Nair, a former student of *Kala-kshetra.* The devotees of Dyana Ashram and the students of the dance school were the visitors to the exhibition. And once again Dance and Prayer coalesced in Kulim as in the days of *Kala-kshetra* in Adyar.

On to Singapore

If France sneezes Europe catches cold. So it is in Malaysia and Singapore. If Kuala Lumpur claps, Singapore welcomes. The exhibition went to Singapore via Penang. In Singapore, we were hosted by the Singapore Indian Fine Arts Society, a pioneering institution for *Bharatanatyam* and the classical dance forms, started in the 1950s. Over the last fifty years, SIFA has rendered yeoman service to the propagation of classical Indian dance and music in Singapore, and is recognized today as one of the premier global cultural organizations of the world. SIFA collaborated with Apsara Arts, which is managed by the Satyalingam couple, alumni of *Kala-kshetra,* to realize the event in Singapore. Satyalingam had learnt music from the great teachers who had taught at *Kala-kshetra* and his wife Neela Satyalingam had her dance training under the observing eye of Rukmini Devi in the 1960s. The Indian High Commission agreed to host the event.

The exhibition itself was presented for five days at "The Substation," recognized as a cosmopolitan hub of the cultural life of Singapore. Located on the famous Armenian Street, next to Orchard Street in Singapore, the exhibition did not just beckon the Indian but the entire multicultural society of Singapore in general. We featured a seminar entitled "*Bharatanatyam* in Multicultural Singapore: Issues and Challenges." Mr. Sommy Lim a *Bharatanatyam* dancer, playwright and actor, Dr. Chau Soo Pong, Southeast Asian theatre person, Mrs. Neela Satyalingam and Dr. Avanthi Meduri presented thematic papers on the global vision of Devi. Both the exhibition and the seminar were well attended and appreciated by all.

Print and electronic Media were responsive to the event and covered it extensively both in Malaysia and Singapore. The Astro Channel, well-known in Malaysia, telecast an interview on the exhibition, and spread the message of the exhibition to the Indian community and beyond. Publications like *Tamil Murasu*, *New Straits Times* and *The Malai Mail* carried extensive reports on the events and helped us carry the message and call the attention of the general public to the event. In Singapore, *Singai Sudar* joined in our efforts to propagate Rukmini's message.

Most importantly at the exhibition venue Satyalingam couple relived their early years of courtship and marriage, in *Kala-kshetra,* like school kids. They named each singer giant and dance maestro who were featured in the photographs. Was this not the purpose of the exhibition—to make the past come alive and live in the present ?

Now to the Young

The day the exhibition returned from Singapore, it had to go from the Indira Gandhi International Airport to New Era Public School, New Delhi for a National School Convention. The event was made possible by the Spic-Macay. The exhibition was mounted overnight, and Shri Vijay Kapoor, the Lt. Governor of New Delhi, inaugurated the exhibition. In a lecture demonstration that afternoon at the Sardar Patel Vidyalaya, New Delhi, Dr. Avanthi Meduri spoke with young children who were eager to learn about Rukmini Devi. It was a heart-warming experience to take the exhibition to young children. How innocent they were! They wanted to know when Rukmini Devi was going to perform in their school! They wanted to go to *Kala-kshetra* to see her and her great Banyan tree. Such innocent questions underscored the need for taking such exhibitions to the younger generation, and sharing with them some information about contemporary cultural history.

On to Sri Lanka: Colombo and Kandy

From Singapore, we backtracked and came home before proceeding to Sri Lanka. The exhibition was to be presented both in Colombo and Kandy. As interest in the exhibition gained, we realized that sponsors wanted the whole package including the exhibition, dance recitals, seminars and talks so that scholars, academicians, children, performers and common folk could participate in what was fast metamorphosising into a social event.

In Colombo, Our High Commissioner, His Excellency Nirupam Sen, carried forward the support extended by Mr. Gopalakrishan Gandhi and helped organize the exhibition in Colombo and Kandy. Indo-Srilanka Foundation provided the gallery and the exhibition was hosted in the India Cultural Centre. Mr. Karusena Kodiwakku, the Minister for Culture Government of Sri Lanka inaugurated the exhibition. From Colombo the exhibition travelled to Kandy and the Assistant High Commissioner hosted the exhibition in *Alliance Française.* Ramakrishna Mission, Colombo, Palayakkad Brothers, Kandy, Standard Chartered Bank, Colombo and Mr Maruti Kumar, Event Manager supported the exhibition each in their own way and made it a reality both in Colombo and Kandy.

Since Sri Lanka boasts of many dance students and dance schools of *Kala-kshetra* style *Bharatanatyam,* it was like a reunion of students around the photo exhibition in Colombo. Ms Padmini Dahanayake Ariyadasa and Ms Harini, the earliest students of Rukmini Devi in Colombo were proud to be present at the exhibition. These 70 plus senior citizens and former students even mooted a plan to discuss the possibility of establishing a network of *Kala-kshetra* students. But this meeting had to be cancelled because Smt. Bhavanaben D.Chikhalia, Minister of State for Culture, Government of India, who was visiting Sri Lanka, graciously agreed to visit the exhibition. In anticipation of her visit, security arrangements had to be put in place, which aborted the possibility of the *Kala-kshetra* student meet.

It was in Colombo that Rukmini Devi Arundale began rolling her dice again, and creating her own community for her travelling exhibition. A young lady student fascinated with the exhibition traveled all the way from Jaffna University by bus to come and see the exhibition. She had travelled 19 hours to reach the exhibition venue! This young college student was so enthused by the exhibits that she pleaded for a record of the exhibition. Sensing her unusual admiration for Rukmini Devi and dedication to Rukmini Devi and dance, we allowed her to video record sections of the exhibition. There are many more such incidents. Spontaneous communities created around the exhibition, both enabled and enriched our engagement with the travelling exhibition. To give an example. M/s Maruthi Kumar and Sivanandan who were strangers to us carried the burden of transporting the exhibition with enthusiasm. They materialized from nowhere because the head of the Ramakrishna Mission, Colombo had desired them to help us. Why? We do not know. But chance encounters and acquaintances like these made the exhibition go places in Colombo and Kandy.

Since we could not feature seminars in Sri Lanka, Dr. Meduri substituted by presenting the Rukmini Devi Memorial Lecture at the International Centre for Ethnic Studies, the British Council, Colombo, and Peradeniya University, Kandy. Mr. Senake Bandarnayake, the internationally famous archaeologist was instrumental in organizing the Memorial Lectures.

When it was not possible to organize dance recitals, Dr. Meduri stepped in and performed *Kuchipudi* dance recitals, endeavoring to trace Rukmini Devi's influence in this other classical style of dance. She gave a performance at Kathiresan hall, Colombo and Indian Cultural Centre, Colombo. The press in Colombo was particularly friendly. *The Sunday Mail, The Island, The Sunday Express, The Veerakesari, The Lankadeepa, The Daily News* and many other dailies pitched in to popularize the exhibition. The services of *Surya TV, FM Radio,* and *Sri Lanka Rupavahini* Corporation were a boon to us.

But the moving moment in Sri Lanka was the visit of the legendary Chitrasena to the exhibition. This 80 plus doyen is to Sri Lankan dance what Rukmini Devi was to *Bharatanatyam* in Chennai. Seeing the pictures and presentations he was moved to tears. He recalled the trials and tribulations of a revivalist in a conservative society. His tears were like the sprinkling of blessed rose-water on our show.

On to London

For almost a year, we had an open invitation from the Nehru Centre, London to present the Rukmini Devi travelling exhibition in the land of theatre and exhibitions. We were excited because the The Nehru Centre is an internationally acclaimed window on Indian culture and Mr. Girish Karnad, sensitive to arts and performers was the Director of the Centre who had promised to make the show a grand success. But how to make the whole thing happen? We had no money, no budget and we were only a fledgling NGO. But we were keen to cross the Seven Seas and take Rukmini Devi Exhibition to every country in the world. All we had was enthusiasm and commitment.

But the dream became a reality when Dr. Avanthi went to present a paper at the Federation of International Theatre Research Conference in Jaipur. Because Rukmini Devi was rolling her dice, Dr. Avanthi accidentally met with Professor Valerie Briginshaw, who teaches at the University College of Chichester in the UK. The latter became enamoured with the travelling exhibition and agreed to host a seminar as an initiative that would be partly sponsored by the Society for Dance Research, Arts and Humanities Research Board, United Kingdom, and the Cross-Cultural Centre for Music and Dance, University of Surrey. Air India stepped in to give wings to the exhibition, and enabled to move the photographs to London as free cargo. So the dream run took off again.

Lord Swraj Paul inaugurated the exhibition, which was a part of Rukmini Devi Week, and included dance and music recitals, seminar, illustrated lecture and memorial lecture. Rukmini Devi was rolling her dice to conjure up a week-long celebration in London. A day of Natyanjali (homage through dance) was curated by Ms. Pushkala Gopal, a well-known dance teacher of London. The Natyanjali featured performances by Ms. Chitra Sundaram, Mr. Unni Krishnan, Ms. Geetha Sridhar and Ms. Anusha. The most memorable part of the event was the presence of Ms. Anandhi Ramachandran, the daughter of Kalki R. Krishnamurthi a famous editor, writer and associate of Rukmini Devi. She was visiting London and generously spared time to participate in the celebrations. She helped Geetha Sridhar choreograph a short piece entitled "Kanmani Pirandhal," written by R. Sundaravalli set in Ragamalika. The number dramatized segments from Rukmini Devi's life. Geetha also performed the *Natabhairavi Tillana* on Rukmini Devi. Mr Unni Krishnan, an alumnus of *Kala-kshetra* rendered an Irish story of a man and his pet in Kathakali style. We all were reminded of Shri Ambu Pannickar's days in *Kala-kshetra,* and how Rukmini Devi had integrated *Kathakali* into her teaching of *Bharatanatyam.*

One evening was devoted to seminar discussions. Ms. Rani Moorthy from Rosa Productions, Manchester, Ms. Vena Ramphal from the School of Oriental and African Studies, Dr. Stacey Pricket, and Dr. Janet O' Shea from the University of Roehampton and Surrey presented papers. Dr.Avanthi Meduri chaired the session. Two evenings were devoted to a music recital by Mr. Prasanjit Gupta and to an illustrated talk by Ms. Shree Devi Nair Pal. Dr. Avanthi Meduri gave a memorial lecture on the last day. Sir Gulam Noon, a noted industrialist of London, presided over the valedictory function. It was a memorable week of celebrations to think back on the legacy of Rukmini Devi living vibrantly in India and in London, in the year of her centenary. And hundreds of visitors from all parts of the United Kingdom, representing several nationalities, paid homage to Rukmini Devi. To our great delight, the exhibition caught the attention of associates of Maria Montessori because Rukmini Devi propogated Montessori Education in India by inviting Madame Montessori to teach in *Kala-kshetra* as early as the 1930s.

On to Japan

After London, the exhibition moved to Japan, thanks to the efforts of the noted painter, Prof. Shin Kitamura. Shin Kitamura is well known in India as the Japanese painter who paints Indian scenes like the beaches of Orissa, and Mahabalipuram, the tribal women of Rajasthan and the fisher-women of the sea-front. Shin Kitamura presents his paintings under the caption "Love India" and has travelled it to New Delhi, Bangalore, Bhubaneswar, Kolkata and Chennai. Since he is a revered painter in Japan, and especially in Gunma Prefecture where he sits even as a Jury member, his interest in the Rukmini Devi travelling exhibition ensured public support for the exhibition.

The exhibition opened in the Miyogi gallery. The gallery is atop a hill and through the huge window panes one could see lush green hills on all four sides. The serenity of the hills, the wafting mist and the crowning glory of nature provided the perfect foil for the Rukmini Devi archive. Of the many galleries in which the exhibit had been presented, this was the best. The gallery not only had the best of exhibition space but also a wonderful human being in its Director General, Mr. Masayuki Shimizu, who galvanized the community of art lovers and his gallery staff to make the show a success.

When I was ushered into the gallery, I even wondered whether we had enough pictures to fill this wonderful gallery. But with the help of a hoard of artists, who responded to Kitamura and Shimizu, the best display of the exhibits was made possible. On the inaugural day, the Vice-President of the Association of Artists Nikkekai (Mr. Kuzuo Kawanishi) and the Mayor of Miyogi along with a representative from the Department of Education, Mr. Takeshi Satoh participated. More than 150 Japanese stood in perfect silence witnessing the inauguration of the exhibition declared open by the lighting of the traditional Indian lamp.

Since the Director of the gallery wanted to feature a dance performance along with the exhibition, Dr. Meduri stepped in along with Ms. Anuradha Ambalapadi to give a *Kuchipudi* dance recital. Dance recitals were also given at (Golf) Green Hotel, Jiangi Temple, Kurosewa Hospital, Gunma Prefecture office, etc. The performance at Jiangi Temple, was the most memorable because it was realized in the glittering presence of ornate gold statues of Buddha, on a temple stage made of shining teak, and bamboo curtains of the kind envisioned by Rukmini Devi in the 1930s. The head priest Mr. Ryoko Yoshi was an ardent admirer of the show. At the Prefecture office in Miyogi, the Governor paid rich tributes to Rukmini Devi, who had visited Japan in the 1960s. Everywhere, the speeches were given in Japanese and by the time we left the country, we were half proficient in the language. We were certainly grateful to Mr Ishi, a Japanese businessman, stationed in New Delhi, who travelled with us and helped us with his translations.

From Miyogi, the show travelled to Tokyo where the Indo-Japan Friendship Association was also celebrating its Centenary year. His Excellency, Mr. Aftab Seth, Indian Ambassador to Japan came up with a plan that would bring together both the Rukmini Devi Centenary and Indo-Japan

Friendship Association Centenary Celebrations. Shri APS Mani and Mr Sasaki, who were committee members of the Indo-Japan Friendship Association, put together a memorable event. Thus the Rukmini Devi travelling exhibition was held in the heart of the city of Tokyo, in the Cho-Yu-Ki ward building of the Tokyo Metropolitan Corporation. The architect of the display was Mr. Sasegawa, the Director of Mithila Museum in Tokamachi, Nigota.

It was surprising to see so many young Japanese throng to the exhibition. Amongst the visitors, there were many who had learnt *Bharatanatyam* in *Kala-kshetra.* In fact, on the last day of the exhibition Mr and Mrs. Sasaki presented a beautiful *Bharatanatyam* recital with four Japanese dancers. It was a traditional *Kala-kshetra* performance. The four Japanese *Bharatanatyam* students from *Kala-kshetra* gurukul gave wonderful performances to the lilting tunes of Tamil songs in Tokyo. It was a fitting international tribute to Rukmini Devi, a pan-Asian personality. Dr. Avanthi was called upon to present a feature from the Indian side, as a gesture of goodwill. So she and Ms Anuradha Ambalpadi presented two *Kuchipudi* recitals.

Two Japanese scholars presented memorial lectures. One of them who had actually translated *Silappadikaram* (The Tamil Epic of Anklet which is a famous Sangam literature discovered by Dr. U.V. Swaminatha Aiyar) into Japanese, described the many, many years in which he had lived in Chennai, and also recounted his numerous encounters with Rukmini Devi. Dr. Avanthi delivered her memorial lecture in the Sofia University, Tokyo to a group of young students. Prof. Valiath, who had completed his dissertation on Vaishnavism at the Madras University, and was serving as Professor in the Sofia University, organized the lecture. He also translated the lecture to the young students who were inspired by the work of Rukmini Devi and her band of dance maestros and music wizards.

The visitors to the exhibition paid the greatest tribute to the memory of Rukmini Devi by carefully going through the details in every panel and every photograph. Some even viewed the photographs through binoculars to catch a glimpse of the great beauty of yesteryears. The exhibition and celebrations in Tokyo was also made possible, amongst others, by Air India. Our thanks to Mr. Roy Paul, Secretary, Civil Aviation, Government of India.

On to Australia

If Japan had been reached, Australia could not be far off. The tryst with Australia became a reality because of the tremendous efforts of Ms. Mano Navoratnam. Ms. Mano is a very enthusiastic social activist who had met us in Colombo when she had visited the exhibition at the Indian Cultural Centre. She was bewitched with the beauty of *Bharatanatyam* and the splendour of Rukmini Devi's vision, and invited the exhibition to Australia. She pursued her initial invitation, extended in Colombo, to its finality when we reached Melbourne. Equally important is the hand of God extended through Mrs. Rathi Vinay Jha, Secretary, Ministry of Tourism, Government of India, who made the trip possible.

The exhibition was opened in Monash University in Drama, Theatre and Performing Arts Centre. It was also a community show for Indian expatriates and Sri Lankan Tamils. The local *Bharatanatyam* dance schools also sent their teachers and students. Some of them even recalled the visit of Rukmini Devi to the Adelaide Festival in 1963.

From Monash, the exhibition travelled to the University of Melbourne. It was presented in Yasuko Hiraka Myer Room at the Sidney Myer Asia Centre, University of Melbourne. Mr. Jim was the Coordinator. As in Miyogi, the gallery space at the Sidney Myer Hall was expansive, well lit, and a great huge square hall. The Rukmini Devi archive seemed to have found an appropriate venue for display. Dr. Avanthi Meduri delivered the sixth memorial lecture in the presence of the

Consul General of India, Melbourne. As in other places, Rukmini Devi materialized two young Australian friends who most cheerfully shouldered the responsibilities. Without the help of Mr. Prasan Kumar, marketing manager Cadbury's and Mr. Vasan, Member of Parliament, whom we met for the first time in Australia, the exhibition would not have been such a success.

Back Home

But we are happy that the archive was on display within India during the famous December Season of Dance and Music at Chennai. Kartik Fine Arts hosted the exhibition and the seminar at the Bharatiya Vidya Bhavan Auditorium, Chennai. On that occasion, the third Rukmini Devi Medal for Excellence in Arts was conferred on Ms. Krishnaveni Lakshmanan, the former principal of *Kala-kshetra.* She is an illustrious student of Rukmini Devi and has participated in almost all her Dance Dramas. She has lived the life of a *Kalakshetra* alumni and dedicated her life to the vision of Rukmini Devi. The highlight of the exhibition was a Sanskrit performance on Rukmini Devi choreographed by Smt. Krishnaveni Lakshmanan. The papers at the seminar were presented amongst others by Dr. Radha Burnier, the International President of the Theosophical Society, Dr. Mrinalini Sarabhai of the Darpan Academy Ahmedabad, Dr. Lakshmi Viswanthan and Dr. Avanthi Meduri. A performance in home ground is what a performer looks for. An exhibition is also a performance and to present it in the home ground, from which it had sprung, is another dream come true.

The Future

Since the exhibition has gone to so many world capitals, we want to take it to UNESCO, United States, Indonesia and Thailand. That is the dream of tomorrow. When will that tomorrow be? Next year, perhaps? For now, the Rukmini Devi archive needs to rest.

This is the saga of a fledgling voluntary organisation pushed into performing a Himalayan task. The story of David and Goliath? Re-visiting the history of one of the great cultural revivalists of India was without doubt a daunting task. Rukmini Devi, besides, was not just a local personality. She worked for global causes, is the subject of research in several prestigious universities, and her students teach *Kala-kshetra Bharatanatyam* in the far corners of the globe. We were perhaps naive in presuming that the history of Rukmini Devi, her dance dramas, her stage mediations, her building of *Kala-kshetra,* her global and national fame, will surpass all difficulties. Travelling exhibition is a new idea in India. But the idea is catching on in India. We were pioneers indeed!

As a newly established non-governmental voluntary organisation, we did not qualify for any government grant and did not get a rupee to date. We had no office, no peon and no stenographer. But the exhibition went from New Delhi, to Kolkata, to Singapore, to Kuala Lumpur, to Penang, to Colombo and Kandy, to Tokyo, and Miyogi to London, and to Melbourne. Several scholars, historians, performers and students gathered around the exhibition. High Commissioners and Ambassadors, Ministers and Industrialists joined us in the celebrations. Thais, Koreans, Japanese, British, Australians, French, Chinese, Malays, Sri Lankans, Singaporeans and Indians have witnessed the shows in hundreds and filled up our Visitors' Book. Elderly people came with binoculars to study minute details of the exhibition; the young and youthful came with a smile and lit up the halls of the exhibition. This was a dream run, and out of this world. It was divined indeed!

PART - II

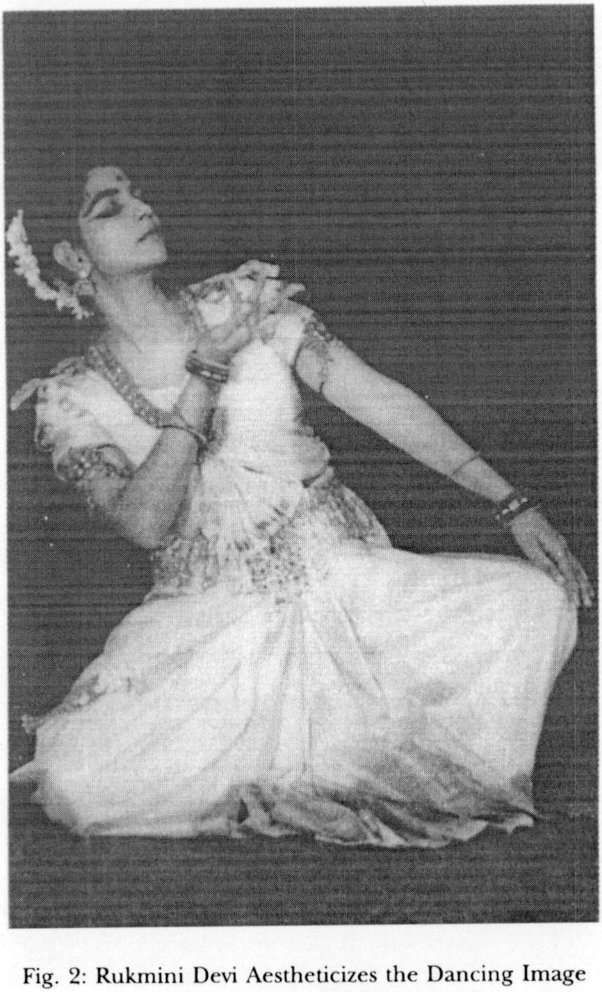

Fig. 2: Rukmini Devi Aestheticizes the Dancing Image

(Photo: C.T. Nachiappan archive)

CHAPTER 3

RUKMINI DEVI AS A TEACHER, GUIDE AND MOTHER

Kapila Vatsyayan

My emotions, feelings and experiences clash deeply with my intellectual and analytical inclinations today. How do I, and with what authority, claim and experience, talk about my mother? Rukmini Devi was a teacher, guide and surrogate mother to me. At that level, the kind of communication that takes place is silent, participatory, and does not rest on explicit articulation but is communicated through the act of silence alone. I would like to emphasize that difference. That is one aspect.

I have had the great privilege of having several mothers in my life. I shall not be autobiographical beyond this, except one last statement, which I shall make later. But amongst those I want to remember are my second mother Kamaladevi Chattopadhyaya and the third, my biological mother. It is these three women in their own unique ways and working in manifold domains, intersecting, disagreeing and agreeing, who broke paths which were not contained, and not thought of in terms of 'box categories'. I want to say that it is this unselfconscious breaking of paths that this generation stood for. They were, unlike modernists or traditionalists, not motivated by thoughts, they just acted.

As we go along, perhaps we should keep in mind the general milieu and, in particular, the intellectual dimensions of that period. I would also like to draw attention to the recent writings on that period, from 1928 to about 1947. In the intellectual discourses there has been a great deal of bashing of the nationalist – ranging from Kamaladevi to Rukmini Devi, Stella Kramrisch to A. K. Coomaraswamy, all of them being branded as people who were constructing a nationalist discourse. That is the other end of a pendulum.

Since that was my childhood, I can tell you about it, whatever may be the opinion of the people who are engaged in the post-modern discourse on the subject (and I have read that literature with care). I want to say very humbly, but most sincerely, that for all these people, this was a search for identity and at no point at all was it merely an intellectual stance or for that matter ideology. I am someone who has known all these people personally and I want this on record today, because there has been so much written of late on the unnecessary nationalist discourse from which a reconstruction unrelated to reality is being made and, in particular, in the political arena. But these women, whether they were in the social fields or in the arts, were exploring different levels. Some like Rukmini Devi returned as pilgrims, thanks to Anna Pavlova (whom I hope we shall honour one day for giving us back our dance and three Indians). Also, the search was one which was not individual or in isolation, nor was it an external movement, and that distinction has to be made.

It is not as if what Tagore did during the same period had not influenced Rukmini Devi in what she did. Again, it was not as if what Vallathol did, meant that Rukmini Devi would follow by saying 'let me also try something'. That happened in the post-independence period, not in the pre-independent era. Nor was the search motivated by personal ambition. For the preceding generation it was in the process of exploration that they got their insight. Illumination came to them through the scattered fragments of a mirror. And they had to piece together that mirror. They knew that what they had were the pieces. Through an enthusiastic but tortuous journey they put it together – whether they merely put it together or they put it in a kaleidoscope to make new images, I cannot say with certainty.

This exploration was not restricted to the fields of music and dance; it was also happening in the fields of literature, painting and the crafts. It was as if those who had been the inheritors of a tradition had found pieces of the tradition. Tradition, we all know, is conservative in some respects, but it also flows. These people possessed a sensibility which enabled them to piece together and rejuvenate a tradition, so that it could breath in open spaces. No doubt they were important constituents of the social, cultural, political and historically contextualized space. It is from the ground of their times that they emerged. Just as students of a particular art get understandably focused on form and technique and a little bit on content, the larger manure which sustains the ground, the tree and its organic growth is not visible, it is the flower that is seen and not the process. Critical appraisal of the period has overlooked or certainly slurred over these aspects.

The third dimension that I would like to speak about which emerges from this is dance, undoubtedly dance; the body, undoubtedly the body and the body alone and all the discourse involving the removing of the dance from the context of the temple and everything that has been written, rewritten including the critique on the history of the *devadasis* or the maharis and so on. What is involved in all this is another kind of discourse that relates at a much deeper philosophic level, to attitudes towards the body and deals with where the dance is located – whether in the context of the temple or outside it. Therefore, the double bind and the paradox of dissociating an art from its immediate context with its sociological background, but retaining the content of dance outside the sociological religious milieu in which it was nurtured, that was the challenge; a challenge of the deepest kind. That which was performed at the level of feeling and emotion was then given an intellectual dimension and then a platform. Sahitya became important in order to sustain the dance; the musical score became important and thus we enter the question of technique.

I cannot elucidate here the changes which ensured from this re-location of space. Instead, I would like to share two reminiscences. I saw Rukmini Devi in 1947 in performance of the *Kumarasambhavam.* I will never forget that curtain and those two feet. As that curtain went up, it was as if Parvathi had come to the earth. Rukmini Devi in that static but fully empowered pose of Parvathi was electrifying. She stood as icon; and soon the icon became the body and flesh. Kalidasa's poem became alive, and Rukmini Devi a legend. This was the beginning of a new journey for my generation. From that day to the many years which followed, there was learning, participation, much sharing, and some disagreements, altogether most enriching. All I can say is that I am grateful and deeply indebted. A book could be written on the many levels of the communication. This is not the occasion even for a summary.

Let me confine myself to significant disagreements. Many decades after *Bharata Natyam* and its dancers had travelled away from both the temple and even *Kalakshetra,* it occurred to me that it was time to relocate the dance in the precincts of the temple. Of course, the *devadasis* were banned, and the Act was not repealed. Kamaladevi, Rukmini Devi and my mother were there as guarding spirits. It was decided to request dancers to dance in the *Tillai* hall. Yamini and Chitra agreed. When I spoke about my intention there was a strong negative response from Kamaladevi and my mother who said, 'you are mad', 'you are not my daughter'. Rukmini Devi said to me, 'is that what I taught you all these years, Kapila? I thought you might even be my successor here and yet you want to go to *Chidambaram* and make them dance as '*seva*', '*nritya seva*'. I said, 'but their dance is all about *Tillai,* and what is *Natanam Adinar;* why should they not have an experience of dancing in *Chidambaram*? This I believe will reconnect them to the source'. There was so much love that there was no question of doubt in anyone's motivations. But I think this was one of the great learning experiences.

All my three mothers were against taking the dance back to the temple. My mother said, 'is that why I started a school in Delhi when no one danced? And you want to go back to where we rescued it from?' Kamaladevi said, 'well, you happen to be Vice-President of the Sangeet Natak Akademi and you can do this, but I am not going, I shall not be seen dead anywhere near it. I am ringing up Rukmini Devi and you should first go and talk to her' - which I did. I tried to convince her. I said, "Athai, I am not suggesting that we attach ourselves to the temples and become part of the whole *Agraharam* and *Devasthanam* system and revive the *devadasi* system. Nor do I intend it as a show. I only ask for them to have that experience, so that wherever they dance it would be Siva as *Nataraja* which would inspire them".

The initiative was a success, altogether too much of a success. The *Arudra* festival became an annual festival. Now it was my turn to disagree with other colleagues and associates. Dancers from all parts of India came. Once a group from Manipur was invited. I love *Manipuri* dance and am a disciple of the great Guru Amobi Singh. I thought it was inappropriate to have a *Manipuri* rasa revolving around Nataraja. Again there were protests. 'Now what has come of her? She is inflexible and conservative.' I argued that I want *Manipuri* in the courtyard of the Govindaji temple and even other Vaishnava sites, but not in Chidambaram. No one understood, they still don't. I wanted to ensure the integrity of each religio-cultural site. Authenticity of experience could only be thus possible.

As for the path finders in the context of *Chidambaram*, I had said, 'You were right when you did it, I am right when I am doing it. That dance which was taken out of the temple has also faced the dangers of dissociating the dancers from the cultural context and thus essence. I want them to reconnect. This is a challenging task. Perhaps an experience of context will enable them to reconnect, even when they dance on urban stages'.

Rukmini Devi, aside from her many other contributions, was chiefly an institution builder. She treated it as not merely a finite structure with a linear progressive movement. Her insistence was on organic growth. She revived textiles; she collected great musicians; was also instrumental in bringing in the U. S. Swaminatha Aiyar Library, among other efforts. The institution thus became a confluence of many streams of the tradition, which had the possibility of revitalisation.

And that brings me to my conclusion. What is the relationship of life and dance for a woman with a holistic vision that was Rukmini Devi. The difference is not whether she came from Theosophy, or some other larger background of values. What matters is the values that this body holds and manifests in time, and the values which the body communicates. Not through the *Sahitya,* not through the great music and not through the *Adavus,* the *Thirmanams* and the *Jathis* and so on. It is communicated through what one is, through what you are. And in this communication is the moment of revelation. Rukmini Devi was life that was whole, whether as *Pranimitra* or a social reformer, as an institution-builder or an educationist; or above all a 'dancer' who facilitated the flow of a tradition into 'contemporaneity' of another kind.

(Dr. Kapila Vatsyayan delivered this keynote address at the the first Rukmini Devi National Seminar, organized by the *Centre for Contemporary Culture,* in New Delhi in 2001.)

CHAPTER 4

RUKMINI DEVI AS A THEOSOPHIST

Radha Burnier

Madame Blavatsky wrote: "Any person of average intellectual capacities, and a leaning towards the metaphysical of pure, unselfish life, who finds more joy in helping his neighbour than in receiving help himself, one who is ever ready to sacrifice his own pleasures for the sake of other people and who loves Truth, Goodness and Wisdom for their own sake, not for the benefit they may confer – is a Theosophist." But ordinarily speaking, the word 'Theosophist' is equated with being a member of the Theosophical Society, although the above description may not apply to every member. In between these two concepts of a Theosophist there can be another definition, based on the literal meaning of the word 'Theosophy', which is 'Divine Wisdom'. Thus, one may say that a person who sincerely endeavours to journey towards Divine Wisdom, and who tries to live according to the principles of the Wisdom Teachings as they have been given in many ages, by many sages and holy men all over the world, is a Theosophist. I believe Rukmini Devi tried to live, to the best of her ability according to the principles of the Ancient Wisdom teachings.

Her father, Sri A. Nilakantha Shastry, was an engineer in government service, and a learned man. He was deeply attracted by the liberal and universal attitudes promoted by the Theosophical Society, after having come into contact with the Founders of the Theosophical Society, namely Madame H.P. Blavatsky and Colonel H.S. Olcott. In order to be closer to the Headquarters of the Society at Adyar, he built a house in the proximity of the Society's estate. His four sons and four daughters were all, in their own way, greatly influenced by Theosophical ideas and the Theosophical Society. The older son, N. Sri Ram, dedicated his whole life to the Society's work and was its President for twenty years.

Rukmini, fifteen years younger, had the privilege of marrying G.S. Arundale, then an ardent Lieutenant of Annie Besant in her varied activities and hence was drawn into the hub of theosophical work and thinking. She was undoubtedly under the lifelong influence not only of Mr. Arundale, but of those who were his elders and leaders, like Annie Besant and C.W. Leadbeater. She was not very much given to the study of the Theosophical philosophy but imbibed its fundamentals from the above mentioned eminent Theosophists and the worldwide contacts she made in the Theosophical world, even when she was quite young by virtue of her life with Mr. Arundale. Towards the middle of her life, she turned to promoting the artistic and cultural traditions of India. It was part of the theosophical view that India had a great message to give, to the entire world, and that the renaissance of India's great cultural and spiritual tradition and values would lay the foundation for this ancient land to play a larger role in the upliftment of all humanity. This led Rukmini Devi to advocate with passion the practice of ahimsa and compassion towards animals and all lesser creatures, thus reflecting in practice the indivisible unity of life, the most fundamental principle and truth embodied in Theosophy. Whatever Rukmini Devi did had a background of the basic theosophical approach to life. These may be briefly listed as (1) universality, which meant absence of prejudice on the basis of nationality, race, religion and so forth, (2) humanitarianism, concerned with the spiritual upliftment of the human consciousness to a state of unity and harmony, (3) dedication to the ideals of compassion and service, (4) recognizing the evolutionary process as a blossoming of consciousness, under the karmic or moral laws of the Universe, and lastly (5) devotion to the liberated beings, who guide humanity towards the light.

George Arundale took office as President of the worldwide Theosophical Society in 1934 after the passing away of Annie Besant. Soon after he encouraged the formation of a Young Theosophists Organization, and Rukmini Devi became its President. Sending a message to Young Theosophists, Rukmini Devi wrote: "To be truly Indian is to be truly international, so none of us must forget the best of our civilization and to live it in our daily lives." This statement implies, that if we do not have an international spirit, then we are not true to our own culture and civilization. Indian culture was always eclectic, welcoming and embracing a variety of religious, philosophical and other points of view. Rukmini Devi's statement of the 1930s given above is most relevant to the situation in India today.

The now famous *Kalakshetra* was named 'The International Academy of the Arts', when it was first inaugurated in 1936, and its two Objects were:

1. To emphasise the essential Unity of all true Art;
2. To work for the recognition of the Arts, as inherent in effective individual, national and religious growth.

She regarded Art 'To be an expression of the power of Universal Life'. Her ideals were high. In one of her earlier lectures, she said, "Just as each one of us should be a real Theosophist, so should each one of us also be a real artist in the various details of living." Rukmini Devi interpreted the Theosophical concept that responding to beauty is a way of uplifting the human consciousness to a state of Unity, as a means of reforming human society. To quote her again, "I feel sure that through Art we can realize more happiness for the world. If we live ugly lives, those around us will necessarily be ugly too. I very strongly feel that cruelty is one of the worst forms in which ugliness expresses itself."

Many persons have appreciated the breaking of age-old conventions by Rukmini Devi, without which the ancient art of *Bharatanatyam* could not have been popularized and made known in the world. It required tremendous initiative and boldness for a Brahman lady in the early part of the 20th century specially when she was below the age of thirty to take lessons from a professional like Gowri Amma or a Nattuvanar like Meenakshi Sundram Pillai. Rukmini Devi was able to do it because every Theosophist of eminence has been a rebel, refusing to accept meaningless conventions and blindly proceeding on ruts of custom. Madame Blavatsky, Founder of the Theosophical Society had such a rebellious spirit that the world reviled her for sins she did not commit. Annie Besant broke from the church, in spite of being deeply religious, when the church insisted that she should ask no questions but simply obey. She had to suffer poverty and abuse as a result. The Theosophical spirit involves questioning superstitions, empty beliefs and out-worn conventions. Rukmini Devi's eldest brother, Sri Ram, (to whom reference has already been made), was regarded in his youth and middle age as a 'black sheep' because he broke caste restrictions, encouraged his mother not to shave her head when she was widowed or wear widow's weeds. There was thus a tradition within the Theosophical Society of a progressive reformist attitude.

Rukmini Devi was supported by Mr Arundale, her family and the membership of the Theosophical Society when she took the necessary steps to reclaim art forms, particularly dance, from the disgrace into which it had fallen. If she had been trapped in an orthodox Brahman family and marriage, the doors of opportunity would have been shut to her. It was only because she was a Theosophist among Theosophists that her talents and ardour were fulfilled.

Not only did she dare to perform in public, but she also refined the art, pruning it of its crudities. Personally I can remember the very early days of *Kalakshetra* when no students were forthcoming, except myself and Leelavati, both from Theosophical families. It required not only faith and persistence but also moral and other forms of support from Theosophists for Rukmini Devi to proceed on.

In conclusion, it may not be far wrong to say that the Rukmini Devi who is known to the world would not have existed if she had not been a Theosophist.

(This paper was delivered at the Rukmini Devi National Seminar, organized by the *Centre for Contemporary Culture* at Chennai in 2003.)

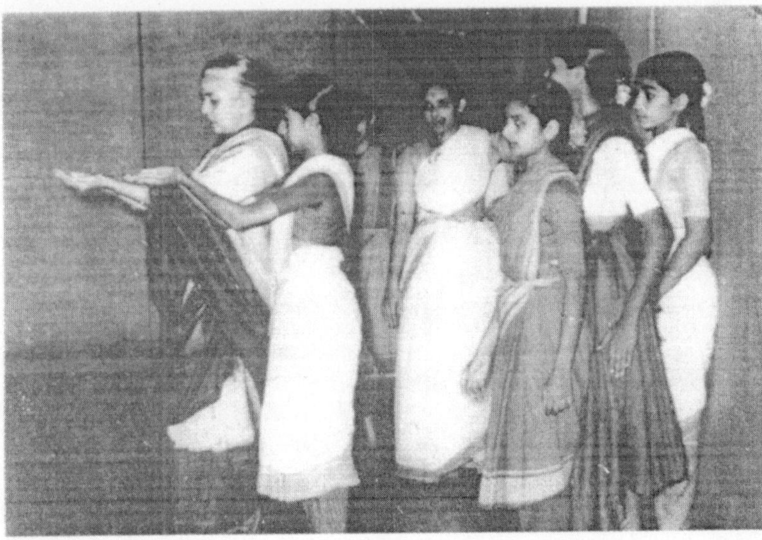

Fig. 3: Rukmini Devi Teaching Dance in Kalakshetra

(Photo: C.T. Nachiappan archive)

CHAPTER 5

RUKMINI DEVI AND ANIMAL WELFARE

Chinny Krishna & Maneka Gandhi

In this centenary year of Rukmini Devi, much has been written and published about her artistic work, especially her work at *Kalakshetra.* Hardly anything has been mentioned about the other passion in her life – animal welfare.

The importance Rukmini Devi gave to animal welfare is aptly summed up in her address to the First National Conference on Animal Welfare in 1971 where she said; "People have often said to me 'What kind of work will you retire from when you are no longer able to carry on?' I can sincerely say that I can retire from all my work except animal welfare because even when there is a little bit of strength in me it would be impossible to pass by on the road and see an animal in distress without feeling that I should do something for it." That she meant every word was proved when she asked that a letter be sent in her name to the District Governor of the Lions International on February 2, 1986, where she wrote: "I am delighted to learn from today's paper that you have organized a seminar on People Caring for Animals which is to be inaugurated this morning by Shri P. Chidambaram at Rani Seethai Hall. I wish I could be there with all of you. Though I am unable to be present, my heart is there with you. With my best wishes. Rukmini Devi." Nothing very special one may feel till you learn that she had asked for this message to be sent while she was in the Intensive Care Unit of a hospital where she had been admitted two weeks earlier and where she passed away after a few days.

In 1952, when she was a Member of the Rajya Sabha, she introduced a private member's bill to replace the existing Prevention of Cruelty to Animals Act of 1890. Her impassioned speech in 1954 when the Bill was placed before the House led to Pandit Jawaharlal Nehru responding by saying: "Of course, it is as well for us, absolutely right for us, to consider the question of preventing any cruelty to animals, not only because of the animals themselves but much more so, as the Honourable member said, because of the human beings involved in it. It is a debasing thing for the person who indulges in this cruelty. If we go back to the history of civilization, it has been one of struggle and one of growth of the idea of compassion. I entirely agree with the Hon'ble member the Mover that one test of civilization – a very major test – is the growth of this feeling and practice of compassion." Pandit Nehru set up a Committee to go into the matter and also requested Rukmini Devi to withdraw her Bill stating that it would be the pleasure of his Government to take up such an important matter. Rukmini Devi graciously withdrew her Bill immediately and a similar Bill was later introduced by the Government.

It was thus that the Prevention of Cruelty to Animals Act, 1960, came into being. For the first time, subjects such as animals in research and performing animals were covered by the Act and a statutory body, the Animal Welfare Board of India (AWBI), came into existence to oversee the animal welfare work in the country and to recommend to the Government various measures to prevent cruelty to and promote the welfare of animals. India is the only country in the world to have such a Board.

One of the provisions of the Act was that whenever found necessary and on the recommendation of the Board, a committee would be set up to look into the use of animals in research and ensure that the research was being done as per the stipulations contained in the Act. In 1964, the AWBI asked that this Committee be set up and the first Committee for the Purpose of Control and Supervision of Experiments on Animals (CPCSEA) was formed with Shri Kamal Nayan Bajaj, MP, as its Chairman.

Rukmini Devi had stated in the Rajya Sabha in 1954 while introducing her Bill that "If people knew the cruelties that really exist in the laboratories, I am sure that many people would shrink from taking certain types of medicines and from tolerating the practice of vivisection. These cruelties can be proved. I can prove it by the statements of the vivisectors themselves. Also, I have met a number of doctors who have personally vivisected, and who have given it up. There is no doubt that these cruelties are going on, and therefore I have said that there should be no exports of animals for vivisection and also that vivisection should be abolished in India." How correct she was can be gauged from the findings of the first CPCSEA, which consisted mainly of the Heads of many Government animal-using laboratories.

In their first report on "Animal Experimentation" they wrote, "Vivisection, or animal experimentation, is one of the most inhuman cruelties against animals, which are being perpetrated in the world to-day. The object of these experiments is said to be in order to advance scientific knowledge, and to undertake research to save or prolong human or animal life and alleviate suffering. In the name of science, however, animals are made to endure the most barbaric tortures ever invented by the human brain, often lasting over long periods and without any sort of anaesthetic. Animals are frozen, boiled, have electric currents passed through their brains or are driven insane, all in an insatiable 'quest for knowledge', which can do nothing whatever to benefit the human race. Many experiments which are successful with animals are a complete failure when applied to human beings. Vested interests, however, make it necessary for the experiments to continue, although what they are showing may be completely useless, or already known. Yet, after this indictment, no follow up was done except to issue a notification containing rules that were never implemented and for the transgression of which no penalties were stated.

Rukmini Devi also campaigned tirelessly to ban the use of animals in circuses; her efforts created awareness of the cruelties involved in training performing animals. She also demanded a ban on the sacrifice of animals in the name of religion, something that is seeing its fruition today. A crusading vegetarian, she was President of the Indian Vegetarian Congress for several years. Her aggressive promotion of this noble ideal made it a goal for all animal welfare workers.

Rukmini Devi was a woman ahead of her times. Her compassion made her the voice of the voiceless, the friend of the animal kingdom. If animal welfare is accepted, even fashionable, today, it is solely her efforts and crusade in the early years of independence that have made it possible. It is important to remember this important contribution of a creative artist as we remember her birth centenary.

In 1964, when the Blue Cross of India proposed that the age old method of trying to control the street dog population by catching and killing them would never work and that the only sensible method was by a proper catch-sterilize-vaccinate and release programme, Rukmini Devi was the only major supporter they had. In 1966, she signed an MOU with the Bombay Municipal Corporation to stop the killing and sterilize all the male dogs caught by them. While this was never implemented after a brief initial spell, it was done a quarter of a century before the WHO came out with their guidelines on stray dog management which stated that only a proper Animal Birth Control program coupled with vaccination against rabies could control the street dog population and bring down the incidence of rabies in human beings.

CHAPTER 6

RUKMINI DEVI: THE DIVINE DANCER

R. Nagaswamy

The history of Tamilnadu, rather the history of India, will never be complete without a reference to this extraordinary personality – Rukmini Devi, a shining example of Indian womanhood. She belonged to the line of *Maitreyi* of vedic age, who were visionaries and immortals. Rukmini Devi was indeed an immortal sage of India, who lived amidst us and showed us what life is meant to be. It is well known that she established *"Kala-kshetra"* at Madras as an institution of dance and music. But for her it was not another institution to train young boys and girls in dance and music to earn their livelihood or material gain. Her vision of *Kala-kshetra* was larger.

Kshetra, in the Hindu context, suggests a sacred space, an abode of divinity, purity and aesthetic environment, not merely to look at but to experience supreme joy on earth. *Siva-kshetra* or a *Vishnu-kshetra* is a space, for instance, where men go on pilgrimage, to experience godliness on earth. This space is different from what we in modern times describe as 'cultural tourism', a descriptive category that can hardly capture what the term *kshetra* means in the Indian context. A centre of cultural tourism is a western notion that is meant to offer material satisfaction while *Kshetra* is essentially meant to elevate human consciousness to a divine level. A visit to a *kshetra* is a visit to God consciousness. Rukmini Devi had deliberated and reflected on these ideals long before naming her institution a *kshetra.* True to her personality, she made it a *Kala-kshetra* – a sacred place of aesthetic becoming. *Kala* is not performing arts but that sphere of aesthetic experience. Indian tradition considered aesthetic experience as – *'rasa - aasvaadana'* as the supreme experience of aesthetic life. The Upanishads declare that aesthetic joy is God itself – '*Raso vai saha*', Rukmini Devi was convinced that every step in music, dance or life led to that experience of beauty and blossoming. The word *kshetra* also meant a temple. By building *Kalạ-kshetra,* she built a "temple of art" as *Kshetra* also refers to a sanctified space. The space occupied by the present *Kala-kshetra* – though now limited by physical boundaries, was an unbounded space for the arts, where everything was steeped in divinity for Rukmini Devi.

As a classical Indian dancer, she visualized and experienced the world as the cosmic dance of Siva himself. The Indian tradition divides dance broadly into four aspects called the four *abhinayas.* Every dancer salutes the Supreme with the following verse:

> *aangikam bhuvanam yasya vacikam sarva ·vangmayam*
> *aaharyam candra taaradi tam mumah saattvikam sivam*

Translated it means: I salute that *Siva* the Supremely auspicious, for whom the whole world is, suggestive limbs *(Aangika)*; all forms of speech, suggestive Music *(Vaacika)*; all the celestials luminaries constituting suggesting decorative costumes (*aahaarya*) and peaceful aesthetics (*saattvika),* the suggestive emotions.

This verse graphically portrays the philosophy of dance through bodily movements *(aangika abhinaya)*, musical articulation (*Vactka abhinaya)* colours and costumes pleasing the soul (*aahaarya abhinaya*), and finally the emotive peaceful content (*saattvika abhinaya*). The philosophy encapsulated in the verse cited above is derived from nature and projected magnificently into Godhood, summing up in a poetic way all that dance stands for today.

Only a poet-philosopher could visualize and experience

such sublime poetry for us and Rukmini Devi was a poet-philosopher of this ancient tradition. She was convinced that all the planets including earth, and the celestial luminaries like the stars remain suspended in a vast expansive space, rising and falling rhythmically in consonance with cosmic time. Uncoordinated movements in space cause uneasy vibrations, resulting in calamities, similar to what one experiences in beholding a dance, described as an "*apa-taal*" or "*apa-sabda*". Only a supreme dancer could visualize the cosmic movement of time in terms of dance. Rukmini Devi was one who did perceive the movement of dance as encapsulating the unfolding of cosmic time.

Rukmini Devi conceived *Kala-kshetra* as the *anga* and *aangika* of the world of Art. She was not one who could build few structures to provide shelter for training, but visualized her *kshetra* appropriately with trees, creepers, flowers, ponds, and birds as the *aahaarya* – the colour and attire of that *kshetra.* She herself enjoyed every tree, creeper, leaves and flowers growing within *Kala-kshetra.* I have seen how on several occasions she would feel hurt if a branch of a tree had to be cut because the trees and plants were living companions for her. The plants and trees were like the natural and beautiful limbs of the *Kshetra* akin themselves to the natural limbs of a beautiful dancer. She thus paid a great deal of attention to the environment in *Kala-kshetra:* designed the buildings in which classes would be held, held prayer and lecture meetings under the huge banyan tree, maintaining all the time that the teaching inside the *Kshetra* should reflect Indian classical ethos and harmonise with nature and the environment of *Kala-kshetra.* The buildings in the *ksehtra* were like the costume and jewellery that adorned the body of a beautiful dancing girl. The devoted students of art and experienced teachers moving around *Kala-kshetra* campus, learning dance, music, theory of dance, etc, were the '*praanas*', the vital breath and the soul of *Kala-kshetra,* the sacred body of arts *Kala-kshetra* was not only a temple of music and dance, but also painting, weaving and crafts.

Since Rukmini Devi was sensitive to harmonious colours, having an instinctive aversion towards gaudy, sparkling and glamorous colours, she created what is called "*Kalakshetra* sarees" that attracted women of cultivated taste. Over the years, she collected both silk and cotton sarees, which not only exhibit serenity but also extraordinary variety. The sarees show how, not long ago, women had very great taste for colours and designs and that sense has dwindled in recent years. Luckily the sarees she collected are still preserved in the *Kala-kshetra* collection and show us her personality. Rukmini Devi believed that both on stage and in life, men and women should pay attention to their dress and display their aesthetic taste. In all her productions, from simple hangings to elaborate scene settings, one could experience serene and subdued colours and designs.

Similarly with jewellery. She never looked at jewellery as a craft, nor valued it for its precious metal and gems. She looked at it as exquisite art, contributing to the totality of aesthetic taste. She did have a very good collection of artistic jewellery of enormous beauty and value. But soon after her demise, her noble successor Sankara Menon was assaulted and Rukmini Devi's jewellery, cherished and preserved when she was alive, disappeared without a trace.

I have had the privilege of taking highly cultured men to *Kala-kshetra*. As one walked through the campus, moved through the trees, creepers and flowers, we could listen to raga *aalaapanas* being taught in a hut and the sweet music of the *Veena* emanating from another hut. As one walked along, the singing echoed through the woods and the *jathis* emanating from the feet of girls and boys learning dance, blended harmoniously with the sound of cuckoos and parrots, fluttering from the tender branches of the trees. Moved by this unforgettable experience, I have heard several dignitaries, exclaim spontaneously "Oh! What an experience! What an environment! I wish we had such an institution amongst us! I must return to this place to spend more time here." A visit to *Kala-kshetra* offered a total aesthetic experience.

If walking through *Kala-kshetra* gave the visitor an immense feeling of aesthetic pleasure and fullness, witnessing Rukmini Devi's dance drama productions offered another kind of aesthetic delight. Rukmini Devi used to make slight changes in the dance-drama productions, but those changes made great deal of difference. Rukmini Devi would select dancers to don the roles of different characters in her dance-drama productions. The dancers would play their role with full involvement, longing to be appreciated by *Athai,* (as Rukmini Devi was affectionately called) for their enactments. A word of approval from *Athai* was everything to them as she was the very Goddess of aesthetic taste. Students adored her, admired, obeyed her commands and lived as she directed. While artists working outside *Kala-kshetra* enjoyed tremendous material gains, those who worked with Rukmini Devi only received seven hundred and fifty rupees a month (artists working outside *Kala-kshetra* received a salary twenty times more than what artists were paid in *Kala-kshetra*). Yet artists continued to work under Rukmini Devi because neither money nor publicity could have given them the joy they derived from serving under her.

I have taken many dignitaries from different countries to see the ballads she produced. They have exclaimed that the recitals they saw were not entertainment but soul elevating experiences. The spectator was transformed. He became one with the enactor – a complete unity of aesthetic experience was achieved. The vocal music, the rhythmic steps, the swaying body and hand gestures, the scenes and environment and above all the communications of *Bhavas* (emotions) by the artists, created a sense of a bygone age. The performance offered a taste of aesthetic happiness – '*rasa-aasvaadana*'.

Rukmini Devi's theatre, likewise, was conceived as a

temple of art. The theatre she built within *Kala-kshetra* was truly Indian. It was designed on the model of *Koothambalam* of Kerala. Seated inside the auditorium, the spectator does not feel himself cut off from the natural environment surrounding him, nor does he feel alienated from the performance. The steps leading to the theatre are also tastefully decorated with traditional *Kolam* and one feels instantly transported to the abode of arts. True to her total philosophy, Rukmini Devi named her theatre *Bharata-Kala-kshetra,* or the temple of Bharata's art. Just as dance is the highest art of suggestive communication, so is the temple of '*Bharata-Kala-kshetra*' a temple of suggestion, where dance itself is worship. No better temple for Bharata could have been conceived and built than Rukmini Devi's *Bharata-Kala-kshetra.*

What made Rukmini Devi's contribution so great, so charming and so divine? For Rukmini Devi, every aspect of life was meant to be lived, appreciated and aesthetically experienced. She had universal love and compassion, as could be seen from her love of animals – including cats, dogs, birds that fascinated her. She served as the Chairman of the All India Animal Welfare Board and strived to alleviate the suffering animal life.

She made me the President of Dr. U.V. Swaminatha Aiyer Library and I remained its *Adhyaksha.* After the demise of Dr. U.V. Swaminatha Iyer, no one cared for Dr. Iyer's collections. It was Rukmini Devi who saved the collection and built a library for it. For over fifty years, she administered and developed it by nurturing it in the campus of *Kala-kshetra.* She continued to be its *Adhyaksha* till her demise. She told me once, that she would like to build appropriate guest houses for scholars to live quietly and work on Dr. Iyer's collection. Her demise deprived us of her dream.

Rukmini Devi was keen to develop a museum – a different type of museum to reflect her ideals. I was made a member of the first museum committee, which drew up a suitable plan of building, and display. Yet the museum project could not be launched, although two attempts were made during her lifetime. I, however, remained a member of that committee till the very end. After her demise, many changes were initiated in *Kala-kshetra.* The Government of India granted 20 lakhs of rupees for building the museum, which remained unutilized for long. But the museum project is underway now and I understand that a building has been erected.

When I served as a member of the Executive Committee of *Kala-kshetra,* under her direction, the University Grants Commission sent a committee to accord 'Deemed University status' to the *Kala-kshetra.* The meeting is still vivid in my mind. There was always a charm in the way Rukmini Devi conducted the meetings, the way the seats were arranged and the way the resolutions were drafted. *Athai* listened carefully to all that was said by the learned Committee members of the U.G.C. who explained at length the benefits that are likely to accrue to *Kala-kshetra,* the prospect of sumptuous University Grants, modernization, etc. *Athai* listened to their exposition and said, "I appreciate your concern and liberality to make this center toe the line of University Grants Commission. But unfortunately your rules and guidelines are diametrically opposed to the ideals of *Kala-kshetra.* For example, your U.G.C. rules would say that one who attains the age of 60 should be retired. But I would like to keep the experienced master till the end of his life to benefit from his wisdom, age and experience. Your U.G.C. rules would say that I should open the school at 10 a.m. and close it at 5 p.m. But in our traditional oriented system we will leave it to the Guru, to teach whenever he felt it good. He may start at 7 a.m. in the day and later continue in the evening till late. I would like to give him the freedom to impart training as best as he can. Those who teach here are *Maha-vidwans.* They are here not for money but out of pure love of their art. Your modernization has no direction. In the name of modernization, I do not want to lose my soul. You may keep your offer and rules to yourself. I would like to run this institution in our own traditional methods, suited to our genius." *Athai* politely but firmly turned down the U.G.C. suggestions.

We were not surprised for we knew *Athai* could not be lured by money, power, status or fame. Did she not turn down the post of the President of India? When Morarji Desai offered her the Rashtrapati post, she told him, she was devoted to her art and would like to serve that. "The post of President of India would not give me that fullness,"she said. No one could imagine that anyone would reject such an important position in the Government. Rukmini Devi did that because she was inspired by Upanishadic ideals: *Na karmanaa na prajayaa dhanena tyaagena ekena amritattvam anasuh* (one attains immortality not by offerings, power over men and money but by supreme sacrifice).

Persons like Rukmini Devi are rightly claimed as *Yuga Purushas* – born once in a millennium. They serve as *Marga Darsis* for us to emulate. Rukmini Devi looked at everything of the world with a poetic vision, with an artist's vision, with a serene and sacred vision. She lived that vision. So she is an immortal *Rishi* for me.

The phone on my table rang. "Sir *Athai* is dead" said a feeble voice from the other end. "She passed away a few minutes before." The next moment I was on my way to Adyar Theosophical gardens where *Athai's* body was lying amidst soft fragrant flowers. I looked at *Athai*'s face. It was the same bright, composed, supremely serene and charming face. She was in her yogic sleep. I only said "*Athai*"! That was my last communication with her. That evening her body was consigned to the flames. There was no huge crowd, but those who stood there were like the congregation of the whole world to me. There were no rites; there were no beaming lights, no video, no flash. *Athai* was lying on the pure pyre in the midst of the nature she loved. Sankara Menon spoke a few words. not about *Athai*'s greatness, fame or work but about immortality. Within those few moments the flames rising over her mortal coil, transformed her into an immortal jyoti. One could see no more difference between her physical limbs and the Supreme jyoti.

Rukmini Devi is no more. Her physical limbs have dissolved into Nature's elements. But her *Kala-kshetra* lives on; the beautiful trees, creepers and the original buildings she beautified, live on. The resonant music and dance she created lives on as *vaangmaya-kosa* or a sheath of melody. The dancers she created live on as the *praana* and soul of the *Kshetra*. While all this is part of her perceptible manifestation, she lives as the all-pervasive subtle mantra – the imperceptible *Paraa-Devataa*, the Goddess in her *Sukshma sarira*. It is impossible to move through *Kala-kshetra* without feeling her presence everywhere. There is a tradition in Indian classical dance to pay obeisance to the *Naatyaadhi-devataa* Goddess of Dance before starting dance, for she remains through out the recitals. Rukmini Devi is the Presiding deity, *Kala-adhi-devata* of *Kala-kshetra*.

What would happen to *Kala-kshetra* after Rukmini Devi? This was the question that was in the mind of all associated with her. *Kala-kshetra* continues to grow and will flourish as long as the ideals she set are upheld and cherished and the strength and vitality of the institution comes from within. However, as one feels the presence of divinity from the micro space of a temple expanding into the vast macro space of the world, so does Rukmini Devi live beyond the boundaries of *Kala-kshetra*, in the heart of all who are steeped in Indian ethos.

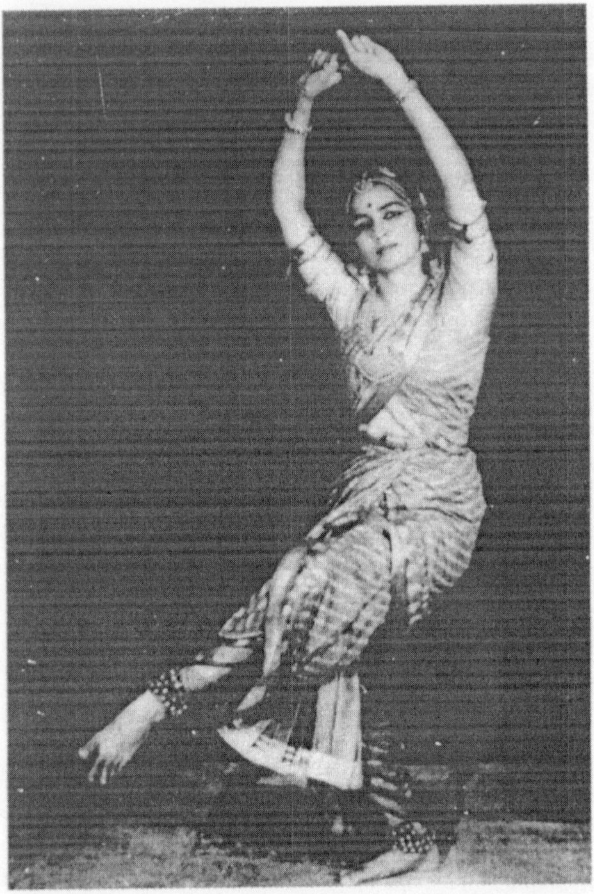

Fig. 4: Rukmini Devi Performing the Dance of Nataraja
(Photo: C.T. Nachiappan archive)

CHAPTER 7

RUKMINI DEVI AND THE VEGETARIAN VILLAGE

Dr. N. Mahalingam

India is part of a rich and flourishing civilization spanning several thousands of years. Fine Arts is part of that civilizational culture. But during the foreign rule, the Fine Arts suffered a serious blow due to lack of patronage

However, great women like Rukmini Devi, revived the performing arts in the twentieth century. They became divine apostles of history. Rukmini Devi was one such divine apostle for *Bharatanatyam.* The dance is unique because it has the capacity to capture the heart and soul of the spectator and elevate his consciousness.

Rukmini Devi was born to Sri Nilakanta Sastri and Smt. Seshammal on 29th February, 1904. She became a revolutionary by marrying Dr. Arundale from outside the orthodox community and by deciding to learn *Bharatanatyam* (which was practiced in temples by hereditary practitioners). *Bharatanatyam* is an aesthetic form of art. Lord Nataraja is the presiding god of the dance, and dances the dance of cosmic creation and destruction. In India, the Gods dance. Lord Krishna dances with Gopies and his flute, and binds the world in his magic spell. Ganesha dances with his elephant head and saints. And Indian poets extol Gods who sing and dance. Because Gods sing and dance in India, dance and music are considered as godly activities in India.

Rukmini Devi belonged to the deep spiritual culture of India. After her marriage, she came into intimate contact and association with two great personalities of our time: Dr. Annie Besant and Dr. Arundale. She travelled throughout the world with them and became associated with outstanding personalities of her time. Because Rukmini Devi moved in elite circles, she was able to win admiration, recognition, acceptability and respectability *for Bharatanatyam.* She was helped in her efforts to revive Indian performing arts by Dr. Arundale, Thiru Narayana Menon, Thiru Sankara Menon and her brother Yagneswara. She was also greatly encouraged by Guru Meenakshi Sundram Pillai, whom she respected enormously.

Theosophy and Vegetarianism, Fine Arts and Blue Cross (love for animals) remained the four corner stones of her life. She served as President of "All India Federation of Young Theosophists (1923) and later as President of the 'World Federation of Young Theosophists (1925). Pavlova, a renowned dancer of Russian folklore, captivated her with her Ballet. In the early period of her life, and before learning *Bharatanatyam,* Rukmini Devi danced Egyptian, Hungarian and South American dances. But under Pavlova's guidance, Rukmini Devi decided to devote her life to reviving *Bharatanatyam.*

With great love and devotion, Rukmini Devi founded '*Kalakshetra*', the 'International College of Fine Arts' where music, dance and drama were taught along scientific lines. She gathered experts in the performing arts and urged them to teach in *Kalakshetra.* Veena Sambasiva Iyer, Mysore Vasudevachariyar, Papanasam Sivan, Veena Krishnamachariyar, Tiger Vardhachariyar, Boodalur Krishnamurthy Sastri, Mylapore Gowriammal, Kalyani Ammal, Pandanallur Meenakshi Sundram Pillai, and many others have served on the faculty of *Kalakshetra.* Thiru Chandrasekhar, Periya Sarada, Sarada Hoffman, Dhananjayan, and Shantha Dananjayan are some of the few outstanding students of

Kalakshetra. The mentioned students maintain flourishing schools in India today.

Students from all over the world come to study in Rukmini Devi's *Kalakshetra.* The Alumni of *Kalakshetra* continue to serve as 'ambassadors' of Indian culture throughout the world. They admire and hold Rukmini Devi in high esteem for her commendable efforts in bringing recognition and respectability to *Bharatanatyam.* Encouraged by Rukmini Devi, Thiru Nachiappa, one of the students of *Kalakshetra,* became an expert in printing and photography. He has worked both in India and the US and has created a large archive of photographs of both Thirumathi Rukmini Devi and her institution. He is now known as 'Nachiappa Swamigal', the Head of Kovilur Mutt in Sivaganga district.

I had the privilege of working with Smt. Rukmini Devi from the moment when *Kalakshetra* was established. It is true that Rukmini Devi enlarged the *Bharatanatyam* dance repertoire by incorporating Sanskrit texts and composing dance-dramas. Enamoured with Tamil poetry, I suggested to her that she might want to compose the *Kamba Ramayanam* as a dance drama. Though I had offered to fund such a venture, it did not come to fruition.

Contribution to Vegetarian Movement

Vegetarianism continued to be practised as a religious movement in India. Rukmini Devi became Founder President of Indian Vegetarian Congress and subsequently President of International Vegetarian Congress. She added a scientific dimension to the vegetarian movement. She explained that vegetarianism is religious, healthy, and economical as the digestive system of the human body is designed for a vegetarian diet. She argued eloquently that the stomach of human beings should not be converted into a burial ground of dead animals. Because of her advocacy, a number of foreign nationals gave up non-vegetarianism and followed the path of ahimsa and vegetarianism. Thanks to Rukmini Devi's involvement in the

Vegetarian movement, it became both a national and an international movement with branches all over the world.

Rukmini Devi Vegetarian Village: A Proposal

Kalakshetra is located on a large campus encompassing over 100 acres. I have suggested that this center be developed into an 'International Vegetarian Township' to honour the memory of Rukmini Devi. It could be developed into a township along the lines of the Aurobindo Ashram at Pondicherry. Theosophists from all over the world might consider settling down in this new place when the infrastructure is developed. About 50 acres of land can be developed into house sites and sold to those who subscribe to the Philosophy of 'Theosophy and Vegetarianism.' A sum of Rs.200 crores can be generated and used as corpus fund to develop the 'Rukmini Devi College of Performing Arts' into a Deemed University. Housing facilities could also be provided to resident artists attached to *Kalakshetra.*

We are fortunate to have Hon'ble Shri R. Venkataraman as President of *Kalakshetra.* He can help us to accomplish the above tasks, which will become landmark events in the world and stand as a tribute to the memory of Rukmini Devi, *Bharatanatyam* and Theosophy all at once.

CHAPTER 8

RUKMINI DEVI: THE EDUCATOR

Sarada Hoffman

Rukmini Devi Arundale's role as an educator was intimately connected with her work in the worlds of art, culture and of spirit. Her approach to education combined progressive ideas with ancient traditions. She sought to develop the full potential of each student providing the stimuli for growth as well as a grounding in discipline opening new windows of thought and experience while teaching reverence and appreciation for our rich Indian heritage. As all the truly great ones do, she distinguished herself by going beyond the mere preaching of these ideals to leading by personal example.

Her legacy of educational work is too vast to be covered in a short article. Therefore, I would like to touch on just two aspects of Rukmini Devi's far-reaching educational ideals. The first is her use of the best elements of the Indian tradition coupled with the latest developments in Western thought, to prepare students to be contributing citizens of the world. The second is the importance she gave to art and beauty as ingredients in a well-rounded education. I have seen these aspects of her approach bear fruit in several students, and have personally benefitted greatly from her efforts.

In many ways, I am a product of her efforts, because for me she was a teacher in almost everything. I learnt throughout my career as an artist as well as in my personal life. This is the model of the *Guru-Shisya* relationship that she offered to her students; it is deeply rooted in India's heritage. To those who had the privilege of such an association with her, Rukmini Devi offered a breadth of experiences that touched many areas of their personality. Two of my earliest recollections are of being in one of her plays, and of seeing her dance.

In one of her first plays, portraying a child of *Siddhartha* (the Lord Buddha), all I had to do was to lie down next to my mother Yashodhara when Prince Siddhartha came to take leave as he left on his quest for truth. Rukmini Devi's husband, Dr. George S. Arundale gave the background narration in his beautiful voice. I learnt a little about being on stage, and a little about the life of Gautama Buddha. When Rukmini Devi gave her first public dance performance, I was a six-year-old girl in the front row, enthralled. I felt the atmosphere created by the performance, and was captivated with the dance. The course of my life was decided.

I soon got Rukmini Devi to promise to teach me the dance when I was ready. I remember the first thing she asked me, when I was six years old: "What is it you want to do?" Without a second thought, I said I wanted to be helpful to others. "Then begin now", she said, and gave me a needle to thread. A guru challenges the student, even if it is just to help in the dressing room before plays. I became her pupil at age ten, and at sixteen, she gave me the responsibility to train young children in the dance. My duty was not merely to conduct dance classes but to be a role model for my students, and to do this, I tried to follow the example she herself provided. In this manner my learning with her continued for the rest of my life. In the Indian tradition, even when one becomes a guru to others, one's own guru remains one's master, an exemplar of possibilities, a guide, as well as a friend. Rukmini Devi was such a guru to me, and to many others. She showed us how to live by her own example, leading a life of simplicity and cultivating noble and helpful thoughts.

While adhering to this most ancient of Indian traditions, Rukmini Devi had her own ideas that she instituted for training. Her exposure to times of great change in Eastern and Western thought, during which movements like the Indian independence struggle and the Theosophical Society were active, and her association with great thinkers of the day like Dr. Annie Besant, gave her a broad view of what Indian culture could offer the world, and what individuals could contribute as its citizens. In her eyes, every pupil was an individual with unique innate potential, which education should help to develop and fulfil. This is still a progressive idea in the educational world today, and to achieve it, what Rukmini Devi showed as most important is the spirit of dedication. Dedication to the pursuit of learning, dedication to those who give knowledge and inspiration, our gurus. Rukmini Devi often demonstrated that Indian culture was capable of being applied to modern situations.

In adopting new ideas for education, Rukmini Devi had the vision to recognise and select the best from the West, and to put it into practice in a manner consistent with Indian culture. During the early 1940s, she pioneered the implementation of the Montessori method of education in the school she had founded in memory of Annie Besant. Maria Montessori herself was living in Adyar as the guest of the Arundales, conducting training courses for teachers from all over India. The Montessori system is free from fear and promotes enthusiasm in learning, and was a complete departure from the oppressive British schooling systems of the day.

New ideas adopted by Rukmini Devi usually received her personal touch, which added an artistic flavour. Such was the case at the Montessori school. Rukmini Devi, at the request of Maria Montessori, conducted art courses so that the trainees would understand and appreciate true arts. She gave lecture-demonstrations in dance and music. Dr. Cousins, a well known poet and the Vice-President of *Kalakshetra,* arranged lectures and exhibitions by great artists such as Nicholas Roerich, Nandalal Bose and others. Rukmini Devi also arranged an exhibition of Indian homes and the Indian way of life. There were village dwellings with simple artifacts like earthen-ware and mats, there was the middle class home with some furniture and metal vessels, and a wealthy home with ornate designs in textiles and embroidery. Every item was elegant and in impeccable taste. It was a beautiful expression of Indian aesthetics, and showed how at every level beauty enhanced the joy of life.

This instance illustrates another key feature of Rukmini Devi's educational philosophy, which was the principle that beauty is essential in life, and that art, by providing a means to appreciate that beauty, is a vital element for the growth of a student. It does not matter whether the student is aiming for a career in art, engineering, medicine, or law. The importance of beauty is the same, because Rukmini Devi's intent was to develop the personality, or spirit, of the student, as much as it was to provide a practical education.

In pursuit of this ideal, Rukmini Devi created beauty in all her endeavours. Walking through the campus of *Kalakshetra* in her days, the sound of music and dancing could be heard from open and airy classrooms, trees and flowers were everywhere, and one could always find a peaceful place for contemplation or study. More beauty was to be found at deeper levels, not so obvious to casual observation. *Kalakshetra* was also a refuge where no living being would be harmed, where the great Indian ideal of ahimsa would be practised, and where young hearts and minds would be spared the trauma of violence. She created beautiful surroundings for places of learning where, in addition to daily classes in the fine arts, discourse on scriptures and on the lives of great souls were provided. Her hope was that by creating the right environment and offering high ideals, young people would learn to respect and value the greatness of Indian culture, making their lives beautiful and joyous.

Perhaps the best known creations of Rukmini Devi are her dance-dramas. When she began her creative work in producing dance-dramas, she used to test the choreography with me to see if it met her standards. She was quite strict and demanding but was a wonderful teacher. I asked her once why she was intent on producing dance-dramas. She said that it was one of the ways to educate people to understand divinity and express reverence.

In so many ways she made it clear that beauty was important to life and the arts were a means to appreciate that beauty. Whether it is dance, music or painting, the presentation must evoke inspiration and happiness. She stressed the importance of attention to every small detail. Harmony in movement, harmony in colour, beauty in sound and music – all were indispensable. To help produce such a result, harmony within the artist was essential. In pushing them towards artistic perfection, Rukmini Devi was educating the personalities of her students.

The proper nurturing of the personality was given such emphasis because education is for the individual to develop into a refined human being. Mastery in skills and scholastic achievements give satisfaction to the mind but inspired intuitive experience gives real happiness. To this aim she dedicated her life's work.

When we reflect on Rukmini Devi's contributions as an educator, we can consider what she did. She offered students progressive learning opportunities while grounding them in the greatness of our Indian culture, and she established institutions where students could develop their full potential in an atmosphere of beauty. We can also admire the driving force behind these accomplishments – a woman whose philosophy emphasised dedication to the pursuit of learning, reverence for our teachers, esteem for our heritage, and the value of developing not just the mind but the spirit. We may also see how these qualities were embodied in her own life, and try to follow her example. When we look for her legacy, the best place to find it is in the hearts and minds of those who passed through her tutelage, and who carry, to whatever degree, a spark of her flame into the world.

(This paper was presented at the first Rukmini Devi National Seminar, organized by the *Centre for Contemporary Culture*, at New Delhi in 2001.)

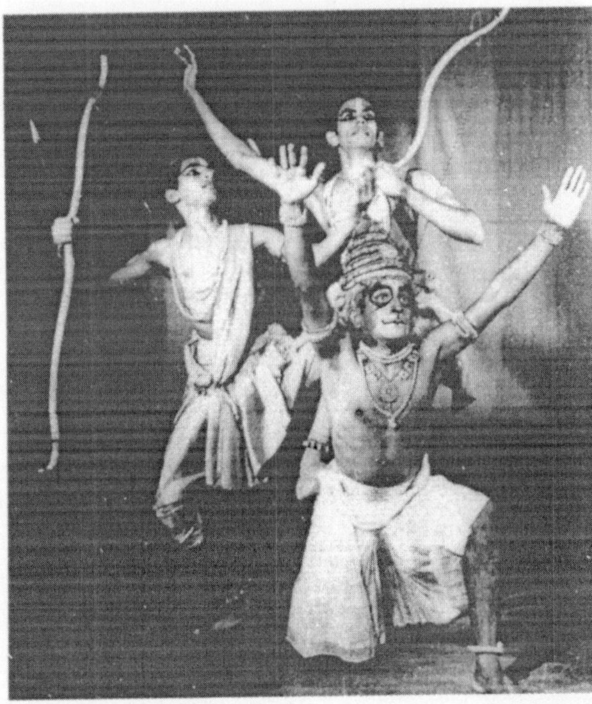

Fig. 5: Rama, Lakshmana and Hanuman Cross the Oceans to Reach Lanka: Photo from Rukmini Devi's Ramayana Dance Drama Series

(Photo: C.T. Nachiappan archive)

CHAPTER 9

RUKMINI DEVI: A BUILDER OF INSTITUTIONS

C.V. Chandrasekhar

I vasudhato bharata sastramunu brabala paratsutakai Kalakstramunu
Vevegame punikato sthapinci palinci Rukmini Devi
Neevanti karunya siluralevaruledanacu madilona dalaci
Vevaganaina navedatirci manamu kapadutuvani vacciti

This was the tribute that the great musician and *vagyeyakara* Sri Veena Krishnamachari paid to Rukmini in his immortal *Tillana* in *Natabhairavi*, which stands synonymous with the great institution that she built, viz., *Kalakshetra*. It reads thus "Laments the art of dance. O Rukmini Devi! When my mind was anguished seeking for a saviour, you arrived and established the *Kalakshetra*, nurtured it with devotion, steadfastness and zeal to make known to the world the art of Bharat and saved me from dishonour".

The *Natya Sastra* of Bharat tells us that Brahma created the *Natyaveda* to redeem the world from chaos, and Bharata and his sons received the same and spread it around the world. By establishing *Kalakshetra*, Rukmini Devi infused new life and sophistication to the art form of *Bharatanatyam*, filling it with spiritual values, thereby saving it from dishonour. This paved the way for the renaissance of *Bharatanatyam*. Music and dance were for centuries transmuted by the oral tradition of the *gurushisya parampara*. Rukmini Devi was well aware of this and the importance of the continuance of the tradition. But she was a *'Deerghadarsi'* or the one who looked ahead of her times. She realized that in times to come it might not be possible for the seekers of knowledge to go to the gurus and she started the reverse process of inviting great gurus to her *Gurukulam*, which she named *Kalakshetra*, "the abode of the arts". She thus sowed the seeds for the institutionalized impartment of knowledge in the field of the fine arts: There was no compromise in the selection of the masters. She brought the best of them to come and live on the campus so that the inmates could breathe their presence. Though associated with an international association like the Theosophical Society from her childhood and married to a foreigner, she was an Indian to the core as she believed in and cherished the past traditions of this great land where spirituality was part of every activity. She had great respect for the religious practices and traditions, which every student was made aware of, but never wanted this to dominate the spiritual path that was beyond all those mundane activities.

Tolerance and awareness of every faith became a part of the process of learning. This attracted great personages and students from all over the globe to come to *Kalakshetra,* which was rightly acclaimed as an international centre of arts. Her vision also saw the need for a campus of its own for *Kalakshetra,* and the present estate, away from the bustle of the city then, was purchased in the middle of the century. Tree plantation was undertaken in a big way and by the time the institution shifted to the new campus, a congenial atmosphere with greenery all around was already in existence thanks to her vision that this temple of learning stands like an oasis in the midst of the concrete desert that has developed around it. There was no disparity between the haves and the have-nots on the campus, which went a long way in creating lifelong associations among the inmates.

There are always financial constraints in running such an institution. But Rukmini Devi's charisma brought in a number of devoted people to work for her, very often without any monetary returns. A simple and austere lifestyle was the hallmark of the campus. For such a living, she realized the importance of the environment, which had to be congenial for the learning of the arts. Love for animals and plants was inculcated in the minds of the young people. One was made aware of anything beautiful and their aesthetic values were highlighted. She believed that a real artiste, be it a dancer, musician, painter, etc. was one who was well aware of all the inter-disciplinary areas. Thus emphasis was laid on the importance of ancient literature to the development of the fine arts.

She nurtured the U.V. Swaminathan Aiyer Library with its collection of manuscripts and rare books as a reference for the future generation of scholars. The study of the *Sastras* was probably introduced for the first time in the curriculum. Many later institutions have followed this. Awareness of the folk arts in music, dance and other allied forms was created in the minds of students. The teaching of folk dance and music was undertaken. *Kalakshetra* was the pioneer in introducing the folk dances of many northern states of the country to the southern audiences. The *Kalamkari*, one of the dying folk arts of Andhra fascinated her and she started a unit for its revival. Rukmini Devi had an aesthetic sense of a very high order and one of her special interests was in textiles. She was one of the most beautifully and aesthetically clad women of the country. With the expert weavers, she established the weaving centre at *Kalakshetra*. The centre brought out exquisite sarees with many rare and lost designs. So much so, these designs were made popular, copied and sold in the name of *Kalakshetra sarees* by the outside designers. Several costumes used in *Kalakshetra*'s earlier dance-dramas were woven at the centre. Many traditional jewellery designs were introduced in the productions.

This was the ambience in which one learnt the arts of music, dance and painting at *Kalakshetra*. The learning process was a deep, but at the same time, a very relaxed one. There was no hurry to complete courses in a given specific time. Diplomas were awarded only when a student was found competent to receive one. The need to study Tamil and Sanskrit literatures was stressed. Great scholars were always available for consultations. Students were welcome in the homes of famous musicians and *vagyeyakaras,* who lived on the campus, to sit and listen to their *abyasa* and occasionally to receive some instructions. North Indian musicians like the Dagar Brothers were invited to come and live on the campus without any assignment to teach. This was just for the students to listen to north Indian music and understand the depth and nuances of that system. Great masters of *Bharatanatyam* and *Kathakali* came to live and teach at *Kalakshetra.* This was a great learning experience for dance students who could see the diversity in the forms while realising that there was much basic unity in the two forms.

Dance training was very disciplined and importance was given to the aesthetics of dance rather than to virtuosity and showmanship. The learning was for the spiritual upliftment more than for mundane pleasures and entertainment. One realises the importance of such training as one evolves and goes into a deep study of the art form. One appreciates how important it is to have an atmosphere, environment and ambience of such variance during one's learning process. Every such institution undergoes changes and *Kalakshetra* is no exception. As mentioned earlier, Rukmini Devi was a visionary and anticipated the inevitable changes that the institution would encounter. She was accepting this change in her own lifetime. But the seed that she had sown sixty-five years ago and the foundation she had laid for an edifice of Indian art and tradition has grown into a great Banyan tree like the one on its own campus, that even earthquakes cannot shatter. The flowers that blossomed there have strewn their seeds all over the world and many of these have already grown big continuing the process of institution building – in the real sense. Some of the best-known institutions, dancers and musicians of the country owe their gratitude to their alma mater – *Kalakshetra.*

Some of the great Gurus who taught and lived at *Kalakshetra*

Dance

Pandanallur Meenakshi Sundram Pillai
Kattumannar Koil Muthukumarappa Pillai
Chokkalingam Pillai
Karaikkal Saradamba amma
Mylapore Gowri amma
Dandayudapani Pillai
Guru Ambu Panikkar
Guru Chandu Panikkar

Music

Sangita Kalanidhi Papanasam Sivan
Sangita Kalanidhi Tiger Varadachari
Veena Krishnamachari
Sangita Kalanidhi Budalur Krishnamurthy Sastri
Sangita Kalanidhi Karaikkudi Sambasiva Iyer
Sangita Kalanidhi Mysore Vasudevachar
Sangita Kalanidhi Mudikondan Venkataramier
M.D. Ramanathan
Turaiyur Rajagopala Sarma
Pudukkode Krishnamurthy
Flute Sri Ramachandra Sastri
Karaikkudi Muthu Iyer
Sangita Kalanidhi Smt. Mani Krishnaswamy

And many others who were lesser known artists but great masters.

Painters

Krishna Reddy
K. Srinivasulu
Dhanapal

Scholars

S.K. Ganapathy Iyer	:	Tamil
R. Viswanatha Iyer	:	Tamil
Adinarayana Sarma	:	Sanskrit
Venkatachala Sastri	:	Sanskrit

There were many others who came to teach and help in the fields of voice production, stagecraft, lighting, and design.

(This paper was presented in the first Rukmini Devi National Seminar, organized by the *Centre for Contemporary Culture,* at New Delhi in 2001.)

CHAPTER 10

RUKMINI DEVI: AN AESTHETIC VISIONARY

Mrinalini Sarabhai

My earliest memories of Rukmini Devi were when she visited my mother Ammu Swaminadhan in our house in Chetpet, Chennai. She was one of the many beautiful and famous women who came to our home. There was Sarojini Naidu, Rajkumari Amrit Kaur, Dhanavanti Rama Rau, Mrinalini Chattopadhyaya and others. At that time we also used to go to the Theosophical Society in Adyar to meet Mrs. Bhagirathi Sriram (Rukmini's sister-in-law) and Malati Patwardhan and also listen to J. Krishnamurthi, whose teachings were just beginning to be known.

It was only after I came back from school in Switzerland where I had been sent due to ill health, that Rukmini Devi came into my life. Since I was a child, I knew 'I was a dancer', and still believe that it was a continuation of another life. I had been dancing with various teachers since I was three years old and now wanted to do it very seriously. My mother immediately thought of Rukmini Devi and *Kalakshetra*. So it was here I began my lessons with Muthukumara Pillai and under the guidance of Rukmini Devi, who I think realized my dedication to the Art and often came around the grounds and would stop in her small car to see me practicing hard under the excellent and stern guru.

She included me in the dance drama she was producing at that time called '*The Light of Asia*', the life of the Buddha. She gave me two roles, one of the queen 'Maya' and the other of 'Sujata', the young woman who took an offering of curds to the Buddha. In between my entrances I would sit with Dr. Arundale and laugh a great deal as he had a wonderful sense of humour, and I too was in many ways very British in my upbringing. I remember clearly the '*Dying Swan'* dance Smt. Rukmini Devi did in the dance drama. I think it was inspired by her meeting with the great dancer Pavlova who was, I believe famous for her dance 'The Dying Swan' which I wish I could have seen.

Rukmini Devi to me represented an ideal of Indian womanhood with her deep interest in the renaissance of the Indian dance form *Bharatanatyam.* When I first saw her recital of *Bharatanatyam,* I was thrilled with her good taste-the costumes and the jewellery and the beauty of the entire performance in which no detail had been overlooked. It was much later that I wore her *Kalakshetra* sarees and understood her passion for beauty which I too shared.

I remember one occasion when I was asked to dance a solo at the Museum Theatre. I was bold enough to ask her to compose something special for me. Though I was young and inexperienced, she took my request seriously and together we created a dance called 'The Rajput Fresco'.

It is strange how so many of our lives are interwoven in the tapestry of the infinite. The musician who played for us was G. Visalakshi also a great friend of my mother's and who later took charge of my music group when I started my regular performances in Bangalore. She stayed with me for many years singing and playing the veena and when she left, her niece Shankari took her place.

After I was married to Vikram Sarabhai and came to Ahmedabad, my sister-in-law Bharatidevi Sarabhai was getting married to an English writer Denis Stoll. The Sarabhais also knew Rukmini Devi well. Bharati thought of having a dance performance by her group which I of course was very glad about. Two of her students danced for us and Smt. Rukmini Devi was an honoured guest. The next morning she asked me with a mischievous look 'Mrinalini, why did you not ask me to dance?' and I replied 'I didn't dare'!

At that time Vikram was a keen photographer and had purchased a cine camera. He asked Rukmini Devi to dance for him so that he could film her. She at once graciously consented and on the terrace of our home 'The Retreat' she danced a *padam*, which he filmed.

Many people perhaps don't know of Rukmini Devi's sense of humour. But I remember exchanging many small jokes with her. One particular joke I remember very well was when she first came to 'The Retreat'. My father-in-law had built this beautiful home for his eight children and everything in it was artistic and Indian, even to the night lamps which were made of bamboo. Rukmini Devi smilingly remarked to me 'I feel I should have brought a carved suitcase when I came here'!

I left *Kalakshetra* as I felt restless in the rather western atmosphere I was growing up in and wanted to go somewhere where I could spend the entire time in an Indian ambience. Spending two-three hours at *Kalakshetra* was not enough for me and I wanted to be in a place where art was a way of life. My mother thought of sending me to *Shantiniketan* which I feel now was a very wise decision and it was here that I really felt one with my own self. I think Rukmini Devi understood my need and gave me her blessings making me promise to come back sometime. But as I have often said 'I have to follow my own star'.

My destiny led me to Gujarat where in my own way I have tried to bring about a revival and recognition for both the traditional Art and folk Arts in Folk Dance and Drama and the Crafts. As Chairperson of Gujarat Handicrafts Corporation, I again met her many years later when she came to Gujarat's Delhi Emporium. I was busy inspecting the handicrafts and arranging them and I saw her come in. She was downstairs and I ran down the stairs, reached her and touched her feet. The people there were so astonished. I had become '*Amma*' to everyone by then, a senior person in my own right and they were in the habit of touching my feet to show their respect. So they found it strange to see me rushing down to touch somebody else's feet! But everyone was glad when I introduced her. I was tremendously happy to see her. We spent a lot of time together later when we both attended the Asian Conference in Delhi. It was a wonderful feeling to sit on the same platform with her, sharing our views.

To me her aesthetic taste was so good and it found an immediate response in me. I think when you are an artist it is not enough to create beauty only on the stage but to represent it even in ordinary life. In your daily routine, you represent something even in the way you dress. I think it is very important to be true to tradition and yet be creative. I know in a strange way we cherished the same ideals of 'Indianness' in bringing out the beauty of India on the stage and in life. The aesthetics of India's arts and crafts, not only the poverty and the suffering. The real beauty of India, which she recognized, and the purity and taste with which she did everything is what I loved and admired and will always remember about her.

(This paper was presented at the Rukmini Devi National Seminar, organized by the *Centre for Contemporary Culture,* at Chennai in 2003.)

CHAPTER 11

ATHAI: MY GURU

Krishnaveni Lakshmanan

Guru is an important person in one's life. The concept of guru is very beautiful and meaningful in our culture. *Maata, pitaa, guru, devam* is the saying of the learned. The parents give birth to a child in its physical form but it is the guru or teacher who initiates the child into a righteous path. The guru moulds the child into a good human being. For every student, the teacher is the role model in every step of his/her life. One should be blessed to get the right teacher. I am fortunate indeed to have had one of the best gurus!

Srimati Rukmini Devi was a friend, philosopher, guide and more! I came to know her when I was a child. I was fascinated with her in every aspect; her beauty, her stature, her commanding personality, her affectionate approach, her dignity, her commitment, and her dedication. As a child I used to watch her practising in a room. I used to look through the window and repeat what I noticed. One day she called me in and asked if I wanted to learn dance. My immediate reply was yes! She then asked me to do a few steps that I had seen her do. Because I did them accurately, she was very happy. Then she decided to have me as her disciple! From that moment on, *Kalakshetra* has been my home and there has been no looking back! From dawn to dusk, I spent my time in *Kalakshetra* campus and the Theosophical Society campus and I grew up amidst the beautiful surroundings of *Kalakshetra* campus. There was no tree that was left unclimbed; no sports without me participating and of course winning! Rukmini Devi used to distribute the prizes at a stretch—at a stretch to me! Yes I used to win in all the games and carry off the championship too! When I grew older, I started to take part in her productions.

My first experience with her was during the production of the first of the *Ramayana* series-*Sita Swayamvaram.* My sister and I played the part of Sita's *sakhis.* It was a small role for me, but I still feel proud as it was composed on us. She took care in teaching me the intricate *swaras* of the song and taught them to me personally.

When it comes to work, *athai* never compromised. She had a special eye for casting a person in a role. She always choreographed the song according to the capability of the dancer, which used to bring out the best from that dancer. While composing she would expect the dancer to be able to grasp her ideas quickly. If the dancer failed to do so she would get annoyed and scold her. *Athai*'s anger was always short-lived! She never failed to appreciate a good dancer. If the dancer lived upto her expectations, she would then give her a big hug with tearful eyes! I have had this experience many a time with my guru. If she was satisfied with our work, *athai* then used to give us each a small gift as token of her appreciation. I have had the wonderful chance of getting gifts twice from *athai.*

For the role of Sita in *Sriramavanagamanam,* she gave me a lovely ring and insisted that I wear it for all the programmes. When I was cast as Sita in *Choodamani Pradhanam,* athai was so happy that she gave me a *Choodamani* (head jewel), which was part of her priceless collection of jewels. She even mentioned this in her speech when I received the *Nritya Choodamani* award from *Krishna Gana Sabha* in 1976. Many of my friends too have received priceless gifts from *athai* in appreciation of their work.

Apart from being a guru to me, *athai* also taught me many things on the personal front. What I am today as a dancer is what she gave me. She moulded me into a performer, composer, teacher and choreographer. I was able to be all this because I worked with her in almost all her productions and was present with her while she choreographed. She would compose the dance on me before she taught it to others because I had a good memory and grasping power and could execute her flowing ideas with ease. I think I had a good rapport with her. I was able to read her mind and do exactly the same *adavu* that she wanted! Our relationship developed because of this and I was with her till her last production. When she was doing a scene she used to consult some of us. She even gave us a few songs and asked us to compose them ourselves. While composing *Shakuntalam*, there was a scene in which *Shakuntala* leaves, after meeting *Dushyanta*, the first time. Love blossoms for her and she pretends as though a thorn has pricked her. To have a last glimpse of *Dushyanta,* she acts as if her saree had got caught in a branch. This sequence was set in *Anand bhairavi* raga in a very romantic tune. *Athai* then asked each one of us to enact in the scene as *Shakuntala.* All of us enthusiastically composed and did according to our imagination. Patiently she watched all of us one by one.

After we had finished she explained the emotion involved in that scene and she enacted the whole song herself. We were awestruck with the way she did the role. Her age and her stature vanished and in that place was a young *Shakuntala* in love! She later gave us all a very constructive criticism of our performance. This is evergreen in my memory.

I should be grateful to *athai* for many a reason. She was the one who brought my father to *Kalakshetra* by letting him teach in the Besant Theosophical High School. All my brothers and sisters were students here. This made all of us to have an open approach in our lives. We gained a lot of experience by meeting many a people who attended the annual Theosophical convention and the art festivals of *Kalakshetra.* Travelling with *athai* worldwide has given me enough knowledge to be on my own!

Athai taught me everything during such tours, which included even table manners while dining with high officials in formal dinners! She always used to say, "learn the good manners from westerners but never give up our own Indian culture and tradition". *Athai* was the same at all times and we all followed her example. Even during long distance travels by road we never used to feel bored or tired as *athai* used to talk to us about various topics. We were also allowed to sing and dance while travelling in the bus! She was good in imitating people and we used to be her regular subjects for a good laugh! *Athai* never used to put on a long face if she was called in for a press conference as soon as we reached our destination. She would go to her room instead, freshen up and return quickly. She would on occasion take some of the seniors to the press meet with her and ask us to answer a few questions. We were thus trained to overcome our shyness, to gain confidence in facing the media, and learned how to speak with them! Even today if someone says that my interview was good, I feel, the entire credit goes to my mentor. Today when I lead my troupe, I follow her teachings and my work is very successful.

During *athai*'s times, *Kalakshetra* artists used to travel continuously for about 2 – 3 months. *Athai* would lead the tour with a tour manager. A lady used to travel with us for taking charge of the girls and costumes. As soon as we reach the hotel, *athai* would allocate rooms for all the artists. Only after we all had retired to our rooms would she go to hers. She used to inspect each room herself. If she were unhappy with the arrangements she would immediately ask the organizers to provide an alternative accommodation. She was very particular that her artists were comfortable while touring.

Athai used to allocate shared rooms for us. She never liked the idea of a young girl staying alone and would ask an elderly person to share the room. She maintained that sharing a room with an elderly person will provide security to the young girl and that the girl on her part could take care of the elder Thus she taught us how to care for older people in our lives. Each one of the girls had to take turns in sharing the room with *athai*. During such times the girl had to wash *athai*'s clothes, fold and pack them back in her suitcase. On these occasions, *athai* used to talk a lot about herself and her personal experiences. She was known to put girls to sleep like a loving mother. Those who have shared the room with *athai* have experienced her love in this way.

Athai was very particular in wearing Indian clothes. She insisted that all women wear only saree or *pavadai/dhavani* and the men, *dhoti* and *kurta*. This rule was obeyed even while travelling. *Athai* had a good colour sense. She disliked a *saree* without a border and *pallu*. If she saw one of us wearing such a *saree* she would ask us why we were draped in a curtain cloth? We used to admire her choice of sarees and jewellery. She always used to dress well. Looking grand but never gaudy. She preferred cotton and silk sarees. She would complement us if we dressed up in silk sarees and the right amount of jewellery. On all occasions she saw to it that her artists were dressed well. She has even lent us a few of her sarees during tours. According to *athai*, anything too much is an eyesore. She believed in being simple yet attractive. Even today, *pavadai dhavani/saree* and *pyjama kurta/dhoti* is the uniform in *Kalakshetra* and its associated schools. *Kalakshetra* designer sarees are world famous now. That was the greatness of *athai* in being a role model for all her students.

Athai always had a soft corner for older people. She encouraged many a great *vidwan* to come and teach in *Kalakshetra*. I have had the wonderful opportunity of learning under such great maestros during my life at *Kalakshetra*: Mysore Vasudevachar, Karaikkudi Sambasasivaiyer, Budalur Krishanmurthy Shastrigal, M.D. Ramanathan, Mylapore Gowri Ammal, Melattur Balu Bhagavathar, Turaiyur Rajagopala Sharma, Chandu Paniker Asan, Ambu Panikar Asan, and Kalyani Kutti Ammal were the noteworthy people who have worked under Rukmini Devi. To have all of them to teach the students is something impossible for an outsider of *Kalakshetra*. In that way all of us were blessed indeed!

Athai used to visit our classes often. When she entered the class, our teachers would greet her cordially and she used to greet them back in the same manner. *Athai*'s humbleness and reverence for elderly people and artists should stand as an example for all the youngsters of today. The teachers respected her for her position as the director of *Kalakshetra* and she gave respect for their age and knowledge. *Kalakshetra* was like a *gurukulam*. We never used to bother about our diploma and *athai* too never insisted on it. We used to attend our classes regularly with our seniors and juniors. My other teachers like S. Sharada, Sarada Hoffman, and N.S. Jayalakshmi used to conduct classes for us. Sometimes *athai* used to conduct the classes herself. We had to be present in *athai*'s class, when she taught the seniors. Though we didn't belong to that class we had to watch *athai* conduct the senior class, which also taught us how to teach and how to learn.

When the responsibility of being the Principal of *Kalakshetra* was given to me, I was nervous because I did not want to disappoint my guru. But then she was the one who shaped me into the human I am. She was the one who taught me to dance, to compose, to choreograph, to conduct, to teach and to administer! I thought the greatest gift I can give to my guru was to continue her work through my divine art. With all her blessings, I have been successful in this field. I thank God for having given me such a priceless guru. What I am today is what she gave me. Till I breathe my last, my guru's teachings will continue through this true disciple. *Sri Gurubhyo Namah*

(This paper was presented at the Rukmini Devi National Seminar, organized by the *Centre for Contemporary Culture*, at Chennai in 2003.)

CHAPTER 12

REMEMBERING AMMA: A BEACON LIGHT

V. P. Dhananjayan

"Look Rukmini, who is coming Viswamitra, Rama and Lakshmana," exclaimed Sankara Menon looking at Guru Chanduppanikkar , Balagopal and myself (Dhananjayan) coming towards the Arundale house in the Theosophical campus in the year 1953 ,October 5th. *Amma* would have got a shock of her life, "what are you talking Appunni ?" she rushed to the door only to see us. We just arrived fresh from Kerala, *Asan* Chanduppanikkar's new finds for *Kalakshetra.* Being the kind of genius that she was, she would have decided then and there that both of us would fit in perfect for the casts of Sri Rama and Lakshmana in her Valmiki *Ramayana-* Part one- *Sitaswayamvaram* being planned to be produced by *Kalakshetra.* Yes, I did play the role of *Sri Rama* till the fourth part – *Sabari Moksham.*

Amma –otherwise called by the name *Athai* had an extraordinary perception of persons and personalities, and her choice of people for different characters in the dance dramas worked perfectly and was unquestionably correct. She had her own reasons, which we could not understand. For instance, in *Aandal Charitam* she chose our Chinna Sarada Teacher as *Aandal* with myself playing the father role of *Periyalwar.* Initially people thought the age disparity between myself and Sarada teacher, who is much older to me in age, would feel a bit awkward. But as days passed by and practice sessions progressed, we felt *Amma* was correct in choosing Sarada teacher as *Aandal.* Her contention being that *Aandal* had an extraordinary birth and was found by Vishnuchittar as a grown up baby, who quickly grew into a youthful young maiden. To delineate such a character, a mature girl was appropriate. When *Aandal* was presented – one of *Amma*'s marvellous choreographic successes, no one questioned the choice of the characters.

Again in *Gita Govindam* she chose a short Sri Krishna (Balagopal) against a taller Shanta as *Radha.* When *Geeta Govindam* was chosen for production all of us thought that I would be the right choice for Sri Krishna, being tall and suitable. But *Amma* belied our expectations by choosing Balagopal as *Sri Krishna.* After we saw the presentation, every one of us appreciated the appropriateness of her choice of characters: Shanta as *Radha,* Sarada teacher as her *Sakhi* and Balagopal as *Sri Krishna.*

In those days, *Gurus* and elders would never praise their students lest they grew proud. They felt that encouraging young students in their own presence would hamper their growth. If the teachers were silent, we assumed that we had done well. Looking back on the past, we now feel that our *gurus* were right because it was their attitude that made us work harder to achieve perfection. Waiting to get a silent nod from our gurus, we were compelled to strive harder and gain the approbation from our elders.

Guru Chanduppanikkar belonged to the category of great teachers mentioned above. In *Kathakali* – the character of *Dharmaputra* in *Krimeera Vadham* was his forte and he was known for his extraordinary portrayal of this character. It took a long time for him to teach that one *Padam* to us, (a very slow tempo *padam.* One day after the class, *Asan* walked away silently and we could not understand what had happened. While walking through the Besant gardens to our boys hostel in Besant school compound, I heard *Amma* calling out to me from the balcony of her office. Sankara Menon was with her. Frightened about being reprimanded,

I slowly went up to meet Amma. At close quarters, I realized she was not in a mad mood, and I calmed myself. (She always spoke to us in *Tamizh* because she detested her students speaking English). *Amma* said." *Asan* came to me just now and told me that you enacted a wonderful *Padam* in *Kathakali*, and he wanted me to come and see you do it tomorrow. So Appuni and myself will come to your class tomorrow," she said. I heaved a sigh of relief.

The next day, nervous though I was, I was asked to perform the *Padam* (it lasted almost one hour or more). At the end of my performance, I could see drops of tears in *Amma*'s eyes, which she wiped away with the tissues that she always carried with her. But she could not cover up her emotion and burst out "you brought tears to my eyes, but the credit goes to *Asaan* who toiled days and months training you all." I felt as if I had won a big, million stars citation or award.

Amma's eyes would not escape any mistakes or irrelevant gestures that we made during the performance. She would spot them individually in a stage production with a cast of forty or fifty. She would also single out these mistakes and correct them the next day. If she was silent after a public performance, and came backstage, we felt reassured because that meant that the performance had gone off well. If she did not come back stage, we knew that the performance had not gone well and would hear from her the next day. Working with her ir each production was a different experience and our batch of students were the most privileged as we had direct interaction with *Amma,* imbibing a great deal from her artistic and aesthetic perception of total Indianness and her art of living.

(A version of this essay was published in the *Rukmini Devi Centenary Souvenir* 2003–04. V.P.Dhananjayan graciously chaired the Rukmini Devi Seminar organised by the *Centre for Contemporary Culture* at Chennai in 2003 and shared these memories as a distinguished alumnus of *Kalakshetra* from 1953 to 1969.)

CHAPTER 13

THE OTHER SIDE OF ATHAI: REMINISCENCES

Shanta Dhananjayan

I felt very strongly that *Athai* had always had a soft corner for me. When I arrived in *Kalakshetra* in June 1952, at the age of eight, *Amma* was not in station. But I had the unique privilege of dancing in her honor after two months of my joining the *Kalakshetra. Amma* was away on a foreign tour and to welcome her back *Kalakshetra* staff and students had put up a cultural program in her honor for which I was quickly trained and put on stage. From that day, her sharp eye fell on me, and she had always cast me in her productions whether it was a small role or a big one. Every one speaks about her greatness as a dancer, choreographer, theosophist, animal lover etc, but I want to just dwell on two incidents, which throw light on her humanness as an ordinary individual. - the other side of *Athai*.

After graduating from *Kalakshetra* and spending 10 years at a stretch till 1962, I left for Malaysia to join my parents. Under the direct umbrella of the Ministry of Culture, Malaysia Government, and under the able guidance of Smt. Uma Sambandan, a Minister in the Malaysian Cabinet, I had started teaching the local Indians and children of other communities.

In 1963 at the South Asia Cultural Festival of Singapore, I had the wonderful opportunity to participate both as a member of the Indian delegation which was represented by *Kalakshetra* headed by Rukmini Devi, and as a member of the Malaysian Indian troupe. As an Indian *Bharatanatyam* dancer,

I had done something totally new by evolving a new concept of choreographing *Bharatanatyam* movements tò a Malay song which was included in the Malaysian presentation. Since this kind of a combination was a new idea, I was not sure if, *Amma* (*Athai*) would appreciate such a venture. When finally *Athai* saw my work at one of the shows, I was extremely nervous about her reaction. To my great joy and surprise when we came back after the show she called out to me and expressed how happy she was to see my new work. She said " Shanta, I never knew you could create this kind of innovative work. How did you learn the local language and interpret the meaning through dance so well. What are you doing in Malaysia, wasting your talent. You must come back to *Kalakshetra* and be with us" Those words were like honey to my ears. She was really magnanimous in appreciating my little work as a budding dancer in a foreign soil. I shall never forget this wonderful experience with *Athai.*

Much earlier to this event I had an intimate experience of *Athai*'s loving care. While we were touring in Assam in 1960, I was privileged to share a room with *Athai* at the house of Sri. Bishnuram Medi, Governor of Tamilnadu at that time. When we came back home after the performance in an open air theatre in a cold winter night in which I did a lot of dancing with fever, *Athai* came to me where I was lying in the room, and touched my feet saying " you danced very well in spite of your temperature Shanta , let me give a massage to your aching feet ?" Saying that, she touched my feet and I got up with a shock realizing *Athai* was touching my feet. There I saw the softness of her heart and I felt so ecstatic. Such a great person behaving like a simple loving mother with care and concern. I can never ever forget that gesture in my life. A great lesson indeed to cherish.

In the year 1959 when *Gita Govindam* was produced I was chosen by *Athai* to do the role of *Radha.* I could not believe the fact as to how I was chosen to be *Radha* when my teacher Sarada Hoffman was to do my *Sakhi*'s role. I had the most rewarding time of my student days in having to learn the part of *Radha* directly from *Athai* . How can I forget the days when she used to take me to her house at the Theosophical Society campus along with Dr. Padmasini Teacher to teach me all the *Ashtapadis* in detail – correcting my postures and *Abhinaya* . I had spent several such wonderful evenings with her watching her sensitive and beautiful *abhinaya* in awe. There I saw in her a true teacher with a lot of commitment and love.

There are many more such incidents to speak about, which will be cherished always in my heart. Here is an example of the another interesting and lighter side to Athai which I will share with you. When we toured Australia in the year 1966, we had great experience travelling the nook and corner of almost the whole continent. Those were the days when very few Indians or Indian food was available there and hence we had to satisfy our hunger by eating fruits and salads along with some kind of concocted Indian curry. That is when we visited several stores looking for stuff like pickles and so on. During the course of travel, I found out that *Athai* had special taste for specific kind of food in spite of being a strong vegetarian. She would pick the most pungent Indonesian s*ambal* (pickle) from the store and invite to share it with her since the other members of our group detested the taste of the sambal pickle. *Athai* also loved varieties of cheese and Chinese and Italian food (of course vegetarian), which I too loved because of my Malaysian background. She would call out to me "Shanta come let us eat this avocado and artichoke...others do not like it." My friends thus used to make fun of me saying "*Athai* and you have some kind of funny similar tastes," and they used to mock me saying "how can you eat that stuff." Thus I got to share a lot of good and interesting food with *Athai* which the other members could not stomach. The interesting thing was that we had very bland food in the hostel. Yet *Athai* loved spicy and *masala* food! And I remember my mother cooking those kinds of food for her when she was invited to my house in Malaysia, which *Athai* enjoyed.

(A version of this essay was published in the *Rukmini Devi Centenary Souvenir 2003-2004*. Smt. Shanta Dhananjayan, was a student and teacher in *Kalakshetra* from 1952 to 1969.)

CHAPTER 14

REMEMBERING A LEGEND

V.R. Devika

Smt. Rukmini Devi Arundale is a legend for reasons more than one. She is remembered for her *Kalakshetra.* She is well known for espousing the cause of Prevention of Cruelty Against Animals. Most of all, she lives through her dance-dramas, including her magnum opus on the *Ramayana.* She realized many achievements in a variety of fields. In her life's journey, she also gathered around her many illustrious and dedicated associates. It is the ability of the great souls to recognize the right associates and inspire them to work for great causes. Mahatma Gandhi had done it, and Rukmini Devi did the same. This is a story about Rukmini, the legend, told from the point of view of Sarada Hoffman and C.T. Nachiappan, the two people that she singled out from among the many that she had nurtured. It tells the story of how she inspired them and propelled them to assume leadership in new fields, and work on behalf of the vision of *Kalakshetra.* Their story, which is recounted here, is also the story of Rukmini Devi Arundale.

Sarada Hoffman:

"I had to stand up and sit down each time I combed her hair and removed the knots. She had such long luxurious hair," says Sarada Hoffman, who had been with Rukmini Devi since her pre-*Kalakshetra* days. Rukmini Devi kept recommending Sarada's name for the President's award from the *Sangeet Natak Akademi* every year. Only in 1997, long after Rukmini Devi was dead and Sarada retired from *Kalakshetra*, was the award given to her for being an exceptional dance guru. With the political developments in the capital, the President of India could not be present in Bombay for the award ceremony in December 1997.

"I had no other life. My life has been only dance and *Kalakshetra.* I feel India owes a great deal to Rukmini Devi. She created an aesthetic climate for dance teaching. The emphasis was on refinement and beauty in simplicity," says Sarada. As a small child in Theosophical Society, Sarada was among the first batch of students with which the Besant Memorial School was begun with the express purpose of giving an artistic education with Indian aesthetic living as the prime goal. Rukmini Devi would produce small dramas with the children in her pre-dance days.

"I was a little girl when I saw Rukmini Devi's first performance and was very happy to have been chosen to play a lotus in a drama. I just had to sit in a basket and be a lotus opening out. The only ambition was to get a nod from her. I was Rahula in the production '*Light of Asia*' and all I had to do was sleep next to Rukmini Devi who acted as *Yashodhara.* With eager eyes, I watched all that was happening around and being asked to remove the knots from her hair in the green room was the greatest joy..."

Rukmini Devi gathered the little children and would tell them stories about the great *rishis* of myths and others. "We sat around her worshipping her... She sat by the steps of the Buddhist shrine at the Theosophical Society. There were lilies in the water tank and the idealism she advocated went straight to our heart," says Sarada.

Chokkalingam Pillai taught Sarada and Radha (later the President of Theosophical Society). "Rukmini Devi would be sitting looking at the papers, but suddenly look up and say that the hand is not reaching high enough. I kept repeating the *korvai tajumta...tarumtha...* from *vasantha jatiswaram* for over two hours. Somewhere she would look up and say all right and then I would go to the next *korvai....*"

After 1939, Maria Montessori, who had been invited to

the Theosophical Society, could not return due to the war. So they stayed on and developed the Montessori method here. Rukmini Devi conducted a course for teachers. She emphasized the need to appreciate beauty and gave lecture demonstrations. She organized an Indian home exhibition to show the Indian way of living. Furniture designed for the exhibition was made at the Society. This was the time that Society made the *kurta* famous. A weaving department was started to make saris. All this was done to relate art to life. "Every detail was carefully looked into," says Sarada. "Artists had the responsibility of helping backstage...helping other dancers in their dressing up and the lighting etc. This was the greatest training given at *Kalakshetra.*" At the Besant Memorial School, the emphasis was not on studying but on idealism and healthy and simple living.

"I had to wait till I was 10-years-old to learn dance but I was very impatient and would go and sit in the classes. *Athai* (as Rukmini Devi was called by everyone) called me on my tenth birthday and formally started classes for me. She would ask us to come and watch her do exercises at six in the morning and teach us to bend, jump like a cat, a horse... She taught us how to relax, how to be light... I still have the vivid picture of the immense grace and beauty of her movements. It was such a special privilege."

"In 1940-41, I went on the first South India tour which was organized to spread the idea of Theosophy and beauty in living. There was an exhibition on Montessori methodology of education, talks on Theosophy, a solo *Bharatanatyam* by Radha, variety dances of *Kummi* and *Kolattam* by us children. This tour brought a lot of children to the Besant School from all over South India, particularly from Chettinad. This was how Nachiappan came to Besant School."

"For my *arangetram* in 1943, she tried different *varnams* on me. I was taught a *todi varnam* which lasted for an hour. She came and saw it and said it did not suit my age. It was to be *mohamana* finally after learning four or five *varnams...* She began to compose new *varnams* after the traditional teachers left *Kalakshetra* just before my *arangetram*. She learnt the *jatis* from *mridangist* Bairavan Pillai and wielded the cymbals herself with Peria Sarada. It was on her birthday that I had my *arangetram...* My family had to move to Madurai after that. *Attai* wrote a letter to me asking me if I would stay and work with her. She said the decision had to be entirely mine and mine alone. You may show the letter to your parents but you must make the decision. I decided to choose what I wanted. Dance and *Athai*, Rukmini Devi Arundale and *Kalakshetra*," says Sarada, smiling.

Nachiappan:

The Dutch commercial artist and photographer, Conrad Woldring, walked into the library of the Theosophical Society (in 1938) and was impressed with the handwriting on the little index cards. He sought out the boy. Young Nachiappan hated the games period and decided to learn art from Conrad. He approached Rukmini Devi and got him special permission to be away from games period to learn photography, commercial art, furniture design and lighting for the stage from Conrad. In 1945, Nachiappan created a makeshift darkroom and began to make prints. He was the first to process an ekthachrome transparency in Madras and the first to start Kodak color processing and printing.

By 1958, the *Kalakshetra* color laboratories became famous in Chennai. Staff photographers for *Time, Life* and *National Geographic* were his clients as were numerous photographers from the Magnum photo agency including the great Henri Cartier-Bresson. *Kalakshetra* printing office also began to print text books and books on Montessori system of education. For *Kalakshetra*, there were text books, dance programme, placards and posters, yearbooks and other work being printed and soon the printing office came to be called *Kalakshetra* Publications.

"By 1975, technology had come to India," says Nachiappan. "All my boys left for other jobs, or opened business of their own. I decided not to turn to the new technology. It cost a lot of money and there was also the *Kalakshetra* philosophy of keeping to traditional Eastern ideas." While the industrial and commercial fell to more technologically advanced printers, a whole new generation of artists, poets and publishers came searching to *Kalakshetra* for precisely what they would not find in modern technology, the handmade quality of craftsmanship that spoke of another era. By stepping back into the world of monotype, collotype, four colour letter press and engraving, hand sewn bindings and the like, Nachiappan and the *Kalakshetra* Publications set the course for a very unique niche in printing technology.

Kalakshetra Publications' most artistic work is the book created for artist Franscesco Clemente called *Udue Clemente Flamina Pulsae.* The illustrations were printed as color plates, tipped into the book using a method of corner slits, similar to the souvenir books sold in temples. Decorative borders surrounding the images were printed in letterpress. The pages were made of thick, brightly coloured paper, made from cotton rags in Pondicherry. The signatures were hand sewn, as is always the case at *Kalakshetra* when they worked on a larger format publication. The binding cloth was handmade Khadi. Franscesco Clemente came back to *Kalakshetra* to work on a larger publication, *Franscesco Clemente Pinxit.* The book illustrated works in a wide variety of media, oils pastel, fresco, sumi ink on paper and one page from Clemente's first series of miniatures made in India. Later, Nachiappan printed over 1,50,000 Hanuman books. Each one set in English monotype, hand sewn, with four colour dust jackets and gold stamping. Forty-eight titles with writings by artists, documents of the Beat generation, overlooked English Sanskrit scholars, Lower East side poets, rock musicians and Warhol superstars were published in miniature format.

Kalakshetra Publications took on many printing jobs including the microfilming for *The Hindu*. Now it still produces Montessori books though on a small scale. Nachiappan has taken *sanyas* and has become the *swami* of the *Kovalur Mutt*.

What will happen to *Kalakshetra* Publications? "Rukmini Devi was deeply interested in *Kalakshetra* becoming a deemed university," says Nachiappan, "She was completely against turning the institution over to the government. It is now 50 years for the *Kalakshetra* Publications; which has done pioneering work in its own areas as the mother institution *Kalakshetra*. Who knows what will happen next?

(A version of this article was printed in *The Hindu*, Sunday, February 22, 1998.)

PART - III

CHAPTER 15

MADE HISTORY AND MADE BY HISTORY: RUKMINI DEVI'S INTEGRATED APPROACH TO BHARATANATYAM

Leela Venkataraman

When history seems to create a stage tailor-made for the talents of a specific person to flourish, one is led to subscribe to the belief of the individual having been born for a purpose, under a special constellation. Such a person was the late Rukmini Devi – artiste, humanist, institution-builder, educationist and reformer. While the circumstances in the country at that point of time were ideal for a person like Rukmini Devi to play a major role in life, it is also true that none but a person of her stature and vision could have filled the vacuum arising during this period. It is interesting to study how the needs of the time and Rukmini Devi's energies dovetailed into each other so smoothly. If history made her, she in turn made history. Her entire approach to the dance, which she wove into a whole lifestyle and pattern of education, had an inevitability about it, given the way life had prepared her.

Looking first at the historical perspective, it appears as if the times almost connived to thrust Rukmini Devi centre stage. One needs to remember the cusp of the century when she was born (29 February 1904, a leap year) when rapid changes were emerging on the Indian scene. She must have been in her impressionable teens when more than the mere rumblings of a desire for self-rule had been set in motion. By her twenties, she had become an active participant in the National Movement, then at its peak, with fervour sweeping all over the country to rediscover India's lost identity. The love for orientalism had already been inculcated in young Rukmini Devi, an ardent activist of the Theosophical Society movement, constantly fed on the fiery oratory of Annie Besant. Classical dance, in particular *Bharatanatyam*, had been pushed to the forefront during the Nationalist struggle, due to the burgeoning swell of censure directed against the hapless temple dancer, hitherto the sole custodian of *Sadir* (later given the appellation of *Bharatanatyam*). Maligned to the point of extinction, the *devadasi* had strong opposition from one who hailed from her own clan in the person of Dr. Muttulakshmi Reddy, spearheading the *anti-devadasi* movement. Later, she was to pilot a bill through the Madras Legislature for abolishing the institution of the *devadasi*. The anti-nautch movement had gathered momentum all over the country. Propitiously, this was the time, when the Madras Music Academy, a cultural offshoot of the Indian National Congress holding its annual meeting in Chennai, then Madras, had as its Secretary, E. Krishna Iyer, a lawyer by profession and a self-appointed guardian of Sadir.

Looking for ways of preserving *Sadir*, which so far had been the sole domain of traditional families of *Nattuvanars* and *devadasis*, E. Krishna Iyer had in earnest begun to educate public opinion in support of the art form, though the battle to save the temple dancer seemed to him, to be already lost, with society having turned its back irrevocably on the institution it had created, nourished and legitimised. The obvious way out of the situation to save at least the art form if not its traditional exponents was to separate art from the practitioner, since it was the person of the *devadasi* that had attracted public opprobrium – affecting in the process the way one looked at the art form. Perhaps understandably, E. Krishna Iyer hailing from a Brahmin background looked for fresh *Sadir* recruits amongst the Brahmin families which had been intimately connected with the art form – but as patrons and never as performers. Lying outside the blamed fold of the *devadasi*, who was regarded as having solicited and become the object of the male gaze, girls from 'upper caste' families had the advantage of their person lying outside of what was being looked upon as a tainted heritage. For E. Krishna Iyer's choice to fall upon Rukmini Devi was natural. A beautiful, talented woman, who by the year 1925 had been given the place of 'World Mother' by none other than Annie Besant (in 1927 *Mother India* published by an American journalist Catherine Mayo had stirred up some public reactions), Rukmini Devi was already President of the All India Federation of Young Theosophists and later also President of the World Federation of Young Theosophists. Her highly publicised and much criticised marriage to an Englishman, Dr. George Sydney Arundale, several years her senior, had also set her apart as a young woman not afraid of unconventional acts.

The E. Krishna Iyer- Rukmini Devi axis would have led to little if it had happened at an earlier time, when Rukmini Devi was in her teens for instance, for she was drawn to the dance only in her late twenties after being treated to a performance of the famous ballerina, Anna Pavlova, at Covent Garden in London, when she was touring Europe with her husband in 1924. It was not till 1928 that chance played a part in her getting closer to Pavlova when the ballerina and Rukmini Devi, with her husband, happened to be travelling by the same ship to Australia. The eventful encounter led to Rukmini Devi beginning to have ballet lessons under Cleo Nordi. Pavlova is credited with inspiring Rukmini Devi, whose eyes by now had been opened to the beauties of dance, to discover more of the dance in her own country. Significantly, Rukmini Devi's stay in Pudukkottai, during her young days, where her father, a construction engineer, was overseeing the building of a new palace for King Marthanda Thondaiman, the ruler of the princely state of Pudukkottai, saw the family living more or less opposite a house where two *devadasis* were being trained under a nattuvanar. The constant rhythm of the *'Tattukazhi'* rent the air with no response from Rukmini Devi. Being treated to a *Sadir* performance inside the Puddukkotai temple too had left her unmoved. But after the Pavlova connection, when she saw *devadasis* Jeevaratnam and Varalakshmi perform, her responses were very different. When E. Krishna Iyer invited her to a performance by Jeevaratnam at the Music Academy, Rukmini Devi, ecstatic about what she saw, was fired by a desire to learn the art form. Her first guru, suggested by Kunjan Raja, a Sanskrit teacher, was Mylapore Gowri Ammal, daughter of Doraikannu of Kapaliswarar Temple. And Rukmini Devi was taught some '*adavus*' and simple items like *Sabdam.* But after witnessing full-blown performances of *Sadir,* she had the feeling that a teacher like Meenakshi Sundram Pillai would be more useful. It was left to E. Krishna Iyer to persuade '*Tata*', which he managed to do with some difficulty, to accept Rukmini Devi as a disciple. Having never taught any student outside the *devadasi* fold, to train one outside this circle and a Brahmin at that, who was all of twenty-eight years in age, was a daunting task. There is little doubt that seeing the writing on the wall as far as the future of the *devadasi* was concerned, the better part of wisdom would have also dictated Meenakshi Sundram Pillai's decision not only to teach Rukmini Devi, but also to move to Madras to do so. A big step for a guru who had functioned only from his home in Pandanallur, where those who wanted to learn from him sought him out. Rukmini Devi's tryst with *Bharatanatyam* had begun.

Gifted with an inborn feeling for beauty and aesthetics, and deeply interested in theatre with which art form she was connected through performances too, Rukmini Devi entered the field of dance, not as the usual six to eight-year-old, submitting herself to all that the guru is prepared to give, but as a mature woman who had seen and experienced art and life. During her very first appearance, as a child, in a Tagore play, *Malini,* for which role her father's reluctant permission had been obtained, her melodious singing in *Kedaragowla* and her dazzling physical presence had attracted attention. It had also led to the father enthusiastically stating that he would have the daughter trained in music. Rukmini Devi was also a lover of music, both Western and Indian – the musical interest being part of her childhood home, thanks to her mother Seshamma, hailing from an orthodox Tiruvaiyaru family, who though not formally trained, could sing melodiously and was knowledgeable about ragas. Thus, Rukmini Devi was bound to bring to the art form her own convictions, unlike the usual young *Bharatanatyam* aspirant whose mind and body can be moulded by the guru.

The father's knowledge of Sanskrit had also instilled in her a feel for classical literature though she was no scholar in the language. The Theosophical Society activity had awakened the spiritual side and while the Hindu in her had been reinforced by this connection, it had also given her a respect for religion without any of the dogma of ritual. Years spent on the campus of the Theosophical Society had inculcated in Rukmini Devi a love for wide, open spaces where one is in constant communion with Nature. With this kind of many-faceted exposure to life, it would have been surprising if Rukmini Devi had looked at classical dance in isolation, as an island in itself. Ever alive to the inter-connections among the various disciplines of life, she patterned *Kalakshetra* as a 'temple of the arts', where dance lived in a total artistic environment absorbing beauty from different fields of activity. Initially set up without much fanfare within the Theosophical Society campus as the International Academy of Arts registered in the year 1936, it was later shifted and housed in Adyar and acquired the new name of *Kalakshetra*.

Dance, for Rukmini Devi, as an expression of the body, mind and spirit, was nurtured by an environment, which acquired its tone and character, through the entire lifestyle. Exposed to both the East and the West, Rukmini Devi's mind was alive to the eternal verities and richness of tradition on the one hand, and to the relevance of contemporaneity on the other. So, for her, the structured essence of tradition had to be accommodated to the compulsions of the present. *Kalakshetra* catered to all these aspects of concern. The multidisciplinary approach could be seen in the number of institutions housed in *Kalakshetra,* which apart from the College of Fine Arts, had a Weaving Section, a Teachers' Training Centre and the Besant Theosophical School.

The bodily training, which emphasised dance technique, came essentially from the traditional gurus. While retaining the best in the intimate teacher/student interaction represented in the *Gurukul* system, Rukmini Devi gave the training an openness in the institutionalised form, somewhat different from the closed-door privacy of the one-to-one teaching system, hitherto practised by the *devadasis.* Great minds like K. Narayana Menon, C.V. Chandrasekhar, Yagneswara, Rukmini Devi's own brother and K. Ramakotiswara Rao were constantly involved in working out the broad patterning of the institution. By bringing into the picture so many non-dance people, she gave to *Bharatanatyam* the benefits of an intellectual approach. She did not believe in the ivory tower exclusivity in which *Bharatanatyam* had been nurtured all these years and wanted public awareness to be built up about the art form. Her fear was that if left to function in a vacuum, the art form would lack an overseeing critical eye, which alone could help ruthlessly weed out the least sign of profanity.

Rukmini Devi's ability to attract the best teachers in the field for *Kalakshetra* seemed endless. Under the renowned Meenakshi Sundram Pillai, Chokkalingam Pillai, Karaikkal Saradambal, and Gowri Ammal were trained the next generation of teachers like Chinna Sarada, Guru Adyar Lakshmanan and others. For *Kathakali,* Rukmini Devi had Ambu Panickar and Chandu Panickar. And in music, which was such an essential part of the training for dance, the stalwarts connected with *Kalakshetra* made people wonder as to what alchemy Rukmini Devi used to make the greatest names agree to work for the institution for little remuneration. Tiger Varadachariyar, Mysore Vasudevachariyar, Budaloor Krishnamurthy Sastrigal, Mudicondan Venkatarama Iyer, Karaikudi Sambasiva Iyer – the list was a Who's Who of Carnatic music. Such wide spread contribution is all the more surprising when viewed against the fact that Rukmini Devi was no musician of stature herself. It was the ambience she provided for their art that made them such willing helpers. In fact, M.D. Ramanathan when once asked as to why he worked so hard for Rukmini Devi, when the compensation in financial terms was so negligible, replied that working in *Kalakshetra* gave him the kind of fulfilment that no money could. At one point of time, the *Nattuvanar* community had begun to resent the withering away of their monopolistic hold over *Bharatanatyam.* Gurus like Chokkalingam Pillai openly voiced their protest about the traditional community of teachers being deprived of their profession, which they said had been appropriated by the Brahmins. Their stand began to influence singers who were urged not to sing for Rukmini Devi. This was the moment when Papânasam Sivan agreed to sing for her, even turning down an award with which he was sought to be lured away. He took the stand that when he had struggled to keep the wolf away from his door, Rukmini Devi alone had come to his rescue, providing him with a haven with all its creative comforts and artistic environment, and his loyalty to her was unshakeable.

With all her reverence and respect for the old masters of dance and music, Rukmini Devi remained very much her own person, and not one who could be exploited by the gurus with whom her relationship had its ups and downs. Her encounter with Meenakshi Sundram Pillai had its share of awkward situations. Her maiden appearance as a *Bharatanatyam* dancer for a Silver Jubilee celebration of the Theosophical Society in 1935, was not agreed to by Meenakshi Sundram Pillai, who either due to reservations about her readiness for a formal recital, or because of pique at being inadequately compensated (both reasons have been cited by knowledgeable persons), refused to conduct the recital. He sent instead Chokkalingam Pillai's son Subbaraya Pillai for conducting the *Nattuvangam*, and Narayanaswami for percussion. When Rukmini Devi's explanations about the recital being an informal, in-house presentation did not change the stand of the guru, she stuck to her guns and went through the entire performance even while shocked elitist leaders like C.P. Ramaswamy Iyer, Rt Honourable Srinivasa Sastri, Sadasiva Iyer and T.R. Venkatarama Sastri boycotted the event. In a similarly determined gesture, she refused to have a formal *arangetram*, despite constant egging from Gowri Ammal. For her, a formal stage presentation did not mean anything, for she was not in the general race for solo performance activities. Her contribution was more as a reformer, and she never tried to project herself as a regular performer. One who at the still-untried age of sixteen had gone through a totally unconventional marriage with a foreigner, who was about forty in age certainly could not be accused of being faint-hearted. Throughout life, she took bold decisions, led more by instinct than logic, and she lived by these.

In art she was guided by her search for beauty in whatever she undertook, and to achieve this end, she never hesitated to make departures from conventional practice. When she had the urge to produce a *Bhagavata Mela* play in *Kalakshetra*, she fell in line with traditional gurus who felt that *Prahlada Natakam* with all its ritualistic associations would not be the right choice for *Kalakshetra*. While agreeing upon *Rukmini Kalyanam* as the play to be embarked upon, she got Balu Bhagwatar and Kalyani Ammal, both from the traditional performing families to teach and guide the students. But she made her own changes – shortening sequences, and making Turaiyur Rajagopala Sarma edit lyrics and even compose new scores. The final enactment, much applauded for its superb artistic vision, however, had one strong critic in her own brother, Yajneswara, who in no uncertain terms accused her of having meddled with tradition. When she felt that *Nattuvanars* were becoming difficult to cope with, she made a person like Sarada do the *Nattuvangam,* and soon specialisation in *Nattuvangam* had become part of the training that *Kalakshetra* provided. The neatly seated musicians on one side of the stage took the place of the traditional practice of the musicians following the dancer as she moved on the stage. There are traditional gurus who claim to have started the practice of seating the musicians on the side of the stage much before Rukmini Devi introduced this practice. But no proof is available of this having been so.

Fearless re-invention of tradition was Rukmini Devi's main trait. She was convinced of art having to be nurtured in a climate wherein creativity could flourish without fear or vulgarity. For this to be achieved, young minds had to be evolved in the right ambience; it is precisely for this reason of spotting young minds which in turn could discover themselves through the art form, that Rukmini Devi decided to educate children. Her contact with Madame Montessori, who came to Adyar for a series of lectures in 1939, gave birth to the Montessori Children's School. A system geared towards leading a child to self-discovery, in place of spoon-feeding with indigestible information, appealed to her. Education for Rukmini Devi was character-building and she was less interested in formal classes than in creating the right climate for building healthy young minds, sensitized to aesthetics. Herself the very essence of impeccable taste, Rukmini Devi shunned ugliness in any form. The way *Kalakshetra* was designed gave ample proof of her extreme concern for beauty. The simple thatched buildings reflected serenity and a highly developed feel for the artistic. The expansive campus and the abundance of trees and greenery were part of inculcating in the young a deep love for nature. If nurtured, nature in turn protected man, and so its creatures were also worthy of the same respect as shown to fellow men. One of the senior teacher/choreographers who graduated from *Kalakshetra,* and also taught there for some time, recounts an incident with *Athai.* "We had just finished our prayer meeting in the morning under the wonderful Banyan tree and as we made our way to the class, we kept trying to shoo away a street dog that persisted in following us. *Athai* happened to see us and called us to her side and questioned, "Why this attitude towards an animal that is not in any way harming you? You just said your prayers for the welfare of all living creatures. The resonance of that does not seem to have lasted too long. That dog, too, is a creature of God. He too has a right to live and he will go on his way soon."

A staunch lover of birds and animals, Rukmini Devi raised her voice against all forms of cruelty to the animal world, like whipping and vivisection. She was filled with the conviction that it was a manifestation of the same Supreme life-force that resided in every living creature. Rukmini Devi's older sister Sivakamu, a great friend of the animal world, was perhaps the one from whom she developed this enormous compassion for what she felt for the much abused animal world. Her vegetarianism, while born out of her Brahmin background, was reinforced by strong convictions against killing any life in order to nurture another. Shobhana Swamy, an old graduate from *Kalakshetra* remembers how on one Christmas day she had greeted *Athai* with a "Merry Chrismas". "For her, all religions were to be revered even though she herself was a Hindu. She returned my greeting and thanked me. And then suddenly broke out, 'How sad that to celebrate a Merry Christmas, by night time today thousands of turkeys would have ended up as meat on the table." One could see the ache reflected on her face. Several of her students testify to the fact of Rukmini Devi's portrayal of compassion in the dance when directed at a bird or any small creature always reflected that extra dimension of intensity. It was an emotion that came from within the deep portals of her heart.

Says Shobhana, "To be beautiful from inside was important to Athai and she educated youngsters by providing the best example through her own life. It was not so much the teacher-imposed discipline in the classroom, as self-disciplining that *Kalakshetra* gave to all of us. *Athai* disliked a wind-blown careless appearance, unkempt hair and unwashed, improperly matched clothes. Even ankle bells casually fastened angered her no end." Shanta Dhananjayan, one of the senior-most products of *Kalakshetra*, still talks of *Athai* never having forgiven her for her ankle bells becoming loose and coming undone while dancing vigorously in her maiden performance. Years later, she would still exclaim "How could she have done this?"

The old students speak of the great sense of equality, which prevailed all over *Kalakshetra*. "There was no hierarchy and all of us were encouraged to finish our tasks and then help the children get ready. It was the same during performances where we all helped one another. We all travelled together by train or road and as soon as we reached the other end, the older students got ready to engage in the tasks of preparing a simple meal for the group. Never has the whole philosophy of simple living and high thinking been so meticulously made into a lifestyle as in *Kalakshetra*." Reminisces another ex-student, "You know the Chettinad princess, Prita, studied at *Kalakshetra* and one cannot remember her being given any treatment different from what others had received. In *Kalakshetra*, one's place was determined by proficiency in art and not position in society."

Discipline was the key to all activities in *Kalakshetra*, and even in the neat rows of footwear arranged outside each classroom, one could see this attention to neatness and order.

Anyone who has spent some years in *Kalakshetra* under Rukmini Devi will vouchsafe for the fact that students were always taught to look at nature with a constant sense of wonder. "Did you notice the new leaves on the tree? Have you seen the flower about to bloom on that plant?" were the questions with which she would greet students. Her own response to nature was so intense that she could not imagine students not being alive to the beauty and harmony of it. The manner in which the entire campus was laid out was itself a constant reminder of being in nature in all her bounty.

Says Shobhana, "The entire atmosphere in *Kalakshetra* made us respect and revere elders. But for this trait in *Athai* herself, how could so many great names have been associated with *Kalakshetra*? To give a helping hand to an old person walking, obeisance to the old, willingness to assist people in any form came so naturally to all the students at *Kalakshetra*. *Athai's* behaviour with the great gurus associated with the institution, was a model for everyone. That feel for selflessness was instilled into all of us."

Rukmini Devi, from another account, was not given to hyperbole and she never singled out any student for too much praise. She was stinting in her show of approval, for the simple reason that she realised how quickly success went to the head. Even if a performance review spoke very highly of a dancer, she would ask in a gentle taunt, "I suppose now you think you are infallible!" The idea was not to hurt or make fun of, but to instill in the student the realisation that there was no full stop to hard work and that one always had to endeavour to seek perfection, which remained an unattained ideal. "Never to lose one's dignity was very important for *Athai*," observed another senior person from the alumni, who had this to say: "None of the eye for an eye and tooth for a tooth philosophy here. On the contrary, I remember Rukmini Devi telling us never to bother to fight back when somebody became belligerent. 'Leave them severely alone,' she would tell us. 'They will soon know that beyond losing their dignity they have gained little'. In fact, while I do not want to be named, it is this passive acceptance that makes people like our Director, Rajaram take every invasive act in *Kalakshetra* from people who have had little to do either with the alumni or with Rukmini Devi, without a murmur". The person continues, "In today's world, the kind of value structure and dignity

Rukmini Devi advocated is not understood. It is people who ride roughshod that get away with whatever they do. We were always told to be gentle. I remember when I was playing a part in a dance-drama and the costume meant for me had the most attractive jewellery to go with it. And just as we were getting ready, teacher said, 'Give that piece to X who suffers from a gross complex about her lack of stage presence. Let us show her that we do not think so, for the best of our costume accessories are being given to her.' I, of course, agreed, perhaps with some regret – which vanished when I saw how much this one act did for that girl's self-confidence. In today's dance scene, with people trying to grab opportunities to put themselves in the limelight, one wonders if *Athai's* philosophy is not an anachronism. But we have also seen some members of the *Kalakshetra* staff going on a strike! I wonder how they feel they are living by *Athai's* principles!"

For Rukmini Devi, dance was an article of faith in a super power. Her attitude to *bhakti*, which supposedly sanitised *Bharatanatyam* of its natural sensuality, has been the subject of much debate. Actually, this was more a controversy stirred by the circumstances of the *devadasi* having lost her monopoly, and the fact that she was considered the queen of *sringara* made out to be the opposite of *bhakti*. And to add to the situation was Bala – a living example of such artistic brilliance in *sringara* that it almost made a mockery of the reaction of society to the *devadasi* and her art. And soon it was made out that the vacuum, in which persons like Rukmini Devi could play a role, had been deliberately engineered. Rukmini Devi, herself, never entered the fray with any notions of giving birth to a new form of *Bharatanatyam*. She, in fact, was an admirer of Bala's art, which she was honest enough to admit could never be emulated by the likes of her who were from an entirely different background. The Sanskritisation and the intellectualisation brought into the dance form as well as the emphasis on the codified geometry of the dance form were Rukmini Devi's contribution. By institutionalising the training for *Bharatanatyam* and by placing the dance on the larger canvas of life, she connected art and life.

In terms of the solo repertoire, she brought in genres like *Keertanams* and Sanskrit passages. And while she did present *Padams* like '*Tamarasakshi...*' and '*Sariga Kongu...*' she was careful while treading into *sringar* areas, not only because her approach to the erotic sentiment was different, but also because cultural memory on what has happened to the *devadasi,* accused of profanity, was still very fresh. The dance had come out of the temple. But Rukmini Devi believed that the stage could be likened to an altar, and if the devotional element predominated in her themes, it was an inevitable reflection of her own attitudes. She had little use for secular *Bharatanatyam,* for she believed that the devotional element enabled the dance to retain its purity and dignity. And for an art form, which used the body as its medium, constant guard against profanity was a must. Her own dance (variously described by different people – her faithfuls going into ecstasies about its beauty and others shrugging it off as just pleasant and nothing extraordinary) was most impressive in its impersonal approach, with no attempt made to draw attention to the person in the dancer– though in Rukmini Devi's case, her flawless beauty was difficult to ignore. Most of the encomia for her dance came from British writers like Barbara Sellon and James Cousin, the Theosophical wicket and her own marriage having brought these people into special closeness with her. Unstinted praise about her personal dance came from professional musicians, who shared her view of the art form being a vehicle for expressing devotion. But most critics, even those who fault her use of *mudras* as being less than perfect, admit that there was an innate dignity about her art and she could enchant the audience with her mesmeric stage presence and aesthetic presentation. It was mainly as reformer whose vision gave *Bharatanatyam* a new lease of life, in a different contemporary manifestation that one remembers Rukmini Devi's contribution. And in the area of the dance-drama, she created a whole new world of aesthetics.

"Rukmini Devi's religiosity had no dogmatic element," says one of the earliest products of *Kalakshetra*, "People who criticise her for being 'Brahminical' are unfair. We had students from all classes and religions being trained in *Kalakshetra* and I remember *Athai* including verses from the Bible or other sacred literature in the prayers. We were all made to know all the stories from mythology. Even our daily prayer had a universal application in its reverence for nature, for the five elements, for the well-being of the whole universe, and so on. There was nothing even remotely parochial about her. Even our costumes were inspired by the best in all of India – there was no special Tamilian bias, though all of us were encouraged to learn Tamil and Telugu (we even had Sanskrit) as the language most connected with the *Bharatanatyam* textual base."

"As if *Athai* could have produced a whole array of dance-drama compositions without *sringara*, people talk without any basis," scoffs Shobhana Swamy. She recollects an exchange that *Athai* had with a foreigner in her presence. 'Do you not think sensuality is important?' asked the gentleman concerned. 'Of course, I think it is important. After all, it is life. But my way of expressing it may be different from others.' Expatiating on the subject, *Athai* continued, 'Imagine two women standing side by side. One who is not afraid to bare her body (and it may be done very artistically) and her dance has an overt unabashed sensuality, which people no doubt respond to. Now the other woman has a body totally covered under clothes, the only part exposed being her feet. And watching those feet with the toe rings and the anklets moving in such grace, the viewer's imagination runs riot on how beautiful and sensuous must be the entire body if just the feet could trigger such feelings. That is my idea of the sensuous, where a hint suffices in suggesting its totality to the audience.' I can never forget that exchange."

Rukmini Devi may have had her individual idiosyncrasies like any human being. But, a woman who flatly turned down the offer to become the President of India because she felt that that would take her away from the attention needed by the institution she had created, could only have been a person of the highest principles. She had a vision and by looking at *Bharatanatyam* in terms of an entire pattern of life, she brought to it a new look of contemporary relevance. She was a revolutionary, and by putting together the best of the old with new inputs, she gave to tradition a new dimension. Perhaps it is because of the entirety of the dance, which she concentrated on that the *Kalakshetra* style, no matter where the ex-student may be placed in the world map, retains its strong identity and stamp. It has not shown the deviations that many schools of *Bharatanatyam* have known like the Vazhuvoor or the Tanjavur styles, which sport as many versions as exponents. But where Rukmini Devi stood for fresh ideas, her own towering personality has made her an icon to be imitated and emulated – and what stood for its revolutionary strength is now looked upon as the most orthodox of styles! Also her approach, so impersonal in its depth, is today largely overwhelmed by her persona and within *Kalakshetra* one cannot see any new artistic vision. The primary aim seems to be to preserve unchanged what Rukmini Devi left as heritage. By showing that art cannot be separated from life and that good art can only come out of pure thoughts and a whole way of life which stresses the right values, Rukmini Devi demonstrated the *Satyam, Sivam, Sundaram* integration.

Rukmini Devi's approach could not have been other than what it was. History, her own talents and how her early life groomed her, combined in an inevitable historical weave.

(This paper was presented in the first Rukmini Devi national seminar organized by the *Centre for Contemporary Culture,* in New Delhi in 2001.)

CHAPTER 16

RUKMINI DEVI'S APPROACH TO TRADITION AND BEYOND

Lakshmi Viswanathan

Transformations in culture are catalysed by events, individuals, circumstances and situations. If one speaks of one individual as a catalyst, it does not necessarily imply that this individual acted in isolation, or was not part of a larger cultural context. Rukmini Devi has to be seen both as catalyst and guru within this perspective. She was the first "*Guru*" of the renaissance, and she has left a trail of influence, which is both phenomenal and vital. She was born in an orthodox Brahmin family and was exposed to Theosophy and its tenets early in her life. She was also greatly influenced by Annie Besant and the "*Swadeshi*" movement.

The first prepared her for a meticulous reverence towards sacred texts like Valmiki's *Ramayana* and Carnatic music. The second gave her not only the Western perspective on ancient Indian art and philosophy, which at the time was fertile grounding for modern Indian performing arts, but also a fresh approach to spirituality without the trappings of ritualistic dogma. The third gave her a mission with a purpose. She symbolised a new-found liberation which women in India had not experienced before.

Sanskrit scholarship and classical music were the soul of her work. Without them, she would have been lost in the unexplored genre, namely the temple/court/boudoir dance. Just the learning of the rudiments, such as the *adavus*, or short pieces which had been urbanised like the *sabdam, padam, tillana,* etc. would not have been enough foundation for her creative contribution to *Bharatanatyam*. She needed material for involving groups of dancers and musicians. With the founding of *Kalakshetra,* she became the Dame Ninette de Valois (the personality behind the Royal Ballet in England) of India.

She approached scholars to help her in her scripts for her dance-dramas and persuaded eminent musicians like Mysore Vasudevacharya, Papanasam Sivan, and a host of other great artists to compose the music for her productions.

These moves were radical in the existing world of dance. If one were to make a careful study of how *Nattuvanars* evolved their repertoire one would see clearly that they followed strictly the *Guru-Shisya* parampara in which transmission of knowledge was an oral tradition. Furthermore, there existed a very distinct professional element which was bound by the caste system. The families involved in dance and music – predominantly *Nadhaswaram* musicians and Odhuvars who were both, like the *Nattuvanars* and dancers, temple employees, were closely knit by inter-marriage. Some of the musicians taught persons outside their families and caste circles, and some of them also learnt from *Vidwans* who were from other castes. This flexibility among the musicians to interact with people outside their circle, perhaps helped the *Nattuvanars* to agree to teach dance to non-hereditary dancers. In their anxiety to preserve their dance tradition in the wake of their being displaced as a result of the banning of dance in temples, the *Nattuvanars* proved to be conservative and sometimes even rigid. Rukmini Devi's scheme of reaching out to the large, wide world with dance needed something beyond the traditional repertoire. Thus she found her role model in the *Bhagavatamela* dance dramas of Tanjore district.

Rukmini Devi established her own new tradition of dance-drama in the *Ramayana* series. There was no dance-drama tradition in South India for her to emulate other than perhaps the odd *Kathakali* play. No manuscripts were available as in the *Bhagavatamela* plays. No musical compositions had been prevalent for a *Ramayana* dance drama although there were some compositions like Arunachala Kavi's *Rama Natakam* which were meant for singing. She had a concept in mind, which would be pan-Indian in reach. She had travelled in South East Asia and seen their *Ramayanas.* That according to my perception was her first inspiration. It stayed in her mind for more than three decades.

"Art has always grown by adding to itself beauty and new influence. South East Asian countries which have their own unique forms of art have developed their uniqueness from one central source. We can see that the central source was India, and the influence is seen in the sculpture, dance-dramas, and even the themes chosen as in Cambodia, Thailand, Indonesia and other countries", she had said. It was a coincidence indeed that almost simultaneously, Rukmini Devi experienced the beauty of Pavlova's dance and the South East Asian *Ramayana* plays. The incongruity of a South Indian woman in a ballerina's garb did not bother her. She wanted to experience dance, and she did what she could.

What remained with her for long after seeing the Rama plays was the ethnic stagecraft of South East Asia. The man who helped her with the subdued lighting technique, was Paul Strom, who was from Holland. An actor and director with more than two decades in the theatre both in Holland and France, he was incidentally born in Indonesia. It is not known whether Rukmini Devi had seen any of the *Kathakali* dance-dramas earlier. After seeing the *Ramayana* in places like Indonesia, she could see its potential in international forums. Showcasing traditional arts and crafts to a national and international audience came naturally to her because of her early Theosophical activities which opened the world to her.

"The peasant equally with the prince delights in the story. Rama and Sita belong to every Indian whatever be his station," she writes. At a micro level, she created a stir among art buffs, equivalent to a modern day producer making a hit serial based on the Ramayana. If Rukmini Devi had been born towards the later half of the 20th century, she may have been the producer of a tele-serial. And how beautiful that may have been!

Rukmini Devi took Valmiki's text for most of her adaptations. With an approach akin to a sacred journey, a longed for pilgrimage, she researched the texts with scholars. She knew that many others knew more about every little Ramayana on paper. With the care of a surgeon she edited a scenario. Thus, she laid the foundation for building up a dramatic unfolding of story and character. The dance content was the shape, the design of this moving edifice. The words of the sages were the pillars and walls, painted, carved, chiselled and polished. And finally the music breathed soul into it, bringing the whole to that shore where *Rasa* awaits a *Sahrdaya.*

Mysore Vasudevacharya began the task of composing music for *Sita Swayamvaram* which was first staged in *Kalakshetra.* This dance drama was the beginning of a new tradition in *Bharatanatyam.* Soon, *Sri Rama Vanagamanam,* and *Shri Paduka Pattabhishekam* followed. She said, "The spirit of tragedy in the *Ayodhya Kandam* invests the whole of the epic with its mantle and sets the tone of the entire story". She, for her part invested each dance-drama with her own creative impulses. For example, in *Sabari Moksham,* which deals with the abduction of Sita, Rukmini Devi brings a specially sensitive angle to Surpanakha. Valmiki never mentions her transformation in order to attract Rama. "My own interpretation of the incident is that Surpanakha was able to understand beauty only in terms of herself, and considered herself to be beautiful. This, I think, must have been Valmiki's idea." A more profound comment on human vanity cannot be found anywhere.

The very fact that Rukmini Devi took it upon herself to explain her thought processes and her act of editing the sacred text was a departure from any known convention in

Bharatanatyam. Which *Nattuvanar* explained to his audience the subtle sub-text of his songs? Perhaps he did not, in his tradition, needed to do this. Her *Maha Pattabhishekam,* afforded an opportunity for her to share some of her thoughts which in more modern times would have been labelled as a glimpse of Rukmini Devi, the feminist. She writes: "Perhaps the unhappiest scene for me to produce has been the *Agnipravesam* of Sita. To me it seems strange and most out of tune with Rama's noble character to show such cruelty to Sita, when he meets her again, in a way that even ordinary humans like most of us would not do. I am convinced that what Dr. Annie Besant, Rajaji and others have said is true that many interpolations have been introduced in the story at various times. Rama says he is after all only a man, yet he does what a normally decent man won't do. He was a great man even prepared to forgive Ravana and took pity on all."

Her choreography of the scene is sensitive, considering she had no tradition to follow in the matter. Perhaps, what she saw in Indonesia or elsewhere in that region, stayed in her mind. That touch of delicacy found in that unspoilt tradition is reflected in her work. Rukmini Devi brings in the symbolism of the *Jeevatma* wanting to become one with the *Paramatma,* through a process of purification by fire.

Vasudevacharya died after composing music for *Sita Swayamvaram, Rama Vanagamanam, Paduka Pattabhishekam,* and *Sabari Moksham.* On the cards were *Choodamani Pradhanam* and *Maha Pattabhishekam.* Within months, she called the young Rajaram, grandson of Vasudevacharya and motivated him to complete the series. "Don't be hesitant or diffident, Raju. *Thatha* (Grand father) is only physically absent, but his soul will never desert us. He alone will carry through his noble mission, but unseen, through you and me. Have faith in his blessings and take up the challenge", she told him.

Rukmini Devi established an approach to dance-drama based on the tenets of the *Natya Sastra.* This was completely new to the genre of *Bharatanatyam*. Whether it was crossing the Ganga or Ravana carrying Sita on a flying machine, she portrayed them in suggestive movements. She has written succinctly, "It is a miracle to see how the human body energised to imagination and feelings can create an illusion by which we can be anything and anyone that we wish to be. The technique in this play is new when we think of *Tillana* and *Varnam*, but every movement is according to *sastra*, though not presented in a stereotyped form."

Who else but Rukmini Devi would have introduced in her cast the following: birds, swan, lotus, creepers, *devas*? She knew the power of imagination and went beyond Sanskrit theatre in her unfolding of the *Ramayana*, through *Bharatanatyam*. Where vigorous action was required, she adapted the *Kathakali* technique. She also took from *Kathakali* the technique of describing nature. She proclaimed that the two styles be kept distinctly separate and had never been mingled together.

In the final *Yuddha Kandam* of the *Ramayana*, she found the best challenges to her inventiveness. With so many varied characters ranging from heroes and villains to *apsaras* and *Rakshasis*, monkeys and monsters, she had to work hard on costumes. Perhaps her best effort in creative design was in her costumes. The fabrics she chose were never seen on the stage before her except, perhaps, in the ancient folk theatre of South India. Guards in Ravana's palace were made to look like the Kondepalli hand-crafted dolls from Andhra. Her magic touch on small details, décor, make-up, etc. was remarkable. Even the crowns worn by Rama and Ravana were crafted with care, drawing inspiration from *Krishnattam* and the trance dancers of Bali. Ultimately, one can say that Rukmini Devi's lasting gift to *Bharatanatyam*, and to the art of India, is her *Ramayana* series.

(A version of this paper was presented in the first Rukmini Devi national seminar, organized by the *Centre for Contemporary Culture*, New Delhi, 2001.)

CHAPTER 17

REVIVING AND REFORMING TRADITION IN CONTEMPORARY CONTEXTS

Gowri Ramnarayan

Holistic. That's the word which leaps to one's mind as one thinks about the contributions of Rukmini Devi Arundale. She integrated everything. She didn't see anything odd in being committed to causes as far apart as animal welfare and Montessori education, Theosophy and *Bharatanatyam* because she did not think like a modernist and see life in compartments and fragments. Rukmini Devi believed that what you wore, the way you talked, your ethical practice, political tenets and social behaviour, were all linked to the whole personality. Vulgarity corroded the individual and the community. It fostered the *rajas* and *tamas* qualities, brutalised and anaesthetised the individual. Sensitivity enriched the individual and civilisation. It promoted *sattvaguna*, gave you courage and compassion. This was Rukmini Devi's large vision of the world.

What better way of banishing vulgarity and promoting sensitivity than through the arts? That is how one reclaimed one's cultural heritage and tried to combat the accelerating global violence, bruising flesh and spirit today. Rukmini Devi's vision, realized most fully in what came to be known as *Bharatanatyam* in her times, was radical. *Bharatanatyam* was not just a performance for her. It was a performance through which young India could be educated. She thus did not think of herself only as a *Bharatanatyam* performer, but more as an institution builder. She believed that through an institution one could also develop a discerning audience without which art wilted and died as in a desert. She wrote, "From the harmony of the environment, the life, the philosophy, the thought and nature all around, with the creative spirit within, inspiration is born, and art is the expression." To her art was not the product of a tortured spirit, but the joyful expression of the exalted soul.

Kalakshetra was not a place where one learned merely to perform on the stage. That was an incidental gain. As Rukmini Devi saw it, the centre produced the ambience and the training where one developed a personality to lead a full life. Dance, music, painting, sculpture, academic education, scholarship, were all means to the end of discovering the self, "the higher soul" as she termed it. She thus reconfigured the *Bharatanatyam* she learnt from Mylapore Gowri Amma and Pandanallur Meenakshi Sundram Pillai to serve this higher purpose. When one looks at the old programmes of Rukmini Devi, one sees a whole range of songs, which accent *bhakti* over *sringara.* We see her having composed dances to Gopalakrishna Bharati's "*Tiruvadi Charanam*", Tyagaraja's "*Ela Nee Dayaradu*", Dikshitar's "*Ananda Natana Prakasam*" along with "*Edukkitttanai Modi*" or "*Baamaro.*" We see how the repertoire was extended to include several *bhakti* poets and saint composers.

Without getting into the *sringara* versus *bhakti* controversies, I would like to say that Rukmini Devi's main focus was to draw young people towards the pan-Indian tradition of *bhakti* which united India in the past across language, creed, class and gender divides. We know she did not eschew *sringara.* But because *Sadir* and *Sringara* were suspicious terms in her times, Rukmini Devi had to project them in subtle sublimated planes in the context of her time. She had to refine and sublimate *sringara* because it had to be expressed, not in stone or on canvas, in spoken word or plays, but through the live human body. What might elevate one to contemplate the divine in sculpture might actually titillate on the stage.

The dance-dramas of *Kalakshetra* provided Rukmini Devi with ample scope to realize her large vision of Indian culture and also to reinvent tradition. Since the dance-dramas evoke aesthetic and ethical values of communities, they transcended the barriers of time and space. Because they focused on myth and archetypical characterization, the dance-dramas also aspired to a universality that was uplifting. But what are the distinctive features of Rukmini Devi's style, the different components of her aesthetic vision as realized in the *Kalakshetra* dance-dramas? Rukmini Devi's aesthetic appears traditional to the core. Yet even when she uses a traditional device like the hand-held curtain (*tiraiseelai*), it acquires fresh meanings and connotations in visual performance. While tremendous teamwork, and all-round research went into the making of each and every aspect of dance-dramas, they were different from what was performed in the temple precincts, because the *Kalakshetra* dance-dramas emerged not from ritual but from art.

Though Rukmini Devi never tired of saying that she wanted to bring the temple to the theatre, the fact is that the modern theatre is not a temple. What you see is *brahmasvada sahodara* as our ancients put it, not *brahmasvada* itself. The *puja* at the beginning of the *Kalakshetra* performance is an artistic device to ensure a calm, contemplative ambience for aesthetic relish. When we describe Rukmini Devi's *Ramayana* plays as building an audio-visual temple to the gods, we are indulging in metaphoric usage. Though Rukmini Devi started with the *margam* of the solo performer, *Kalakshetra* is today best known for its dance-dramas. Scholars have pointed to the impact of Western ballet on her work. But for those of us who have seen her dance-dramas, there is nothing more Indian in content and style. And yet, its aesthetics and architectonics are vastly different from existent genres like *Bhagavatamela* and *Kuravanji.* Rukmini Devi used *Kathakali* techniques, especially for the anti-heroes, but her dance-dramas are not imitations of *Kathakali*, or any other mode of presentation.

She once wrote: "It is a miracle to see how the human body, energised to imagination and feeling, can create an illusion by which we can be anything and anyone we wish to be".

Rukmini Devi choreographed 25 dance-dramas between 1936 and 1986. Yet all the dramas were diverse in theme, characterisation, musical score, poetic idiom, dance style, language, costume, stage décor and lighting techniques. The stories are drawn from many sources – from several parts of India. You have poets from *Valmiki* to Rabindranath Tagore, speaking in many tongues, from different ages and regions. The music is classical, mainly *Carnatic*, but Rukmini Devi also used *Rabindra Sangeet* and Hindustani, with folk strains for contrast and effect. Some of it is old, as with the *Bhagavata-mela* productions, learnt painstakingly from sources like Balu Bhagavatar. Most of it is new, composed by some of our maestros, from Tiger Varadachariar to M.D. Ramanathan.

The dance-dramas highlight different *rasas* – *Sringara* in *Shakuntalam, Karuna* in the *Ramayana, Santa* in *Buddhavataram, Adbuta* in *Kurmavataram, Vira* in *Minakshi Kalyanam, Bhakti* in *Andal* and *Meera.* Through a mesh of allied and contrastive emotions, of *sthayi* and *sanchari bhavas,* each dance-drama maintains a dominant mood of its own. But as in all art, merely nominating the *rasa* falls terribly short of the complexities involved. Both *Gita Govindam* and *Rukmini Kalyanam* evoke *sringara* with *Krishna* as the *nayaka.* But the *sringara* portrayed is vastly different in the two productions! Why, the six parts of the *Ramayana* with *soka* as the *sthayibhava* vary the treatment so that you get a different feel of *karuna* as modulated in each.

All the dance-dramas are alike in one feature. They are all born of a highly-charged, profound emotion and inspiration. But an art-work needs to objectify the emotion by using form and technique. "In educational and creative work, it is vital to be constantly on the lookout for new expression", she said, adding that there was no need to copy and lean on others for this new thought or expression. In the process of finding and crafting this new expression, she revolutionised the *angika, aharya, vachika* and *sattvika* aspects of stage presentation. Some of these features are so widely accepted now that we have forgotten who invented them! *Dhvani* was the basic principle, not only with the intangibles, but also the tangible aspects of objectification.

Aharya

Rukmini Devi had already designed costumes reminiscent of temple sculpture for her solo dance. But her imagination had full play in designing costumes for a bewildering range of human and non-human beings, gods, animals and birds – real and legendary. The end result seems so traditional that we often don't realise the striking inventiveness here.

Take the first dance-drama she created – *Kuttrala Kuravanji*. The *devadasi* performances she saw of this over 300-year-old genre seemed to have lost their poeticity and spiritual tone. To recover that ambience she not only needed melting music, both classical and folk, composed by Veena Krishnamachariar, she also needed a new visual aesthetics starting with the costumes. She designed them in deep-toned *Kancheevaram* silk and *Sungadi*, with jewellery and hairstyles to match.

Rukmini Devi had an unerring sense of the colours that evoked the essential traits of the *alambāna* and *uddipana vibhava* (character and situation). The blues and pinks and creams of *Gita Govindam* take us into a river-twined woodland pastoral, wafting romance with every swirl. The backdrop and costume are inspired by *Kangra* paintings. And take *Sita* in each of the *Ramayana* segments. Her cream and orange proclaim her the princess of *Ayodhya*, but the olive green in *Asokavana* and single braid reflect pathos and despair.

Since the box stage was inadequate for her purpose, at times she had used open air spaces under the trees in her shows at the Theosophical Society. But the sophisticated dance-dramas needed an area with multi-levels and possibilities for multi-directional entrances and exits. Ravana comes through the audience to fight Rama, Meera dives off the stage into the river. The God of Fire rises from underground at the back, and the monkeys build the bridge across the straits by throwing stones out of stage space up front. Today the special stage devised in *Kalakshetra,* with the apron and two side openings for exploring different kinds of vertical and horizontal spaces is part of the big theatre on the campus. Everything is designed for drawing the *rasika* to participate in the art experience.

The backdrops differ to highlight the colours of the costumes in each drama. The props are spare, minimalist. But a single state umbrella can usher in might and magnificence. As we know, colours change, sometimes drastically, under different kinds of lights and filters. Rukmini Devi paid meticulous attention to shades and hues as seen under the stage lights. With the help of experts like Alex Elmore and Paul Storm, she pioneered the use of lighting designs to suit each play.

Lighting underscores the dialogue, conflict and mood. The stunning effect of Rama and Sita rowed across the river by Guhan, is due to the semi darkness of the stage, and the picking out of the upper portions of the moving figures at the back. You forget there is no board or oar, no rope or water for that matter! Hanuman flying with Rama and Lakshmana on his back, or setting fire to Lanka are feats of lighting.

Angika

Lighting is crucial to the sequence where the *apsaras* emerge from the Ocean of Milk in *Kurmavataram.* But *aharya* is not enough, it is +*angika abhinaya* which makes them glide into ethereal motion. A breath-stopping moment in *Paduka Pattabhishekam* has Rama, Lakshmana and Sita describing the lofty *Chitrakuta* mountain, with eye movements first, followed by gestural and body movements. Then they move back as light-footed *kinnaras* appear dancing on the peaks. This long shot has always been sheer enchantment for me. The raga *Naganandini* has a celestial ring, the translucent scarf that the dancers hold in their hands adds to the mystique.

Rukmini Devi's amazing creativity in *angika abhinaya* is a challenge to the performer, demanding that he put something of himself into its nuancing, by "energising the body with feeling and imagination". It is this *angika* which makes the dance-drama appear new each time you see it.

The *patra pravesam* is rivetting, whether the gorgeous Mohini or a poor devotee. Think of Vaali's militant entrance with the war cry, to an upward rush of melody in *Mohanam*. In contrast, wife Tara enters slowly, her very movement in simple *naatadavu* images her untold apprehensions. Think of the charm of Krishna's entrance under a canopy, held by the *gopis*!

Rukmini Devi's *nritta* passages are marked by a crisp, definitive sharpness. They are never just fillers or frills. *Nritta* can be choric, it can evoke ambience, initiate you into character, or situation. Non-human characters like *Jatayu* or *Sugriva* come alive through *nritta*. It can also depict a whole action sequence as the gods and demons churn the Ocean of Milk to extract nectar.

Scholars speak of *masruna* and *uddhata nritta*, which carry the emotion with them. Rukmini Devi could make *nritta* an extension of the *bhava*, as in the movements of Sita when she spurns Ravana. The short *nritta* passage races through a gamut of feelings from anger, sorrow, fear, contempt, sarcasm, irony, world weariness, despair and revulsion.

Space was defined, designed and given dimensions by the dance itself. I wonder if anyone has excelled Rukmini Devi in the visual framing of groups – she had a bias for what I may call "organic asymmetry" as of nature. She brought off brilliant formations with odd numbers. Her formations – still or moving – gave ample scope and visibility to every dancer on the stage, whether in a coronation scene with 20 artistes, or in the forest where an aggressive *Surpanakha* storms in, or a gentle *Sabari* ambles through. For spectacular visual effects you remember the Goddess *Minakshi* practicing the martial arts.

This accent on *angika abhinaya* enabled the choreographer to give a new dimension to male dancers, with or without the admixture of *Kathakali* methods. It also devised ways of making minor characters buttress the narrative, accelerate plot and action. Sometimes minor characters are vital to unravel action. A dance-drama depends on the networking of emotions but it does not offer the freedom of solo dance. And yet, she managed to conceive each role fully, where each glance and stance bristles with possibilities.

The mood is defined by the physical movement. Take *Andal* as she asks the *Panchajanya* about the fragrance and sweetness of the Lord's lips – "*Karpooram naarumo, kamalappoo naarumo*"? Her contoured movements across the stage shape the sensuous conch.

Vachika

Starting with the placement of the musicians at the right end of the stage, Rukmini Devi made *vachika abhinaya* integral to her vision of the dance-drama. Every *Kalakshetra* production stands out for its music, no two alike. Even when she revived an old genre like the *Kuravanji*, the music had to be scored afresh. Research, editing and sharp cutting were needed when *Bhagavatamela* music was taken up as in *Usha Parinayam*, or the *bhajana paddhati* in the south for *Gita Govindam.*

Persuading great masters like Tiger Varadachariar and Papanasam Sivan to compose the music was to ensure a textured authenticity in the emotion. In *Kumarasambhavam* it is enough to hear the *ghanapanchaka* ragas at the start to feel awed by the theme. The stalwart musicians of *Kalakshetra* knew how to highlight the *sahitya* and the *bhava*. So you hear familiar ragas revealing manifold and sometimes unfamiliar moods (just examine *Kalyani* or *Khamboji* as they occur in different contexts). Rare *ragas* come into their own. The use of *vivadi* ragas is something you will never come across anywhere else.

I think we can say that the *Kalakshetra* dance-dramas have extended the scope of *Carnatic* music in very special ways, a subject for research for students of dance and music. No account of Rukmini Devi's work is complete without discussing the contribution of Mysore Vasudevacharya who created inspiring music for the first four *Ramayana* productions. He knew that composing music for a dance drama was very different from composing music for singing, or even for solo dance. The *raga* and the *laya* had to suit the changing events and occasions, depict the actions and the feelings of the characters. This meant that the composer had to identify himself with the character like an actor so that the verse could be made to reflect the inner states, turmoils and contradictions of the character in changing situations. I confine myself to a single example where Rama tries to persuade Sita to remain in Ayodhya, and she insists that she will accompany him to the forest. Vasudevacharya makes the old *Anandabhairavi* yield a wealth of *sanchari bhavas* in their interaction. There is strength here, as also delicacy. Where old ragas did not serve, he created new ones, like *Chittabhramari* for Dasaratha's bewilderment and *Gangalahari* for crossing the Ganges.

(The paper was presented in the first Rukmini Devi National Seminar, organized by the *Centre for Contemporary Culture*, at New Delhi in 2001).

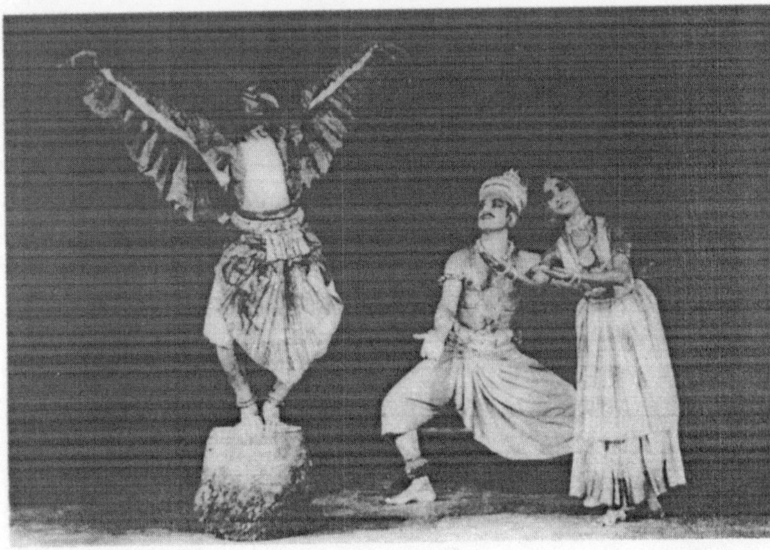

Fig. 6: Jatayu Fights Ravana: Photo from Rukmini Devi's Ramayana Dance Drama Series

(Photo: C.T. Nachiappan archive)

CHAPTER 18

RUKMINI DEVI ARUNDALE: HER NEW VISIONS IN HER DANCE DRAMAS

C.V. Chandrasekhar

For centuries the devout have been visiting Kashi for a dip in the holy *Ganga* and a vision of *Vishvanatha*, its presiding deity. By environmentalists' standards it is one of the most polluted cities. But the stream of pilgrims continue to visit Varanasi, although they are only marginally comfortable, compared to the days of *Adishankara*. Why? It is because of the greatness of the abode, its air, its aura – that is the '*Sthala Mahima*'. A '*sthala*' (place) attains its '*mahima*' (glory) by the visits and presence of great souls within its parameters. It becomes a '*Kshetra*' – a holy abode. By the same yardstick, this 'abode of the Arts' – the *Kalakshetra* has become a centre of pilgrimage to the cognoscenti of the arts. The presence here of its founder Rukmini Devi and the greatest of artists, and other noble souls who have treaded the portals have made this place incomparable to any other. I will share with you some of the most beautiful moments which we have all experienced watching the creations of Rukmini Devi in her dance-dramas, not just as an alumnus of *Kalakshetra* but a real *sahrdaya*.

The Stage

Rukmini Devi gave the best aesthetics for the stage that she created for her dance-dramas. The colour-smeared drapes of the backdrops, the flies and wings neatly pleated with a central hanging lamp and the entrance were designed by her more than 60 years ago for a solo performance and no better alternative has been found to date. The cloth temple pillars for *Kutrala Kuravanji*, the Himalayas painted for *Kumarasambhavam* and *Meenakshi Vijayam* have taken us to those abodes. The use of the gauze curtain (probably used by Rukmini Devi for the first time), which brought an ethereal vision of the mountains, made one feel like being in *Kailasa* itself. The doorframes on either side were put to fresh use in every production. The bright and colourful *Kathiawadi* front curtain opened out to a serene setting behind. Lighting techniques best developed during Paul Storm's stay in *Kalakshetra*, play a major role in the productions. The inner chamber where Sita watches the '*dhanusha yajna*', the crossing of the *Ganga* in *Rama Vanagamanam*, the ocean in the *Chudamani Pradanam*, *Sita's agnipravesham*, in *Maha Pattabhishekam*, Siva descending to the earth from *Kailasa* in *Meenakshi Vijayam*, are some of the memorable marvels of excellent lighting. The '*pusta*' or the stage property used for the various dramas were small seats and thrones symbolically represented. The ambience of *Kalakshetra*'s theatres added so much to each production. So much so one often felt that the productions of Rukmini Devi were meant only to be staged in these theatres. Staged elsewhere one misses something of the original.

Patra Pravesas

It is said that a single grain of rice can certify the quality of a meal. The *Patra Pravesas* that Rukmini Devi created were unique to each of the dance-dramas. The painstaking attention paid to the first entry reflected the quality of the entire production. The importance of rehearsing the holders of the *Tirasila* or *Tiraskaranis* was strongly felt; the two men holding it had to be present at every rehearsal and know the line of the song thoroughly in order to pull away the curtain at the right point. A finesse was brought to the movements of the dancer behind the *Tiraskarani*. She later used different materials as *Tiraskaranis* with dancers holding them and manipulating them to form beautiful patterns. The entries of Rukmini, Andal and Yasodara were marvels of imagination. I am sure she must have had sleepless nights creating those visuals. The entries and exits of every minor character were meticulously planned.

Groupings

One could write an entire thesis on this aspect of Rukmini Devi's dance-dramas. Right from *Kutrala Kuravanji* to *Meera of Mewar,* I do not think there was any repetition of patterns. The corps de ballet were not just to decorate but were very often the main stay of a scene. Parvati's, Rukmini's and Sita's weddings were all different though the ritual was the same. She used space in such a way that at no time was any one dancer covering another. They were everywhere but never dashing against one another, all the while executing a perfect *adavu.* One found a lot of asymmetry in her groupings. The entire formation became a larger body but remained a single entity. In *Andal,* the personification of the conch became the extension of one character. Watching *Geeta Govindam,* one feels that Rukmini Devi had brought the miniature paintings to life. The cut out in the backdrop signifying a bower was a rare feat of imagination. The scene when *Radha* and *Krishna* enter the bower with the other dancers turning their heads and looking down, taking different postures, create a sense of privacy for the divine couple, which was choreography at its pinnacle. The group dances of the retinues of Guha and Ravana in the *Ramayana* were highly stylized pieces bringing out the characteristics of the forest dwellers and the demonic kingdom. The *Sangara Varnana* and the *Setu Bandhana* scenes were again *Sarirabhinaya* of a very high order. One cannot but recall the *Samudra Manthana* scene in *Kurmavatara.* One wishes Bharata were alive to witness Rukmini Devi's production of Kalidasa's *Shakuntalam* which distilled the essence of complete theatre.

Costumes

Rukmini Devi's aesthetic sense found total expression in the costumes she designed for the characters. She wholly relied on pure silk and cotton handloom fabrics which she used judiciously. She respected and adored the artisans and knew the value of their creations. She disliked tight-fitting dresses and all the costumes she designed had a flow giving them movement as the dancers moved. When *Kalakshetra* could not afford expensive costume jewellery, she had macrame jewellery made, painted with gold paint. The designs were eye-catching. She recreated traditional jewellery studying the ornaments of the temples as well as designs from the sculptures. She would never settle for anything but the best. She generally avoided black for the costumes but used them prolifically to represent *tamasic* characters in combination with red and gold. Cotton fabrics from Gujarat, Rajasthan and Orissa found new aesthetics in her hands. She created special headgear for each of the characters that were never repeated. She relied on *Kathakali* makeup for many of the animal and bird characters while adding her own inputs. She never used the *Nattu* (the nose ornament) as she felt it concealed the expression on the face.

Choosing of Dancers for Different Characters

Rukmini Devi had the unique ability of choosing and picking the right dancers for a particular role. She choreographed each role keeping in mind the potential of the dancer chosen. Though she had the last word, she had great faith in her main dancers and appreciated their own inputs. The characters of Hanuman, Kannapar, Ravana Sanyasi, Bharat or Vidushaka in *Shakuntalam* were it seems specially created with Balagopalan in mind. She was aware of his *abhinaya* talents and he did not disappoint her either. I have heard people in the audience remark that he could never be replaced. Top-class dancers like Sarada Hoffman, Krishnaveni, Leela Samson, Santa, Dhananjayan, Janardhanan, and Kunjhiraman have literally lived their roles adding new dimensions to every production. Who can forget Pushpa Shankar's *Shyama* and Surpanakha or the simple Kurathi enacted by N.S. Jayalakshmi? Sometimes she was criticised for choosing wrong dancers for a particular role. But she always had valid reasons to defend her choice. The beauty of a dancer was not her only criterion for selection. The dancing ability was the prime concern. She would say everyone looked beautiful on stage and they all did so too.

The Musical Scores

Rukmini Devi was very fortunate to have had the music composed for her dance dramas by some of the greatest names in the field of Carnatic music of the 20th century. Stalwarts and Vagneyakaras like Papanasam Sivan, Mysore Vasudevacharya, Tiger Varadachari, Veena Krishnamachari, M.D. Ramanathan, who were all attached to Kalakshetra at different periods, contributed to the uniqueness of the dance-dramas. One really wondered as to how Rukmini Devi was able to rope in such musicians to compose music for dance at a time when most senior musicians thought it below their dignity to do so. It was again her charisma that made it possible. Each one of these composers had a different style which gave variety and an individual stamp to each production. Rukmini Devi's demands were not easy to fulfill but the rapport that developed between the choreographer and the composer was always total. The challenge to each one of them was so big that very often some of her scores were composed at odd hours of the night. Tiger's score for *Kumarasambhavam* was of a very gamaka-oriented chaste Carnatic style, both difficult to sing as well as to put it into dance. Music for *Kutrala Kuravanji* was an excellent amalgamation of the classical and the folk mode. Vasudevachar's presence was felt in each of the songs of the *Ramayana.* His choice of ragas for each mood was a great inspiration to the choreographer and the dancer. Sivan's music for *andal* and *Geetagovindam* could not have made the *Alwars* of the *Divyaprabandham* and Jayadeva more proud. The recitation of the mnemonics is *Sruti* became a specialty in *Kalakshetra*'s repertoire. It was Rukmini Devi again who had the '*mukhaveena*' (a small-sized *nadaswaram*) as the only accompaniment other than the *mridangam, maddalam*, etc. The flute came in later and violin much later. The *mukhaveena* is now hardly heard of and I am sure dancers and musicians of the present generation are not even aware of its existence.

Kathakali and Other Inputs

Rukmini Devi felt that *Kathakali* had great potential in the realm of acting and used it very judiciously to enhance the dramatic element of a particular situation. It was mainly the male roles, which essayed this style as it suited many of the *Uddhata Prayogas.* Chandu Panikkar who lived, taught and also danced in Rukmini Devi's earlier productions contributed substantially in training the male dancers for their specific roles. Dancers received training in *Kalaripayattu* for Meenakshi Vijayam much before this Kerala art form received recognition. The battle scene danced in the above dance-drama was a true demonstration of '*Nyaya*' (art of fighting) as mentioned in the *Natya Sastra.* In *Buddhavataram* one could see flashes of classic ballet in the movements of the swan. The *Bhagavatamela* tradition found new freshness in the hands of Rukmini Devi in *Usha Parinayam* and *Rukmini Kalyanam.* She stressed the need for '*auchitya*' – propriety – in introducing techniques other than *Bharatanatyam* to enhance the beauty of a production.

There are innumerable observations like these which have been guiding and inspiring us, her followers, through the decades to continue her work to the best of our ability. This is the deepest homage we can pay to her at this hour of her centenary.

(A version of this paper was presented at the Rukmini Devi Seminar, organized by the *Centre for Contemporary Culture,* in Kuala Lumpur in 2003.)

CHAPTER 19

KURAVANJI: DANCE-DRAMA

Dr. Sunil Kothari

The tradition of *Kuravanji* dance-drama appears to be nearly three hundred years old. Like *Bhagavatamela Nataka*; the *Kuravanji* is also a continuation of the *uparupaka* tradition. The *chitrakavya* variety of *uparupaka* could be seen in *Kuravanji* dance-drama, in particular, in the delineation of *vipralambha sringara*. The influence of *Gita Govinda* [1] is easily discerned in the role of the *Sakhi*, the confidante, whom the *nayika* requests to convey the message to the *nayaka*. The *Kuravanji* dance-dramas were performed by women only. However, the role of the *Kattaikkaran*, the herald, used to be played by a male dancer.

The dance tradition in the temple and the historical evidence indicate that the *Kuravanji* dance-dramas were performed by a group of female dancers attached to the temples. It also appears that the technique employed was the classical *Bharata Natyam*, known then as *Dasi Attam*, and *Sadir Nautch*. The security and fillip that the resilient Hindu chiefs of the South from the Vijayanagar times onwards gave to Hindu religion and culture helped the continuous growth of the performing and the plastic arts.

The tradition of the cultural richness of this area goes indeed to the Chola times and even earlier, but due credit must be given to the successive rulers who realized the value of this culture and not only preserved it but enriched it considerably. If the Nayaks reinforced it with elements of value from Andhra, the Marathas breathed some fresh life into it with the elements from Maharashtra. In arts and letters, devotion and spiritual endeavour, the culture of the

Kaveri delta attained a marvellous complexion, varied, brilliant and uplifting.

Similarly the institution of the *Devadasis* has contributed in a significant way in preserving and perpetuating the art of dancing in the temples. They were employed by the temples to perform rituals. The Brihadishwara temple at Tanjavur is considered a symbol proving at once the growth of the Chola power into a formidable one. Befitting the place of the great temple in the social and religious life at the capital, a strange migration of musicians and dancers was ordered by the Kings of Tanjavur. We have inscriptional evidence[2] from the Brihadishwara temple dated in the 21st reignal year of Raja Raja I, which lists the names of the dancing girls who were brought to Tanjavur and allotted one *veli* of land per head. Four hundred *devadasis* from various neighbouring temples were transferred to Brihadishwara temple. These *devadasis* danced in the temple and it is probable that later on their descendants performed the *Kuravanji* dance-dramas. To this day one can see a specially built platform in front of the temple where the *Kuravanji* dance-dramas used to be performed during the reign of the Maratha rulers (A.D. 1674-1854).

Ekoji was the first Maratha ruler of Tanjavur. His son Shahaji (A.D. 1684-1710) won fame as 'Aparabhoja' for his patronage of letters. It was during his times that *Thyagesar Kuravanji* used to be performed at Tiruvarur temple in praise of Lord Thyagesa. He was a great patron of arts and therefore, the poets, men of letters and artists found favours with him. *Shahendra Vilasa* by Shridhara Venkatesa [3] refers to a picture of plenty and all-round richness of life that was vouchsafed to his subjects in Tamilnadu.

Shahaji was succeeded by Sarfoji I, Tookji, Bavasaheb and Pratapsimh. However, it was during the reign of the last two rulers, viz., Tulaja (A.D. 1765-1787) and Sarfoji II (A.D. 1798-1832), that the tradition of *Sadir* and *Kuravanji* achieved a remarkable artistic growth. Tulaja's *Sangitasaramrita*[4] is a treatise on dance and music and throws light on the contemporary practice of *Sadir* nautch which has now gained the name *Bharata Natyam.* For example, he explains how tatta adavus are to be executed; how *dhi dhi thai adavu* should be practised and so on. These references indicate a living tradition with which we are now familiar. This technique was employed by the *devadasis* for solo as well as for *Kuravanji* dance-dramas of *Brahmotsava* or annual festivals.

The origin of the *Kuravanji* dance-drama is traced to some sort of dances performed by the *Kurava* tribe. In Tamil, the term is derived from two words, *Kuravan* and *Vanji.* The word *Kuravan* refers to a tribe and *Vanji* means a woman of the hilly tract who practices fortune telling. In due course the term was used to denote composition wherein the character of *Kurathi,* a gypsy woman, figures.

The *Kuravanji* dance-drama belongs to Tamil dramatic literature. It also combines three aspects of Tamil literature, viz., *Iyal* (poetry), *Isai* (music) and *Natkam* (drama). The *Kurattippattu* songs pivot round the palm reading by the *Kurathi* or the gypsy woman. The classical Ula and Kuram Types of Tamil literature have influenced the *Kuravanjis.* In Kuram, the verses contain dialect of the Kurathi. Minakshiammai Kuram, Draupadi Kuram, Bhavani Kuram appear to be predecessors of *Kuravanji. Kulavanatakam,* another type of *prabandha,* along with *Kuram* shaped the genre of *Kuravanji* dance-dramas. The characters of *Singan,* the gypsy, and *Singi,* the gypsy woman converse with each other in an interesting dialogue which is musical.

The Kuravanjis are also included in the list of *prabandhas* although they differ from the sacred *Vaishnava Nalayira Divya Prabandhas.* However, they compare favourably with *Ārupadai* in Tamil.

Tirukuda Rasappa Kavirayar wrote *Kutrala Kuravanji*[5] in praise of Lord Tirukoodanathar in the year 1720. The author was born at Melakaran, a village near Kutralam in the

Tirunelveli District. The name Tirukuda Rasappa Kavirayar has been given to every successive grandson in that family ever since. It is said that nearly a century ago this *Kuravanji* was performed at the Kutralam temple, though only at the time of the annual festival. For many years it was also staged during the Navaratri festival at the Brihadishwara temple at Tanjavur. However, with the introduction of the Devadasi Bill the practice was discontinued.

Kuravanji was revived in the year 1944 by Rukmini Devi as a dance-drama production which she choreographed at *Kalakshetra.* She herself used to dance the principal role of Vasantavalli, the *nayika* of the dance-drama.

All *Kuravanji* dance-dramas have a set theme. The *nayika* of the *Kuravanji,* a young charming princess sees the Lord of the place to which she belongs, in a procession and falls in love with him. She pines for union with him. She is unable to bear the pangs of separation. Seeing her plight, her friends, the *sakhis,* try to entertain her and assure her that her wish will be fulfilled. Meanwhile one *sakhi* brings the news that a Kurathi, the gypsy woman who reads the palm, is visiting the town. She is summoned to read the palm of the princess. The Kurathi after invoking the gods and performing the rituals and the rites, forecasts the happy union of the lovers. She is given precious gifts by the princess at the auspicious and happy forecast. The *Kurathi* wishes her well and leaves singing and dancing.

In some compositions we notice an appendage which is light and brisk. The *Kuravan,* the gypsy and his wife the *Kurathi,* the gypsy woman, go for hunting. They are also known as Singan and Singi. This episode is full of mirth and merriment. Singan is waiting and looking for Singi. He is annoyed at her late arrival. However, his anger vanishes when he sees her loaded with valuable presents. They engage themselves in a fine dialogue which appeals to the laity.

There are more than sixty Kuravanjis written in various languages including Telugu, Malayalam, Marathi and Gujarati.

The Kuravanjis as a rule are in praise of some deity. In *Kutarala Kuravanji, Thyagesar Kuravanji, Kumbesar Kuravanji, Azhagar Kuravanji,* the theme of the first half reveals the undercurrent of divinity and *madhura bhakti.* It has at its base the pining of the soul, *jivatma,* for union with supreme being, *paramatma.* This was also the result of *Bhakti* movement and the literary compositions revealed the influence of the same in several Kuravanjis that were written during this period.

Thyagesar Kuravanji belongs to the group of sacred *prabandhas.* There is some controversy about the authorship of this work. A great Tamil scholar, Muttu Kavirayar[6] who adorned the court of Shahaji, is believed to have composed it. This particular *Kuravanji* used to be enacted until recently in the *Devasiriya mandapam* near the eastern gopura in the Thyagesa temple at Tiruvarur during the Brahmotsava festival for three nights. Till recently one of the songs, 'vasalidu vasalidu' in *Nadanamakriya raga* describing the glory of the temple and the city of Tiruvarur was being sung by the *Devaradiyar* standing near the *jali* (window) on the southern prakara adjoining the garbhagriha (sanctum sanctorum) of Shri Thyagaraja Swami, during the rituals and special ceremonies.

Whereas most of the Kuravanjis are Shaivite in theme, the *Azhagar Kuravanji* by Kavi Kunjara Bharati (1810-1896) is *Vaishnavite.* The author was the samsthan vidwan in the courts of Ramanad and Shivaganga. He composed the Kuravanji in the year 1840. The story centres round Sundaraja Perumal, the presiding deity of Azhagar kovil in Madurai District. The *nayika* of this Kuravanji is Mohanvalli who sees Malazhagar in a procession and falls in love with him. Thematically it resembles other Kuravanjis. It is said that it was first performed at Shivaganga. Kavi Kunjara Bharati is famous for his Skanda

Purana *kirtanas.* His songs are noted for their enchanting music, sweet diction and poetic flights.

Kumbeswara Kuravanji, the work of a Tamil composer Papanasam Mudaliar of the eighteenth century in praise of Kumbeswara, the deity of the Shiva temple in Kumbakonam, is another noteworthy composition. It used to be performed in Soolamangalam village during the years 1835-1875 on the fourth day of the Vasantotsavam of the local deity. It used to be staged by the *devadasis* when the *bhagavatas* were presenting the Bhagavatamela Natakas. It suggests that nearly a century and half ago these traditions were at their peak.

Sendil Kuravanji centres round the theme of the Lord of Tiruchendur shrine in Tirunelveli District. After the usual invocatory verse, the *Nayika* Madanamohini appears on the scene and sees Lord Murugan coming in a *pavani* (procession), and falls in love with him. In this *Kuravanji* as an appendage the episode of the *Kuravan* and *Kurathi* is woven, which evidently aims at pleasing the common masses.

Of all the Kuravanjis, one which differs from the set pattern is *Kannappar Kuravanji* composed by Navalar of Tozhuvur in 1880. It is in the style known as Kuravanji *pan-kirtanam,* which means that it was intended to be used as a dance-drama, in singing and in *kathakalakshepam.* It is about a hunter being enlightened through his devotion; though born low, he becomes purified, so much so that he is included in the set of *Shaiva* saints – the *Aruvattimuvar* and is cited as a bright example of Shaivism and compassion. Such a theme is very well worked out in the frame-work of *Kuravanji,* as all the characters, except one, are *kuravas* – hunters and gypsies. The language is a mixture of classical and colloquial Tamil. Instead of *Sringara, bhakti* is delineated. Kannappar, the *nayaka* of the Kuravanji, a great devotee of Lord Shiva shows his dedication to the Lord with intensity of a true bhakta.

While surveying the *Kuravanji* compositions it is noticed

that a few court poets and authors composed the *Kuravanjis* in praise of the patron kings, the nayaks and the zamindars. In *Viralimalai Kuravanji,* the *nayaka* is a mortal human being. Though ostensibly written in honour of Subrahmanyam Mudaliar a descendant in the line of the great Tamil poet Sekkizhar, and a minister of Raghunath Tondiman, ruler of Pudukottai (A.D.1730-1769),[7] the dance-drama has always been construed as written in praise of Lord Murugan of Viralimalai.

Sarbhendra Bhupala Kuravanji is in praise of King Sarfoji of Tanjavur, written by the court poet Kottaiyur Sivakkozundu Desikar. Sarfoji II(A.D. 1798-1832) was a scholar and patron of fine arts, music and dancing. Thanks to his interest in literature, the Saraswati Mahal Library at Tanjavur, which started with a small nucleus in the time of the Nayak rulers, today stands as a magnificent tribute to the king's love for learning. There are preserved manuscripts of rare merit and precious documents which throw light on the cultural era of past several centuries.

In this Kuravanji the poet has interspersed prose speeches with *viruttam, agaval* and *venba* giving to the entire composition a kirtana form. Many Sanskrit words are used in this *Kuravanji.* It also contains the names of nineteen of the sixty years from the Hindu calendar. They are cleverly interwoven in the *sahitya* in a meaningful manner. It furnishes an instance of *samvatsara mudra.* The excellence of the musical and dance features of the composition is ascribed to the celebrated Ponnayya who was the palace musician and *nattuvanar.* This *Kuravanji* used to be performed regularly at the Brihadishwara temple during the Brahmotsavam festival.

Natyasastra refers to two aspects of sringara: *sambhoga* (union) and *vipralambha* (separation). In the *Kuravanji* dance-dramas, the *nayika* after seeing the Lord in a procession suffers pangs of separation and pines for the union with the

Lord. Therefore *vipralambha shringara* finds sufficient scope for delineation. In the chapter on *Samanyabhinaya*[8], Bharata mentions how a *vipralabdha nayika,* separated from her lover should depict various stages to enhance the *virahatapa* and achieve *rasanishpatti.* Since the *nayika* is also *mugdha,* who has not experienced pleasure of love *(rati),* she has to represent love in ten stages.[9] Of the ten stages, *abhilasha,* longing arising from efforts born of desire and wish for the beloved, leads to the means of meeting him. The *nayika* goes out to see where the beloved was seen first, and speaks to the female messenger *(duti),* or *sakhi,* as to how could she unite with her Lord. She sighs and reminisces about him only. This is the second stage called *anusmriti;* being engrossed in thinking about him she does not attain composure in sitting or lying in bed.

When the *sakhis* try to comfort her by putting new ornaments and jewellery, she finds it meaningless as her lover is away; another *sakhi* plays on musical instruments but it enhances her agony; she loses appetite; cannot bear the cool breeze; the sandal paste anointed by her *sakhis* has no effect on her; the rays of the moon strike her like arrows and she blames the moon for being so ruthless *(Chandradushanam);* blames Kamadeva, the Lord of Love *(manmathadushanam)* and with various *sanchari bhavas* depicts her plight with consummate artistry.

The scheme of *abhinaya* is more or less repeated in all the *Kuravanji* dance-dramas with literary conceits, metaphors, images and poetic fancy. But they all aim at one thing: the delineation of *shringara* in its varied hues and shades. The *abhinaya* to the songs is performed, as per the technique laid down in the *Natya sastra* with the use of *drishtis, mukhabhinaya,* and the *hastas.* The overall impact is that of the agony caused by separation.

The classical Carnatic music and the *ragas* used have a powerful appeal. The *ragas* are *rakti ragas* which suit the mood and the situation. Genuine folk tunes are employed for the character of the Kurathi. The sequence of *jatis,* the rhythmic sol-fa passages, interspersed in between the *sahitya* at appropriate places enhances the appeal of the dance.

Like *Bhagavatamela Natakas,* the *patrapravesha darus* in *Kuravanji* dance-dramas are used to introduce the characters from behind a curtain held by stage-hands. The verses occurring in between the songs serve as narrative links between the different *darus* of the story. Some of these verses are sung in *Saveri raga* without *tala.* The choice of *Saveri raga* for the verses is very apt, as it fits in harmoniously with any part of the night. *Kuravanjis* also have *samvada darus* when the characters are engaged in conversation.

Adi tala, Mishra Chapu tala, and *Tisra Eka tala* are the time measures most commonly met with in the majority of the *Kuravanji* dance-dramas. *Tisra Eka tala* is also referred to as *Rupaka tala* in some of them. The *Mishra Chapu tala* has been preferred to all other *talas* for most of the *darus* of the main characters. It is also eminently suited to the songs in *vilamba kala.*

The *takita ta ka dhimi* rhythm figures invariably in Kuravanji dance-dramas as in the Bhagavatamela Nataka. Of the three degrees of the speed usually employed *vilambita laya* and*madhya laya* are more frequently used. The *anupallavi* is sung in *Madhya laya.* In Bhagavatamela Nataka also the *darus* of the minor characters are sung in *Madhya laya.*

The Tamil verse forms that occur in the *Kuravanji* dance-dramas include *Viruttam, Kochchagam, Agaval, Chindu, Venba, Asiriyappa, Kanni pattu* and *darus* in form of *khandikas.*

As noted earlier, Rukmini Devi contributed in reviving this tradition by choreographing *Kurala Kuravanji* in the year 1944. From the temple records of Brihadishwara, we gather that from 1942 to 1946, *Sarabhendra Bhupala Kuravanji* was revived and that Kuppaiah Pillai of Tiruvidamarudur was asked to conduct the *nattuvangam* and present it. One of dancers Rajamma, Kuppiah Pillai's disciple who used to take part in the *Kuravanji,* has now retired and lives at Tiruvidamarudur. These *nattuvanars* and the artistes are perhaps the last repositories of traditional *Kuravanjis* as they were performed in the temple. For a long time *Sarabhendra Bhupala Kuravanji* was considered the property of the Tanjavur palace and no outside body was permitted to perform it. It was late R.K. Shanmukham Chetty, one time President of the Tamil Isai Sangam, who had this stipulation removed. In the year 1950 the Tamil Isai Sangam produced it in Madras with the renowned Balasaraswati playing the role of *Kurathi.* Later on Mrinalini Sarabhai presented it in major cities of India and abroad. It forms one of the major dance-dramas in her repertoire.

Following Rukmini Devi, the well-known *nattuvanar,* the late Dandayudhapani Pillai, had written and choreographed *Chitrambalam Kuravanji,* which was staged many times in Madras in the 'fifties.

Besides *Kutrala Kuravanji,* Rukmini Devi has produced *Kannappar Kuravanji*(1962) and *Krishnamari Kuravanji* (1971), for which the late Papanasam Sivan had composed the music. Some well-known dancers like Kamala, Vyjayanthimala, Padma Subrahmanyam, and others also have choreographed the *Kuravanji* dance-dramas. Kamala presented in 1964 *Azhagar Kuravanji* and in 1970, *Thyagesara Kuravanji.* Vyjayanthimala's choreography and presentation of *Azhagar Kuravanji* in 1965 were spectacular. From the younger generation of contemporary dancers, Padma Subrahmanyam has choreographed *Viralimalai Kuravanji,* with the help of Shyamala Balakrishnan and old devadasis from Viralimalai. The latest *Kuravanji* produced in the north was *Chandramaulishwara Kuravanji* in Gujarati language. It was written, choreographed and composed by Anjali Merh, a disciple of Rukmini Devi, in 1977. Anjali Merh had followed the example of *Kutrala Kuravanji* in which she used to dance as *sakhi* along with Rukmini Devi. This is the first ever

Kuravanji written in Gujarati. Anjali Merh had also composed the music for this *Kuravanji* in praise of the presiding deity of Somnath in Saurashtra.

(A version of this article is included in Dr. Kotharis' *Bharatanatyam: Indian Classical Dance* published by *Marg* Publication. Dr. Kothari presented excerpts from this paper, at the first national seminar on Rukmini Devi, organized by the *Centre for Contemporary Culture,* in New Delhi in 2001. He has given us permission to reprint segments from his published article. We thank him and *Marg* publications for extending this courtesy to us.)

Notes

1. See *Kalakshetra Quarterly* (1986: 118-119), for a chronological listing of the awards conferred on Rukmini Devi.
2. Kothari, Sunil: The Dance-Drama tradition of Kuchipudi, Bhagavata Mela Nataka and Kuravanji, with special reference to the Rasa Theory as expounded in Bharata's Natyashastra, thesis submitted to M.S University, Baroda (1977), Vol. II, pp.507-510.
3. South Indian Inscriptions, Vol. II, No. 66.
4. Venkatesh, Shridhara: Shahendra Vilasa, Ed. Dr. T. Raghavan, Saraswati Mahal Library, Tanjore. See his detailed Introduction.
5. *Sangitusaramrita of Tulaja* Ed. S. Subrahmanya Sastri, The Music Academy, Madras (1942).
6. Tirukkuttrala Kuravanji, Kalakshetra Publication, Madras.
7. *Thyagesara Kuravanji,* Ed. V. Premalatha, Saraswati Mahal Library, Tanjore.
8. Shyamala N: A Survey of Folk Arts of Tamil Nadu, 1962, Report submitted to Madras State Sangita Nataka Sangam.
9. *Natyashastra,* Part III, Chapter XXII, on *Samanyabhinaya,* G.O.S. (1954). See also Abhinavagupta's commentary in *Abhinavabharati.*
10. *Ibid,* Shlokas 169-190.

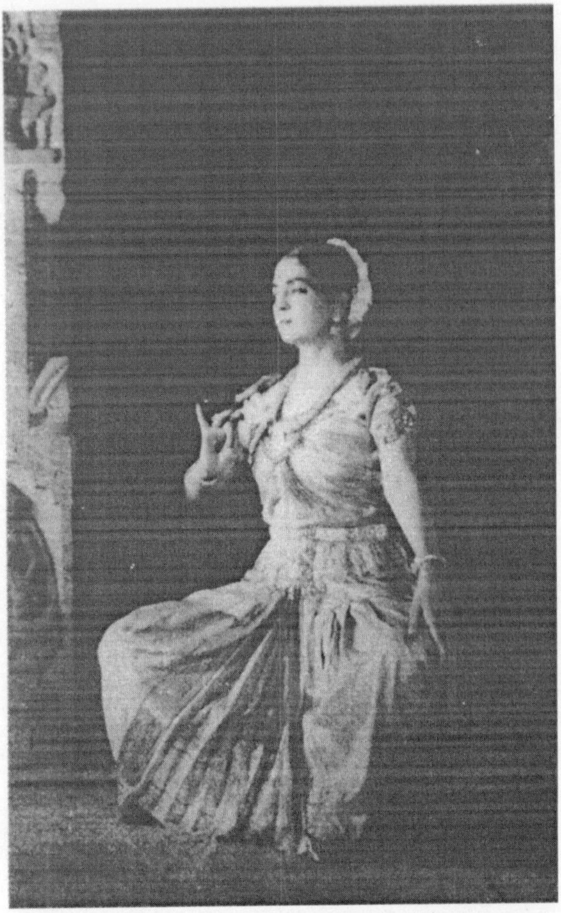

Fig. 7: Rukmini Devi - The Divine Dancer
(Photo: C.T. Nachiappan archive)

CHAPTER 20

THE BIRTH OF BHARATANATYAM AND THE SANSKRITIZED BODY

Uttara Asha Coorlawala

The body construct of the dancer in the classical Indian dance forms today can be perceived as an accumulation of the values held by migrating peoples from the civilizers of the Indus valley, through the Islamic and British influxes. Certain core concepts persist while others transformed. In this paper, I will focus on the early twentieth century circumstances inscribed on the body as presented by dancers of classical Indian dance. I argue that these traces are not only evident but are still formative as we move into the twenty-first century, that we need to understand the current effects of this history if we are to move on. I write not so as to point a finger at this or that personality or trend, but rather with a view to understanding the human interactions, expectations and habits that inscribe the dancing body and the body of classical Indian dance, and which inform the way the dancing body is read.

I will argue here that Rukmini Devi Arundale evolved what became a prototypical format for '*Sanskritization*' that has been taken up by several dance traditions as they transitioned from local dance to "classical dance."[1] This process or sanskritization, is most evident in the Post-Independence retrieval and reconstructive phase (1953-1990). In order to contextualize this argument, I will need to very briefly revisit oft-told tales so as to track how certain perceptions of the dancing body persist.

The history of the institution of the *devadasi* and her dance is not the neat linear progressive deterioration from temple to courts and from courts to streets, as mythologized.[2] Scholars have shown just how complex this story can be.[3] There were from ancient times, many kinds of dancers. Kapila Vatsyayan maintains that ancient texts and law treatises indicate that secular art dance and religious dance existed simultaneously and were distinct and that there was a social space for dancers whose services ranged from dance as art to dance as a pretext for solicitation.[4] Leslie C. Orr's detailed study of the status of temple women in medieval Tamilnadu clearly contra-indicates a notion of "a pan-Indian and transhistorical *devadasi*" and notions of consistently degenerating agency for temple women.[5]

We are still discovering different localized histories of dance traditions. Pan-Indian influences such as the Golden age of Sanskrit classicism, the colonizations of the Islamic rulers and the British, the *bhakti* movement may have interacted with all of these narratives, but not necessarily in the same way. Yet all the dance stories are still bundled together into one simplistic story of women as passive victims and ritual symbols. This tale of exclusion and otherness is still deployed by the dancer today and arouses audiences. I wonder if this is so because English became the main language of narrating the story, and very early on, one narrative came to dominate the discourse?

By the late nineteenth and early twentieth century, in India, English had become the official language of higher education and with that ideas of the west were being accessed.[6] Indigenous customs and institutions were being re-perceived in the light of the new Victorian and rational approach. For example, medical publications cited objective and scientific evidence on the physiological repercussions of child marriage to convince the public of the need to reform this practice. Administrators, missionaries, women's rights activists and doctors instigated considerable concern and activity towards raising the age of consent to marriage for minors.[7]

The gender inequities of this period had convinced women rights activists of the necessity for either single monogamous marriages and of the need for celibacy for working women. Such progressive persons (both Indian or non) expected the *devadasi* to live by puritanical ideals of asceticism associated with celibate Brides of Christ, with Jain and Buddhist monk's Hindu widows.[8] The zealous reformers could neither comprehend the *devadasi,* nor her function, (to facilitate auspiciousness in the present) nor the sensitive socio-historic structure of sponsorship that enabled her to devote herself to perfecting her art.[9] Again, she came to be perceived as exploited. Several researchers as Kothari, Khokar, Srinivasan and others have named some of these women activists and their roster is international from a British Miss Tenant, to Dr. Muthulakshmi Reddy from within the Tamil Isai community itself, and Americans as Dr. Clara Swain,[10] Katherine Mayo and her more recent incarnations. Of their intentions Veena Oldenburg writes:

"Katherine Mayo, allegedly an American feminist, was expressly recruited by a defensive colonial government in India in the 1920s, to journey through India to produce a book at least as negatively compelling as her earlier malevolent book on the Philippines, that would discredit the nationalist movement in India. In *Mother India,* published in 1927, Katherine Mayo surpassed both herself and the zeal of her colonial sponsors."[11]

This perception of exploited womanhood was furthered by shifting power structures within local Indian politicians who used the controversies over the female dancing body to further their own agendas. The presence of the *devadasis* in temples was cited as evidence of the "corruption" of Hindu religious institution and that a "pure" custom had been polluted and must be cleansed. A campaign, the anti-Nautch movement, was launched to discredit the *devadasi*'s person and lifestyle.[12] Inherited Brahminical convictions about the need for ritual and personal purity based upon caste-based functions had become conflated with Victorian convictions regarding social purity where respectability was based only on gender politics and represented in as monogamous marriage (within patriarchy) or as celibacy for working women.[13]

Dancers know of how E. Krishna Iyer campaigned actively to draw attention to the beauty and integrity of the form by presenting performances himself and also by presenting prominent *sadir* artists at the Madras Music Academy. (Controversial then, because the Music Academy was and still is considered to be an institution of "high" art something dance could never be...) He initiated what became a historic debate that raged in local newspapers and in legislative circles[14] protesting that generations of aesthetic tradition would be lost if morals and art were to be conflated. The debate resulted in a series of laws intended to protect women from victimization; yet, female institutions such as dowry, virgin-widowhood and child-marriage persist even today. Looking back, one notices that only the institution and person of the *devadasi* were effectively discredited. Dowry still markets woman's body and sponsorship is still tied in with access to the performing body. Scholars who have researched this situation extensively, agree that although a small section of the traditional community offered entertainment along with the person of the dancer, this local situation was exaggerated (perhaps conflated with situations elsewhere as for example in Kerala) with excessive consequences[15].

Nevertheless, narratives on the dance in India (not just *sadir* or *Mohini Attam*) during this period, continue to proclaim that the dancing body and the body of dance had become debased, almost nonexistent and this, despite our knowledge of ongoing genealogies of gurus, dancers and dances.[16] Could hearsay have caused this perception to reify into belief? Could it be possible that what has really changed globally is perceptions of what is moral with regard to the female body, especially the one on display? Could it be that with the rise of nationalism, our own appreciation and awareness of the art has changed? In fact, it has recently been argued that the popularization of *Bharatanatyam* has resulted in lower standards of artistry than in the pre-Independence period of supposed paucity in this art.

The Prototype of Sankritized Dance

This is the stage where Rukmini Devi Arundale re-enters this narrative of perceptions, as an active participant (among others of her generation in India) re-asserting women's independence and freedom to dance. Pattabhi Raman has always argued that Kamala Laxman's appearances in films greatly spurred popular national awareness of *Bharatanatyam* and there is no doubt that Balasaraswati's international appearances revolutionized (at least in the United States) perception about the dancing body and the art of *Bharatanatyam.* However, I argue that Arundale's vision of the dance and the dancing body remained contained by the patriarchy that she so actively negotiated.

In an article by Rukmini Devi written before 1957,[17] Rukmini Devi claimed that the dance form, *Bharata Natyam* was the quintessential dance described in the *Natyasastra* and that other classical forms as *Kathakali* and *Manipuri* were its variants.[18] Earlier in the same article she stated that *Bhagavatamela Nataka* and *Kuchipudi* also "come under the category of *Bharata Natyam.*" Thus she argued for the aesthetic priority and dominance of *Bharata Natyam.* If she meant that *Bharata Natyam* generically included all the dance forms that subscribe to the canon of Bharata, then this thought presaged the scramble to Sanskritize.

In relation to dance, sanskritization has become a legitimizing process by which dance forms designated as "ritual," folk," or simply insignificant, attain social and politico-artistic status which brings the redesignation, "classical."[19]

Whereas in 1958 it was thought that there were four classical dance forms in India,[20] the number has more than doubled as "classical" dance forms are recovered from oblivion in different parts of India. The term "sanskritization." originally designated a sociological process described by M.N. Srinivas in 1956, whereby lower castes emulated the customs and culture of upper castes in order to upgrade their social status.[21] 'Sanskritization' had come to denote a deliberate self-conscious return to ancient Vedic and Brahminical values and customs from a new intellectual perspective, (often but not necessarily in response to "westernization"). The term is often used synonymously with brahminization, because Sanskrit had been the exclusive preserve of brahmin males.

The *Kalakshetra* method of organizing and transmitting the practical and theoretical aspects of the dance evolved gradually into a model not only for teaching and institutionalizing dance training but also for retrieving or reconstructing other endangered traditional forms. This revival has been misconstrued by some scholars as a reconstructive process of restoring lost movements, patterns and repertory. Such a process may be part of the research of dancers working in other sanskritized forms as *Odissi, Mohini Attam* or *Satiriya* but *Bharatanatyam* inherited a wealth of repertory evolved over generations within the *sadir* tradition. Although the extent of reconstruction and transformation varied in the sanskritizing processes of different forms, the prototypical model of our early post-Colonial history of institutionalizing dance continues to offer common themes that inform the way we dance and read the dancing body.

To disassociate the dance from the stigma attached to its earlier names, Sadir was renamed *Bharata Natyam.*[22] The renaming linked the dance with the *Natyasastra* whose authorship is attributed to Bharata, and the principles of *Bha-va, Ra-ga* and *Ta-la* of Indian *sangeet,* thus establishing the dance as possessing an ancient spiritual and aesthetic heritage, and as an equivalent to the British art of Classical ballet.[23] This renaming also established *Bharata Natyam* as a shastric dance tradition, an indigenous equivalent of the status of classical in the western tradition. Further, since Bharata is the Sanskrit name for India, the renaming also linked the dance to nationalism.[24] Thus the dance of Tamilnadu could be historically validated and represent unified India. Later scholars and dancers would continue this linking of dance with continuous lineages of oral practice and written texts in a search for legitimization as high art.

Sanskritized dance points to an authoritative text to validate its authentic antiquity in terms acceptable to newly embraced western scholarship. In the 1970s, almost every dance form claiming classical antiquity and sophistication, pointed to references to itself within the canonized *Natyasastra* and demonstrated how its postures, movement units and narrative techniques were organized according to this text. Given the comprehensive inclusivity of that text, it is not the purpose of this study to investigate Arundale's or other such claims, but merely to demonstrate how urgent was and is the need to legitimize hitherto oral traditions by association with an ancient revered text.

In addition to in-body practices, learned from members of the former *devadasi* community, at *Kalakshetra,* the curriculum was modelled after (British) academically rigorous text-based methods and included a study of the musical accompaniments to the dance and aesthetic theory from Sanskrit texts as in Nandikeshwara's *Abhinaya Darpana.* This shift initiated radical repercussions regarding control over the dances and dancers that are still playing out. While this may not appear to be a radical strategy, it has had radical consequences. Previously lineages of male teachers controlled access to the repertory, monitored the art and established continuity. As the focus shifted to institutionalized education, the guarded possession of a dedicated few became accessible to all. As dancers mastered the theory and music of the dance, authority to validate transformations could now shift from the inheritors of the tradition to texts. Established gender, caste and linguistic hegemonies were and are still being challenged. It is no co-incidence that the first wave of creative choreographers were predominantly women who challenged the right of the male *nattuvanars* and gurus to dictate their repertory.

With Sanskrit, a root language for many dialects and dance languages across India, and English as a medium of communication in *Kalakshetra,* this local dance form could be accessed by students from diverse geographic regions of India and eventually this curriculum would become the global model for academic certifications in *Bharata Natyam.*[25]

Shifts from ancient oral traditions with their own inbuilt controls of access and *dakshina* to western and now global legal systems of intellectual property ownership based on texts and copyright have had lethal consequences for those *natuvanars* who did not learn to negotiate the changes brought in first by this shift from individualized practical training to institutional instruction and later by recording and filming technologies that would replace their very presence and embodied knowledges.

Antony Seeger writes: "There is a colonial aspect to the copyright laws. A creator takes unprotected, public domain materials and creates something "new" from them that can be protected. Anyone who wishes to use the adapted original materials must pay the "improver" for them, not the original creator or his or her heirs." He goes on to argue that this abuse of the bearers of tradition who are not remunerated while the appropriator is, will eventually result in the extinction of the traditions....

The Sanskritized Body and Dance

Rukmini Devi believed that the confrontation between the pro and anti nautch movements necessitated a reversal of emphases; that dance could only survive by purging all references to sexuality or even sensuality. She forbade dancers to use the poetic texts of their dances to solicit even imaginary lovers. *Sringara,* was reinterpreted only as *bhakti* or devotion to the Divine form.[26] Balasaraswati, rooted in her integrity as a secular performer with deeply personal devotion to Krishna, continued to resist these trends. Expressing her dismay at the developments around her, she did not hesitate to delve into the personal losses and joys of women through *sringara* in public. Much has been argued and documented about the secular versus sacred interpretations of *sringara* of these protagonists.[27]

In sanskritized dance, body is the central object and the word "pure" the ultimate arbiter that is applied to interpretation of emotions, selection of appropriate themes, authenticity of repertory, classicism in technique and costumes,—all must be refined and purified. In terms of repertory it means that any elements deemed external to the particular style and lineage being performed must be purged. Sanskritization involves *samskriti,* or refinement. Emotions as lust, sexuality, greed (anything exciting by contemporary television standards...) are to be avoided. Technique and lines of the dancer must be pure. The hip deflections of the Chidambaram temple karana sculptures are "purified" out making way for the 'pure' triangular form of the *ardhmandi.* This is Brahminized dance still carrying its fear of being contaminated by association with *devadasis.*

Rukmini Devi called upon archetypal images of empowered women from India's mythical past. She spoke persuasively of "the woman as she was in ancient India, not as she is today; the woman who was the Warrior, the True Mother, the Priestess, the ideal for the World"[28] Indian dancers continued for many generations after Rukmini Devi Arundale to embody powerful images of womanhood, both in their dances and public persona (as when they take on the appellation "*Devi*" or Goddess) Since then, dancers have been appropriating the power relationships between dance and temple rituals that had been symbolically ascribed to them by male imaginations.

Only two generations ago, it was inconceivable for women of upper-class families to perform publicly. Today, most dancers hail from high castes and wealthy families. Dancing has clearly involved empowerment for them for their privileges recall those of the early historical dancing women who could read, write, pursue a vocation and skills while these were inaccessible to other Indian women. In a socialist pre-global country where not many people could afford to travel, the star dancers of the seventies accompanied by musicians were constantly travelling, both domestically and internationally as cultural representatives.

Where for most Indian women even into the eighties, the Law Codes of Manu,[29] were still considered household wisdom, (*"Na stri svatantryam arhati"* or woman is not fit for independence!). Post-Independence dancers were embattled and committed to keep dancing. In 1977, a public confrontation between bureaucracy (bastion of conformity and male hegemony) and three leading dancers, received widespread coverage in all India's newspapers and sparked much discussion, which resulted in reformed cultural policies.[30]

For Rukmini Devi, *Bharata Natyam* embodied "the very essence of India itself."[31] So effective was Rukmini Devi Arundale's vision in her time, that she was nominated to the position of President of India, though not selected for this post.[32] For a nation rediscovering and redefining itself after nine centuries of Islamic and British domination, undoubtedly the arts of India have a special psychic value. This is apparent from the post-Independence institutions set up by the government. The Department of Culture handles domestic issues concerning patronage and encouragement of the arts and two additional departments within the Foreign Service exclusively handle the presentation of the Indian performing arts outside India. These are the specially appointed Festivals of India Committees, and the Indian Council for Cultural Relations.

The Pandanallur tradition of dance taught at *Kalakshetra* involves geometric precision of shapes, austere and vigorous dynamics. The torso actively extends the lines of movement into space, a practice well suited for proscenium stages. However, today, dancers in India vie with each other for introducing surprising virtuoso combinations of rhythmic complexity. As speed increases, the movements of the torso are abbreviated. Thus the focus on the moving body shifts to a focus on the body as a virtuoso rhythmical instrument. While some read this change as laziness, for others, it signals middleclass housewifely respectability.

Deeply ingrained in some levels of Hindu society is the idea that physicality is contradictory to refinement. Dance, because of its association with the body, has often been described as subordinate to music.[33] By extension, musicality and rhythmic complexity offer reliability as markers of the dancer's proficiency.

Dancers of the Pre-Glasnost/early Independence era blatantly used gender to negotiate their power. Costumes of the classical dance still emphasize gender and surface. If the dancer is not as shapely as convention demands, (mango breasts, wasp waist, and elephant hips) a little padding is built strategically into the pre-sewn costumes. If the dancer is dark skinned, a base make-up is applied to lighten the skin tone. The persistence of equating beauty with fairness today points to deep-seated racist concerns for *varna* (or skin colour was traditionally an indication of caste). The use of authentic silk and gold costumes and real jewellery associated with south Indian brides, denote a full and loving offering/ sacrifice to the deity of the dance; yet, strangely the use of artificial flower braids in the hair for the sake of convenience is not perceived as contradictory to the spirit of making offerings. One can only conclude that expensive authentic sarees and jewellery are indispensable perhaps because they announce respectability, even as they ensure the spectator's visual pleasure. That even dance critics are not immune to the charms of appearance, is evident from Sadanand Menon's scathing condemnation of what he calls the "Her large-liquid-eyes" School of Dance Criticism"[34]

In the 1990s, as Indian dance entered its post-revival phase, the consequences of the overvaluation of classical dance manifested. In the winter performance season of 1995-6, apparently 334 dance and 1283 music performances took place in Madras alone[35]. Despite the presence of participants and observers from all over India, North America, Europe and the Far East, the majority of the performances were poorly attended and heavily subsidized by cultural institutions and by the performers themselves.

Dance has become a very expensive hobby. The government patronizes and subsidizes only the most recognized, who by teaching and touring make a good living. For an impressively vast majority of dancers, the bottom line is the prohibitive cost of performing and researching new dances. When resources run dry, dancers face the choice between housewifely chores or seek a "sponsor" as their forebearers did. As India's socialist economy moves into international markets and capitalism, the dancing body though glorified, and exalted, has in actuality, been reduced once again to the status of negotiable commodity.

While the Sanskritized dance insistently proclaimed its true spirituality and ability to uplift both practitioner and audience, it took many years before anyone could openly acknowledge that the contradictions inherent in sustaining a dancing career in a capitalist world market, compete with the ego-eliminating processes demanded for the dancers spiritual and artistic progress,[36] Long term connoisseurs of *Bharata Natyam* in India, have often lamented that the recent global popularization *of Bharata Natyam* has resulted in lower standards of artistry than in the pre-Independence period of supposed purity in this art; that dancers lack the discipline to maintain the proper posture, that repertory tends to be simplified for accessibility to non-indigenous audiences, and that the complex of the layered associations, references and psychological odysseys, tend to be ignored.[37]

To summarize, in response to a complex of colonial misperceptions, gender and caste interactions, *sadir,* was buried so that *Bharata Natyam* could be birthed. This re-incarnated dance was validated by its link with ancient texts and upgraded by yogic refinement. Sanskritizing a dance form involves relating current oral tradition with texts and either re-discovering or re-inventing its methodology. It involves "refinement" a process of adapting costume, repertory and technique to sophisticated urban sensibilities. The dancing body and its control was the central issue around which this radical shift took place. In Post-Independent India (1948-89) dancers acquired a kind of independent and prestige way-beyond their counterparts in the United States. However, as the post-reconstruction period (1990's) dawns, dance and the dancing body in India, have again reverted to negotiable commodities.

Today the dancing body of the dancer and the body of Indian classical dance, bear inscriptions of Orientalist discourse, caste, nationalism and intercultural hegemonies. The dancing body serves as a vehicle for praising deities, as ritual aid to acquiring power (*shakti,*) as rhythm instruments culture-bearer and as diplomatic bargaining tool.[38] When the body is a body, it is a commodity.

If this summary seems too stark, too harsh, I would like to point out that my conclusions only underline the admirable consistency with which the dance reflects the Hindu perception of the body. When belief in rebirth is the norm, bodies are temporary vehicles. Whereas in America, dance celebrates the body and life, it is no empty cliche that Indian dance celebrates freedom from the body, an ultimate state of bodilessness.

Here I have described the dancing body in Indian classical dance from the perspective of American modern dance. Should and can one apply the criteria of one world view to the dance of another? If such interactions are an unstoppable inevitability in these times of collapsed space, then what might be their repercussions? The interaction between Indian and western cultures initiated a plunge down the abyss of degradation for the dance that preceded *bharatanatyam.* What do Indian dancers today stand to gain by imbibing the world/body-view of their western sisters? As Indian dance re-encounters again and again, the sisterhood of dance of other cultures, the negotiation remains both fertile and destructive.

(An earlier version of this paper was presented in 1996, at the Congress On Research in Dance, held at the University of North Carolina, Greensboro and published in the Proceedings of the same).

Notes

1. For definitions and issues relating to classical dance as a high art please see Coorlawala "Classical and Contemporary Indian Dance: Overview, Criteria and a Choreographic Analysis." Ph.D. Dissertation at New York University 1994 and Coorlawala "The Classical Traditions of Odissi and Manipuri" in Dance Chronicle 16/2. New York, 1993.

2. See Judith Lynne Hanna, "Classical Indian Dance and Women's Status" in Dance Gender and Culture ed. Helen Thomas (New York: St. Martins Press 1993) 125-6; Projesh Banerji's *Erotica in Indian Dance* (New Jersey: Atlantic Highland, Humanities Press, 1983) 144.

3. See Amrit Srinivasan, "Temple Prostitution and Reform" Dissertation, 1984, and Meduri dissertations of which this is barely a selective summary of their in-depth research.

4. Vatsyayan names dancers whose services were attached to temples, *devadasi* who could service men of equal and higher castes only and according to institutional restrictions; high art dancers or *nartaki*, courtesans or *ganika* prided themselves on their dance as high art. Vatsyayan, *Classical Indian Dance in Literature and the Arts.* New Delhi Sangeet Natak Akademi, 1968 p.162, 178-9; Srinivasan 7.

5. Leslie C. Orr, *Donors, Devotees, and Daughters of God: Tamil Women in Medieval Tamilnadu*, South Asia Series, ed. Richard Larivere, University of Texas Center for Asian Studies and Oxford University Press (New York and Oxford) 2000.

6. In 1835, The Government began to support the use of English as a medium for higher education. See Ainslee T. Embree's *India's Search for National Identity* (New Dlehi: Chanakya Publications) 2nd ed. 1988 Ṣ 1980 p.5.

7. For the effect of Victorian feminist activities on social reform in India in the early twentieth century, see: Amrit Srinivasan, 184-216 and Uttara Coorlawala "Ruth St. Denis and India" Dance Chronicle Vol.15,No.3. 132.

8. In the ballet 'La Bayadere' and Delibes opera 'Lakme', the *devadasi*, the central figure is a 'vestal virgin'! Srinivasan 285. See also Saskia C.Kersenboom, "The Pulse of the Art: Asia Confronts Europe in South India" *Ballet International* 11'90. 15-16 and Kersenboom "Devadasi Murai" in Sangeet Natak Akademi Journal 96, April-June 1990. pp.44-54.

9. It was then the custom for the *devadasi* (servant of God) to be consecrated to the temple at a pre-pubertal age through a symbolic marriage ceremony to the deity, and another ceremony initiated her training. Initiation enabled her to devote herself to her art without the distractions of household obligations usually expected of women. As the economic supporter of the household, she was its legal head and property was inherited matrilineally. Unmarried, she lived with the children of her liaison as designated by strict social and religious codes. See Srinivasan 1984, 161-181.

10. Dr. Miss Clara Swain the first woman physician with a medical diploma was sent to India by the American Methodists Foreign Missionary Society. Srinivasan p.47.

11. See Veena T. Oldenburg, "Elisabeth Bumiller, May You Be The Mother of a Hundred Sons: A Journey Among The Women of India" in Manushi; A Journal About Women and Society (New Delhi), No. 84 (September-October 1984), pp. 39-43.

12. The Justice party legislated for raising the age of consent, (1924) and to reduce Brahmin monopoly over temple finances, (1923). This political group joined forces in 1938 with the non-Brahmin self-respect movement to form the radical *Dravida Kazhagam* which in 1949 became the Dravida Munnetra Kazhagam. Srinivasan 14-15.

13. *Bharatanatyam* dancer Srividya Natarajan writes of how a text *Radhika Santvanam* by Telugu writer Muddupalani in the early 18th century was rediscovered and republished in 1910 only to have the books seized by the Police Commissioner Cunningham, because of the erotic content. See *Sruti* 80, May, 1991.

14. See Sunil Kothari *In Praise of Bharatanatyam* (Bombay:Marg Publications) 1979.

15. G. Sri Hari, "A Rich Dance Tradition in Andhra Pradesh" in Deccan Chronicle, (undated)

16. See B.V.K. Shastry, *Sruti* 99/100 p37-8; Kothari in *Bharata Natyam, Indian Classical Dance Art*. 125-32. Coorlawala, "St. Denis and India's Dance Renaissance". 129-137. Indrani Rehman also reminisces that she was told Mohini Attam was not existent when she was in Kerala. See Indrani Rehman, "Revival of Odissi Dance" in Annual Broc hure of Kala Vikas Kendra, Cuttack, Orissa, c.1990.Dr. Kanak Rele "Sensuous but not Sensual' in Times of India June 17, 1989 *Sruti* 67, Feb., 1990 "Historic Seminar on Bharatanatyam Dance Traditions".

17. See Rukmini Devi, "Spiritual Background" in and reprinted in Sunil Kothari's *Bharata Natyam Indian Classical Dance Art* (Bombay:Marg Publications) 1979. p.13.

18. Rukmini Devi, "Spiritual Background" *In Praise of Bharata Natyam*, Bombay, Marg Publications, 1979. p.15.

19. "The very survival of some dance forms in post-colonial India without its royal patrons, has hinged on their being recognized as classical, a perception that is brought about through repeated performances in theatres in cities, in cultural programs, in scholarly research, and in re-presentation of the living tradition. Uttara Asha Coorlawala "Odissi and Manipuri" in Dance Chronicle 16/2. p. 270.

20. M.N. Srinivas, "Sanskritization and Westernization" and V. Raghavan, "Variety and Integration in the Pattern of Indian Culture" in *Far Eastern Quarterly* 14, No.4, Aug., 1956. pp. 481-495, 496-505.

21. Richard Schechner *Between Theater and Anthropology*, Philadelphia University of Pennysylvania Press Fourth edition, 1994. p.69, 78 Here Rukmini Devi's role is misapprehended. See also Richard Schechner, in *Rasa: The Indian Performing Arts in the Last Twenty-Five Years*. Vol. 1 Calcutta, Anamika Kala Sangam, 1994. p.209,210.

22. Rustom Bharucha cites scholar and Sanskritist Dr. V. Raghavan as stating that he came up with the name. Chandralekha (New Delhi: Harper Collins 1995), p.343.

23. Her admiration for Anna Pavlova and her dance art is well documented...

24. See Srinivasan. Meduri nuances the argument further. She argues that the name Bharata is linked to Sanskrit history of *Natya Sastra* but also to Coomaraswamy's Dance of Shiva, to a pan Indian nation that could still celebrate notions of diversity, regionalism and particularism as in the name *Bhava, raga, tala* which referred the dance to itself (pages 269-273).

25. The Imperial Society of Teachers of Dancing syllabus for *Bharatanatyam* for example has to fulfill criteria equivalent to levels of accomplishment expected in other British forms similarly examined. The *Kalakshetra* syllabus was most suited for this kind of institutional adaptation. See Stacey Prickett's "Techniques and Institutions:The Transformation of British Dance Tradition through South Asian Dance" Unpublished MS. Also personal interview with Anusha Subrahmanyam.

26. "When *bhakti* is to be conveyed, the selected composition should contain the best of sublime truths. Those passages derogatory to the gods should be omitted. ...:Reject those works which are likely to kindle the baser instincts in man. Only those compositions which elevate human nature should be chosen..." "Advice from a Veteran," an interview with S.(Peria) Sarada, a veteran teacher, at *Kalakshetra* in *Sruti* 136, Jan. 96, p.9-14.

27. O'Shea, Mathew... RGK "Amazing Grace" in *The Illustrated Weekly of India* Feb., 22, 1987. p.50-51.

References

Allen, Matthew, Harp, "Rewriting the Script for South Indian Dance" *TDR 41/3* Fall 1997/T155 63-100.

Arundale, Rukmini Devi, "The Spiritual background of Bharata Natyam" in *Classical and Follk Dances of India,* Bombay, Marg Publications 1963 and reprinted in Kothari, Sunil. *Bharata Natyam* Bombay, Marg Publications 1979.

Kothari, Sunil. *Bharata Natyam Indian Classical Dance Art,* Bombay, Marg Publications, 1997.

Aslecha, Ram, The Mad Mad Madras Season" *Sruti* 137, Feb., 1996.

Balasaraswati, T. "Bala on Bharata Natyam" *Sruti* 4 Madras, March 1984.

Banerji, Projesh *Erotica in Indian Dance.* New Jersey: Atlantic Highland, Humanities Press 1983.

Bharucha, Rustom, *Chandralekha.* New Delhi:Harper Collins 1995.

Coorlawala, Uttara Asha, "Ruth St. Denis and India" *Dance Chronicle 15/3.*

Coorlawala, Uttara Asha, "The Classical Traditions of Odissi and Manipuri" in *Dance Chronicle 16/2.* New York, 1993.

Coorlawala, Uttara Asha, *Classical and Contemporary Indian Dance: Overview, Criteria and a Choreographic Analysis.* PhD Dissertation at New York University 1994.

Doniger, Wendy. *The Laws of Manu* (New Delhi: India Penguin Books 1991).

Embree T, Ainslee. *Inda's Search for National Identity* New Delhi: Chanakya Publications, 2nd ed. 1988 S 1980.

Erdman, Joan. "Who should Speak for the Performing Arts? The Case of the Delhi Dancers." *Pacific Affairs 56/2.* Summer 1983.

Hanna, Judith Lynne, "Classical Indian Dance and Women's Status" *Dance Gender and Culture* ed. Helen Thomas. New York: St. Martins Press 1993.

Hari, G. Sri, "A Rich Dance Tradition in Andhra Pradesh" in Deccan Chronicle, (undated)

Indu, (Pseudonym) "Advice from a Veteran," an interview with S. (Peria) Sarada, a veteran teacher, at *Kalakshetra* in *Sruti* 136, Jan. 96. p.9-14.

Kersenboom, Saskia C. "The Pulse of the Art: Asia Confronts Europe in South India" *Ballet International 11'90.*

Kersenboom Saskia C. "Devadasi Murai" in *Sangeet Natak Akademi*, Journal 96, April-June, 1990 p.44-54.

Kothari, Sunil. *Bharata Natyam*, Bombay:Marg Publications, 1979.

Kothari, Sunil. *Bharata Natyam Indian Classical Dance Art*, Bombay:Marg Publications, 1997.

Meduri, Avanthi, New York University PhD. Dissertation, 1996.

Menon, Sadanand "Her large-liquid-eyes" School of Dance Criticism" in *The Sunday Observer*, Feb. 5, 1984, India.

Natarajan, Srividya "Bharatanatyam: Its Relevance and Future. *Sruti* 80, May 1991.

O'Shea, Janet, "Traditional Indian Dance and the Making of Interpretative Communities" *Asian Performance Journal 15/1*. University of Hawaii Press Spring 1998.

Oldenburg, Veena T. "Elisabeth Bumiller, May You Be The Mother of a Hundred Sons: A Journey Among The Women of India" in *Manushi A Journal About Women and Society, No. 84* (New Delhi), (September-October 1984).

Orr, Leslie C., *Donors, Devotees, and Daughters of God: Tamil Women in Medieval Tamilnadu*, South Asia Series, ED. Richard Larivere, University of Texas Center for Asian Studies and Oxford University Press (New York and Oxford) 2000.

Prickett, Stacey "Techniques and Institutions: The Transformation of British Dance Tradition through South Asian dance" Unpublished MS.

Raghavan, V. "Variety and Integration in the Pattern of Indian Culture" in *Far Eastern Quarterly 14*, No.4, Aug., 1956.

Rehman, Indrani. "Revival of *Odissi* Dance" in *Annual Brochure of Kala Vikas Kendra*, Cuttack Orissa, c.1990.

Rele, Kanak "Sensuous but not Sensual' in *Times of India*, June 17, 1989.

RGK "Amazing Grace" in *The Illustrated weekly of India*, Feb. 22, 1987.

Schechner, Richard. Between Theater and Anthropology Philadelphia University of Pennysylvania Press Fourth edition, 1994.

Schechner, Richard. "Restoration of Behavious" Rasa: *The Indian Performing Arts in the Last Twenty-Five Years*. Vol.1, Calcutta, Anamika Kala sangam, 1994.

Shastry, B.V.K. *Sruti* 99/100. p.37-8.

Shringy, R.K. trans. *Sangita-Ratnakara of sarngadeva Vol.I. Treatment of Svara,* Delhi: Motilal Banarsidass, 1978.

Srinivas, M.N. "Sanskritization and Westernization" *Far Eastern Quarterly* 14, No.4, Aug., 1956.

Srinivasan, Amrit "Temple Prostitution and Reform Dissertation, 1984.

Sruti staffer, "Historic Seminar on Bharatanatyam Dance Traditions" *Sruti* 67, Feb., 1990 .

Vatsyayan, Kapila, *Classical Indian Dance in Literature and the Arts.* New Delhi, Sangeet Natak Akademi, 1968.

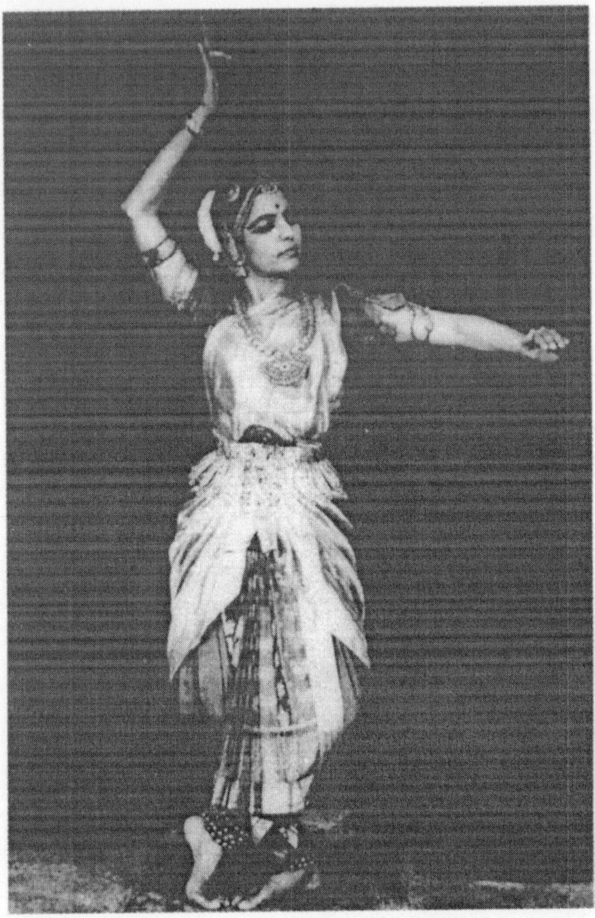

Fig. 8: Rukmini Devi's New Costume for Bharatanatyam

(Photo: C.T. Nachiappan archive)

CHAPTER 21

RUKMINI DEVI AND 'SANSKRITIZATION': A NEW PERFORMANCE PERSPECTIVE

Dr. Avanthi Meduri

From the time of the demise of Rukmini Devi in 1986 to the present day, there has been one main criticism of her aesthetic vision circulating both in the public domain of the arts and in scholarly circles: all have maintained that Rukmini Devi textualized and Sanskritized *Bharatanatyam*. Amrit Srinivasan raised this criticism in the mid 1980s. She argued that Rukmini Devi textualized and sanskritized the history, technique and content of Sadir, which had been embodied by *devadasis* till the1930s (Srinivasan 1985:1874-5). Srinivasan maintained that the use of Sanskrit aesthetic theory, including the study of Bharata's *Natyasastra* and Nandikeswara's *Abhinaya Darpana*, enabled Rukmini Devi and other urban, upper caste women dancers to learn the dance and to project themselves not just as dancers but also as interpreters of the dance. She argued that this emphasis on textuality disabled *devadasis* as they could not use Sanskrit aesthetic theory to legitimise their dance, which was essentially a regional (Tamil) practice preserved in *guru-shisya* systems of oral transmission.

Srinivasan condemned the textualizing imperative in the *Bharatanatyam* dance revival because it disempowered *devadasis*, removed these women from the revival, and relegated them to the margins of history. She explains the problem in this way: "classical Sanskrit literature was invoked not just as a means to purifying the classical traditions but as also reviving lost forms.... What was significant, however, was that the texts were considered as authoritative and carried out in the name of improvement of the art or the regeneration of its lost classicism... The art of *Bharata Natyam* is now monopolized by Brahmins in Tamil Nadu who clearly see themselves as having rescued the art from the fallen prostitute—the *devadasi.* Yet in a very real sense it is only the art of the *devadasi* that they are perpetuating " (1985: 1874-5).

Srinivasan launched her influential critique without recognizing that Sanskrit texts actually played only a secondary role in the dance revival as they were not used literally but metaphorically and thus divested of the pedagogical (*sastric*) authority associated with literary texts. It is well known that Rukmini Devi did not herself study the *Natyasastra,* nor did she apply the text in her own re-creations. Gowri Ramnarayan explains that Rukmini Devi did not study the ancient text with the intent of translating theory into practice. She quotes Sankara Menon who said categorically ... "Rukmini Devi did not study the *Natyasastra*" (Ramnarayan 1984c: 30). Yet Rukmini Devi maintained that the *Natyasastra* was the source text of all Indian dancing, and that "*Bharatnatya* is the root and origin of all dance in India. Essentially all real dancing is *Bharata Natya.*"(Devi n.d: 22). Rukmini Devi went further and stated that the "*sastras* do not discourage creativity or new expression. I can say this positively as I can prove that it is possible to be creative and yet adhere to the *sastras.* The important thing is to catch the spirit of the *sastras* and to keep this at a high level. In fact this spirit is the fountain source of creative expression" (Quoted in Kothari: 28).

Taking their cue from Srinivasan, scholars argued that Rukmini Devi privileged Sanskrit texts and did so without examining how she actually used these texts in her own revival of *Bharatanatyam.*[1] Not only did Rukmini Devi supplement and displace the authority of Sanskrit texts by privileging the oral traditions of *gurus,* but she also used Tamil, and other multilingual literary texts in her revival. It is well known that Rukmini Devi nurtured the famous Dr.U. V. Swaminatha Aiyar collection of palm leaf manuscripts, converted it into a public library and made it available as a rich resource to Tamil scholars and writers. Rukmini Devi, in other words, was committed to preserving the regional Tamil history of *Sadir* as also the Sanskrit history of the *Natyasastra,* which according to scholars like Kapila Vatsyayan, was always already part of the practicing history of the dance (Vatsyayan 1974: 14).

Srinivasan, however, did not recognize the multilingual commitments in Rukmini Devi's revival because she articulated her critique from the standpoint of an anthropologist rather than a dance scholar. Yet Srinivasan was reflexive about the alien point of view that she brought to bear on the study of the dance revival, drew attention to it by explaining "her ignorance of dance practice, of the complexities of Sanskrit studies and art analysis and her lack of stake in academic discourses other than the anthropological"(1984: 7). Her disclamations notwithstanding, Srinivasan's critique found favour with a host of international scholars working in diverse disciplinary fields ranging from dance, ethnomusicology, cultural and literary studies. Endorsing Srinivasan's theory of Sanskritization, international scholars, since the 1980s, have replicated her simplified critique in their own elaborations of the dance revival. [2] In order to propose a more nuanced critique of the revival, one that does not privilege Sanskrit texts, I will describe how Rukmini Devi used 'Sanskrit text' in her revival, and inscribed *Sadir-Bharatanatyam* in a triple reed Sanskrit, Tamil, and oral history simultaneously.

This essay is divided into three parts. Part 1 provides a brief discussion about the name *Bharatanatyam,* describing how it textualised *Sadir* and facilitated textual and anthropological studies of Indian dance. This will be followed by a discussion revolving around the two complementary streams known as the *tala* (percussive)and *bhava* (expressive) elements that combine in *Bharatanatyam,* which Rukmini Devi had to conjoin to realize her own dance revival in the 1930s. Part 2, focuses on Rukmini Devi's inaugural performance, describes her staging techniques and how she constituted a three pronged God, *Guru* and *Natyasastra* frame for *Bharatnatyam.* I conclude by urging that we re-examine Rukmini Devi's three-pronged aesthetic constellation in order to understand the marginalization of *devadasis* and also to historicize the vibrant practice of *Bharatanatyam,* circulating in the local and global flows of modernity today.

PART 1
Triple Reed History for *Sadir-Bharatanatyam*

To critique the textualization of *Bharatanatyam* one would have to begin not with Rukmini Devi as Srinivasan does, but with the renaming of *Sadir* as *Bharatnatyam* because the new name proposed a Sanskrit history and identity for the dance.[3] Although Venkatrama Sharma was the first to use the name *Bharatanatyam* in the 1930s, most scholars and practitioners aver that it was Dr. V. Raghavan, a revered scholar and executive member of the Madras Music Academy, who conceived the new name. V. Raghavan did not deny this perception, but downplayed its significance by saying that "there was nothing new or incorrect about it as it ... invested the dance with the requisite status, which was needed in the circumstances of the revival. And served to underlie its classical moorings. The name at once established the form in a historical continuity, which went up to Mohanjedaro and Rig Veda" (Arudra1986/87d: 31).

Some scholars have argued that the new name sought to legitimize the dance by associating it with the name of sage Bharata, the author of the *Natyasastra,* and thus with Sanskrit

history(Coorlawala 2004: 173-193; Ramphal 2004 247-258).[4] Others have suggested that *Bharatanatyam* was really a Tamil name referring to *Bharatam* and the Brahman dance masters who taught the dance to *devadasis* in South India (Arudra 1986/87d: 35). Padma Subrahmanyam explained that *Bharatanatyam* was a really new name that was given to the dance in the twentieth century (1977:76). And scholars like Vatsyayan denied the legitimacy of the name by suggesting that "*Bharatanatyam* is perhaps the oldest among the contemporary classical dance forms of India. Its claim to antiquity rests not on the name, which is derived from the word Bharata and thus associated with the *Natyasastra,* but on the overwhelming, literary, sculptural and historical evidence available"(1974: 15). *Bharatanatyam* then was an inclusive name that spoke to multilingual spectatorial communities, encompassing old and new, Sanskrit and Tamil versions of Indian cultural and dance history.

The new name was prophetic because it enabled scholars like V. Raghavan to locate *Sadir* within an indigenous classificatory system known as *marga* and *desi* categories. Indira Peterson explains that *marga* is usually described as "that which is governed by country-wide common rules i.e., that which is universal, whereas *desi* is that which varies from place to place, i.e., the local or regional (1998: 41).[5] Because V. Raghavan was a Sanskrit scholar, he located *Bharatanatyam* both within the *marga* and *desi* categories, and described *Sadir* as a classical (Sanskrit) and a regional (Tamil) dance both at once. But V. Raghavan did more in that he also pushed the boundaries of Sanskrit textual studies by combining it with what we might today describe as anthropological studies of culture. He developed this new research initiative by prioritizing T. Balasaraswati as a hereditary *devadasi* practitioner, promoted her point of view on the dance and co-authored a book with her entitled *Bharatanatyam.* He was also instrumental in founding a school in the Madras Music Academy, where T. Balasaraswati taught

for many years.[6] V. Raghavan, in other words, pioneered a new genre of dance studies that privileged literary texts, albeit, from an anthropological perspective and facilitated new studies of Indian dance from within textual and anthropological frames of reference as early as the 1930s.

E. Krishna Iyer (1897-1968), another important figure who stood behind the revival of *Sadir* in the 1930s, (Arudra 1986/87d: 32-36), repeated V. Raghavan's double conceptualization by inscribing *Sadir-Bharatanatyam* within a literary history of Tamil source texts, including the *Silappadikaram,* which he claimed was comparable to the *Natyasastra* (1957: 11). Yet, he too privileged hereditary practitioners and endeavoured to bring *devadasis* and male dance *gurus* into the mainstream revival in the 1930s. T. Balasaraswati, on her part, maintained that the *Natyasastra* was the large conceptual frame for *Bharatanatyam.* Yet she prioritized Tamil texts like the *Silappadikaram* (Balasaraswati 1988: 38), while also describing *Sadir-Bharatanatyam* from within the oral traditions of her *guru* and her own family of musicians. Finally, Rukmini Devi also reclaimed *Sadir* from within the textual history of the *Natyasastra,* affirmed Tamil texts by reviving Tamil literary performance genres such as the *Kutrala Kuravanji,* while also prioritizing traditional dance and music gurus, from whom she learned the dance in the 1930s.

All four pioneers of the dance revival, including V. Raghavan, E. Krishna Iyer, T. Balasaraswati and Rukmini Devi used the name of *Bharatanatyam* creatively, did not deny the legitimacy of the *Natyasastra* as souce-text, affirmed Tamil source texts, and reclaimed *Sadir* with the help of heriditary *gurus.* Suffice it to say that this triple- reed approach prevailed in the scholarship and practice of *Sadir-Bharatanatyam* until the demise of T. Balasaraswati and Rukmini Devi in the 1980s.[7] Soon thereafter Indian and international scholars came forward to press forth new,

exclusionary claims on behalf of *Sadir* as a Tamil form.[8] Thus began the radical process of disengaging *Sadir- Bharatanatyam* from the triple reed Sanskrit-Tamil and oral history in which it had been nurtured for over fifty years, and a separate regional history and identity was constructed for the dance in the manner proposed by Amrit Srinivasan.

Rukmini Devi's Problematic

Much has been written since the 1980s about how Rukmini Devi textualized, sanskritized, spiritualized and masculinized *Bharatanatyam.*[9] But scholars have not focussed any attention on another key issue, revolving not around textualization or Sankritization, but around the splitting of the *Sadir* dance into the *tala* (rhythmic) versus the *bhava* (musical or expressive) traditions. Whereas Indian scholars have worried this question (Ramnarayan 1984b: 24), international scholars have not dealt with it in any meaningful way. Since Rukmini Devi recognized the *tala/bhava* dialectic as being the central thematic of the revival, I shall focus my discussion on this problematic.

It is well known that Rukmini Devi began her dance training with Mylapore Gowri Amma, who hailed from a well-known family of traditional *devadasi* dancers attached to the Mylapore temple in Madras. Gowri Amma was noted for her *abhinaya* and musical talents. But in 1933, on an invitation from E. Krishna Iyer, Rukmini Devi went to see the dance performed by two *devadasis* in the precincts of the Madras Music Academy. She was enamored with the dance and said this of the performance: "I could see that the dance was highly classical, but there was not much *bhava.* Gowri Amma was the expert in *Bhava.*"(Ramani 2003. 37).

Rukmini Devi marveled at the rhythmic virtuosity displayed by the two *devadasi* dancers. But she also recognized the lack of *bhava* or emotional feeling in the performance. Despite this shortcoming, Devi decided to

learn the dance from Shri Meenakshi Sundaram Pillai, the renowned male teacher who tutored the two *devadasi* dancers. One could fault Rukmini Devi for shifting her loyalties from Gowri Amma to Meenakshi Sundaram Pillai, and for not recognizing the gender politics in the revival, debated openly in the English langauge newspapers of the time.[10] Yet Rukmini Devi explains her decision in this way: "it seemed perfectly natural that I should wish to learn from two sources of pure tradition, one enriching the other, especially as they were complementary, Gowri Amma's guru being Meenakshi Sundaram Pillai...." (Ramnarayan 1984b: 19).

By shifting from one source of tradition to another, Rukmini Devi pointed to the stylistic differences embodied in the *devadasi* style of dancing and contrasted this with the style represented by the male teachers. She articulated the difference as representing two different orientations to the study of *Bharatanatyam*: the *tala* or percussive approach to the study of dance, represented in Meenkshi Sundram Pillai's style of dancing and contrasted this with the musical(*bhava*)based approach to the study of *Sadir-Bharatanatyam* represented in the style of Gowri Amma.

Rukmini Devi, in other words, pointed to a structural problem in the revival, namely, that Meenakshi Sundram Pillai possessed the percussive knowledge base of the *Sadir* dance whereas Gowri Amma held the expressive emotive techniques of the dance in her custody. Was the *tala* base necessary for the revival of *Sadir-Bharatanatyam*? Or could the dance be revived from the musical source? Urban practitioners from the 1930s, continuing into the present, did not raise this question but sought out male dance teachers to learn the rhythmic aspects of the dance, and *devadasis* to learn the musical and *bhava* naunces in the dance. Devi likewise did not ask herself why the *tala* base was important, but recognized intuitively that she could not revive *Sadir* without this knowledge base.

Any critique of the revival, then, should recognize this *tala/bhava* splitting, and not textualization, to be the fundamental, structural problem in the revival. It is this splitting, I want to suggest, that disempowered *devadasis*, because urban dancers who desired to learn the *tala* knowledges, sat at the feet of the male teachers, and idealized them as their *gurus*. *Devadasis* were thus rendered marginal to the revival as their use-value as expressive and interpretive dancers was supplanted by urban women dancers. Male *gurus*, on their part, were reluctant to teach *devadasi* women and more than willing to teach their *tala* knowledges to urban women in the 1930s.

When Rukmini Devi began her revival in 1933, her task was not that of choosing between a Sanskrit versus Tamil history for *Sadir-Bharatanatyam*, as argued by O'Shea (2001: 24). Both histories had been conjoined in the very renaming of the dance. Rukmini Devi had to yoke the *tala/bhava* traditions, which as I have argued elsewhere had created new patriarchies in the dance practice of the nineteenth century (Meduri 1996: 40-48). But how was Rukmini Devi to yoke the expressive and percussive streams of the *Sadir* dance when it was not customary for *devadasis* to teach the dance and when male dance teachers were neither great dancers nor musicians?

It was the gendering of the *Sadir* dance tradition, which stipulated that *devadasis* could be singers and dancers but not teachers, as opposed to textualization, that was the real practical problematic that Rukmini Devi had to grapple with in the dance revival of the 1930s. She resolved this problematic by enunciating the dancer-teacher category in her *Kalakshetra* arts institution and by imparting instruction in music, combined with the learning of *tala* techniques to *Kalakshetra* students as early as the 1940s. (Meduri 1996: 366-376). She thus eroded the gendered division of labor that had fetishized *devadasis* as dancers in the nineteenth century, and enabled the democratization of *Bharatanatyam* in the 1940s.

PART 11

Devi's Inaugural Constellation

Since mainstream national institutions like the Madras Music Academy had inscribed *Sadir* within the triple histories of Bharata's *Natyasastra,* Tamil literary histories and *guru-shisya* geneologies described above, Rukmini Devi accepted this mainstream history and repeated it in her own revival of *Bharatanatyam.* But what was unique about Rukmini Devi's revival is that she visualized the triple reed history by using the three symbols of *Nataraja, Natyasastra,* and *Guru*[11] theatrically in her debut recital of 1935. If *Nataraja* was described as the cosmic dancer and presiding deity of the *Natyasastra,* the *Natyasastra* was posited as the source text for *Bharatanatya,* and sage Bharata the author of the *Natyasastra,* was described *as* the *'Adiguru'* or first *guru* of dance and drama.[12] Rukmini Devi visualized this triple-reed, conceptual history by identifying them as the foundational symbols of the revival. She then knit the three symbols into a visual cluster and used them as stage props to envision a contemporary classical and traditional performance history for *Bharatanatyam.*

Rukmini Devi worked within the phenomenological world view of her multi-pronged constellation through her long and distinguished career between 1930-1980. Scholars and dancers use Devi's multisited frame to research, practice, teach and perform *Bharatanatyam* both locally and globally because it continues to be posited as the smallest and largest historical worldview of *Bharatanatyam.* Yet Rukmini Devi envisioned this multisited frame improvisationally and with no grand design other than to provide a historical and theatrical frame for *Bharatanatya.* Here is an eyewitness account of her historic performance:

> Nearly a thousand people were seated under the great rain tree, through whose giant branches glimpses could be caught of the stars in an almost purple sky. The stage

was at first in semi-darkness: *on one side the ensemble of musicians, including her guru, were seated on rugs, with their picturesque instruments*; on *the other a group of young men appeared chanting in unison a most impressive dedication of the dance recital Bharata Natya to Nataraja, that aspect of Divine* life. The music grew stronger, and the lights came on and against the green curtains of the background, Rukmini appeared in her archaic white and gold dress, looking like some *temple carving*, full of arrested movement.... For more than two hours she danced with scarcely a pause and all the time the audience sat spellbound absorbed by the beauty of movement, no less by the telling of beloved stories in voice, gesture, and expression (Ramnarayan 1984b: 21). [Italics mine].

Nataraja in a Civilizational Frame

It is important to note that Devi began her revival by dedicating her dance to *Nataraja,* the cosmic dancer, whose presence she invoked by having a group of young men chant verses in praise of him.' The invocation associated Devi's *Bharatanatya* dance recital with the name of sage Bharata, the author of the *Natyasastra,* and also with *Nataraja,* the presiding deity of the *Natyasastra* both at once. One might argue that by using Sanskrit chants in the frame of her inaugural performance, Devi spiritualised and transcendentalized her temporal recital. But the chanting did not just elevate Devi's dance, it also temporalized Bharata's cosmological conceptualisation of *Natya,* juxtaposed the cosmic dance of *Nataraja* with a temporal recital of *Bharatanatya,* and counterpoised Bharata's originary status as *adiguru* with Devi's real *guru,* who was seated on the urban stage and presented as the living, hereditary teacher of the dance.[13]

Devi's doubling devices—which juxtaposed the ideal teacher (sage Bharata) with real teacher (Meenakshi

Sundram Pillai), and *Nataraja's* cosmic Dance with the real *Sadir-Bharatanatya* recital might appear facile on the face of it. Yet the staging techniques were successful because this history was being disseminated in mainstream national institutions like the Madras Music Academy in the 1930s. The doubling techique worked also because they inscribed the dance in a historical continnum, and enabled the idealization and particularization, metaphorization and historicization, abstraction and temporalization of *Sadir-Bharatanatya* all at once.

Because Rukmini Devi staged *Sadir-Bharatanatya* symbolically and by combining textual with visual (real) images, she was able to performatively visualize the (textual), anthropological(*guru-shisya*),and sculptural histories of *Bharatanatyam* and imprint this multipronged history in the mind of the urban spectator. After 1935, Rukmini Devi could reclaim *Sadir-Bharanatya* from three sources of Indian tradition — art history and sculpture, Sansksrit aesthetic theory, and *guru-shisya* genealogies all at once. After 1935, Rukmini Devi plotted not one 'Originary' textual source for Indian dance, as argued by O'Shea (2001: 24), but at least three historical sources for *Sadir-Bharatanatya.* After 1935, scholars and practitioners could describe *Bharatanatyam* from within the dramatic theories of the *Natyasastra,* from within anthropological genealogies of hereditary teachers and practitioners, and from within sculptural histories of the Hindu temple simultaneously.

Devi's debut was momentous because she enlarged the regional worldview of *Sadir* not ideologically but from within the name and history of the new name *Bharatanatyam.* We can perceive the art historiographical and Sanskrit textual frames that Devi envisioned for *Bharatanatyam* as representing two new hueristic frames that spatialized the history of the dance. If *Nataraja*'s cosmic dance helped envision a timeless, civilizational, spiritual and divine history for the dance, the *Natyasastra* placed *Sadir-Bharatanatya*

within the history of a classical literary and textual history and the *guru* located the dance within an anthropological history of guilds, and lifestyle practices.

Yet the dance itself was perceived as being contemporary because it was presented on the modern dance proscenium, with 'green back curtains,' was lit with stage light learned from British stagecraft, and performed not just by *devadasis*, but also by urban women in the 1930s. Yet the contemporaneity of the form did not impress itself on the imagination of the urban spectator because Rukmini Devi staged the dance within the two symbols of god and *guru* simultaneously. The urban public watching Rukmini Devi's inaugural performance endorsed her theatricalization techniques because they were continuous with scholarly and popular understandings of Indian dance: a history in which gods danced, and *gurus* were revered as repositories of ancient knowledge. By staging the dance in this way, Rukmini Devi envisioned a dialogical and polycentric aesthetic for *Sadir-Bharatanatyam* that was civilizational, classical, traditional and contemporary all at once.

Guru in an Anthropological Frame

It is well-known that prior to *Sadir*'s arrival on the urban stage in the 1930s, *nattuvanars* (dance teachers) used to walk behind *devadasi* dancers even as they danced. The legendary T. Balasarawati explains:

> You must understand why in the old days the *nattuvanar* and the musician used to walk behind the dancer in a performance. The audience used to be positioned on all sides of the performer. There was no power amplification and the dancer couldn't hear the musicians properly. Since the song and the rhythm must be heard by the dancer, the supporting cast used to move back and forth along with the dancer. It may present an amusing picture to you today, but we shouldn't laugh at it. Our elders didn't do anything foolishly (Raman and Ramachandran 1984b: 21).

Rukmini Devi changed this conceptual worldview in which the teacher imposed his physical presence on the dancer and the dance in each and every act of public performance. She transformed this vision by first separating the teacher from the dancer, and by seating the teacher and his ensemble on beautifully laid out rugs. Devi explained:

> The musicians would follow the dancer with their music and drumming as she moved about the stage... I wanted to change all that. I made the musicians sit on the side of the stage. I also stopped having the Harmonium and the Clarionet as accompaniments, choosing instead the softer musical instruments *Mukhaveenai,* Flute, etc. I designed my own costumes, Madame Cazan who was good at tailoring and Mary Elmore helped me put my ideas into proper shape. Conrad Worldring, a remarkable young musician, who was a wonderful technician on stage, Alex Elmore who was a lighting expert, all of them did a marvelous job even with the limited equipment we had. All these things made a profound impact and presented the despised *Sadir* in an entirely new way. (Ramani 2003: 45).

The staging devises worked magically as the urban spectator could suddenly behold the 'despised *Sadir*' clad in new clothes, lit by new light, and freed of the conservative presence of the male teacher who loomed behind the corporeal form of *Sadir* and the body of the *devadasi* dancer in performance. Yet Devi did not desire to sever *Sadir* from its moorings in tradition and history because the *gurus* were the keepers of the *tala* traditions. She thus seated them on the stage and referred her revived *Sadir-Bharatanatya* to patterns of ideas associated with hereditary teachers and *devadasi* dancers, interpreted her own cultural and aesthetic practice in relation to those other traditions, and inscribed the revived dance in *guru-shisya* genealogies of performance.[14]

Gowri Amma and Meenakshi Sundram Pillai were to Devi what the native informant was and continues to be for the traditional Anthropologist.[15] She thus envisioned a music and dance *gurukul* or community comprising of dance and music teachers. She realized this vision by inviting traditional teachers to teach in *Kalakshetra* and adorned her institution with a galaxy of great traditional teachers. Like the traditional anthropologist, she idealized the teachers and projected them as the guiding metaphors and spirits of her institution.[16]

Natyasastra in a Historical Frame

Devi also enlarged her ethnographic revival by providing verbal and textual commentaries that referred the dance, albeit metaphorically, to the *sastric* values embodied in Bharata's *Natyasastra.* She explained that "*Bharatnatya* is the root and origin of all dance in India. Essentially all real dancing is *Bharatanatya.* The most ancient authority on Indian dance is the *Natyasastra* of Bharata" (Devi n.d: 22). As already mentioned, Rukmini Devi did not herself study the *Natyasastra,* nor did she translate aesthetic theory into practice. Her English husband likewise did not refer to the textual rules of the *Natyasastra* in the verbal commentaries that he provided for Devi's dance recitals (S.Sarada 13-14), but simply alluded to the antiquity of the dance and described it poetically as an emotional interpretation of the 'aspirational outpourings of the Soul, and an ecstatic identification of these with the very Soul of the Universe itself, the merging of the individual soul in God.

> Every movement, every gesture, every pose, each song, expressed an aspect of such union, so that the whole dance became an intricate yet beautifully rhythmic symbol of a soul's awakening to its divinity. Yet emotional in structure though this particular Dance undoubtedly was, it had a very high intellectual content, appealing

no less to the mind than the emotions themselves. (1936: 19-20).

The Sanskrit text impinged on the mind of the urban spectator merely as a metaphoric text because few had really read the *Natyasastra* in the 1930s. Yet all concerned with the revival were aware of the associative links between *Bharatanatya* and Bharata's *Natyasastra* because of the uniquely performative manner in which Devi used Sanskrit chanting—"*with a group of young men, chanting in unison a most impressive dedication of the dance recital Bharatanatya to Nataraja, that aspect of Divine life.*" Thrilled by these associations, made real with the help of dramatic techniques including the projection of voice, and use of choral effects, critic after critic described Devi's debut as conveying an otherworldly experience "a sacramental and spiritual experience, such as the dance-dramas in their original purity were intended to convey."[17]

The urban spectator, witnessing the revival, did not desire to know if the Sanskrit *sloka* that Devi used in her inaugural performance was a verse from Nandikeswara's *Abhinaya Darpana*, or Bharata's *Natyasastra* as one Sanskrit text was interchanged with the other. Sanskrit texts ceded their pedagogical authority as they were transformed into performance texts, and became part of the performance. Literary texts, transformed into Sanskrit chants, combined with the dancing bells and with musical renditions, created a contemporary, cosmological universe that was visual/textual/and aural all at once. While the dancing bells grounded the revival in the truth metaphors of the real history of the dance, the Sanskrit chants created links with ancient pasts and with notions of antiquity. The new associations between history and antiquity that were realized in the domain of performance and the eye/I of the urban spectator, democratised the revival and made *Bharatanatya* "accessible and acceptable to everyone" (Ramnarayan 1984b: 24-25).

Where was the *Natyasastra* in performance? What was its authority? Invoked in the beginning of the performance, present as invocation in the name of the dance, it was suddenly manifest in the hand gestures or *mudras* of the dancer, recognized as such in the eyes of the spectator, but was quickly supplemented by the iconography of *Nataraja*, interchanged with the guru, with the sound of the bells, then with the music, and finally with the dance itself. The spectator/reader could not focus selectively on the *Natyasastra* because it was not used pedagogically as a source text but rather as a performance or metaphorical text to forge real and imagined connections with ancient and contemporary notions of antiquity. [18]

What enabled the textualization of *Sadir* ? Did the name of *Nataraja* emerging from the textual folds of the *Natyasastra* enable the textualizaion of *Bharatanatyam*? Did the new name of *Bharatanatya* textualize the dance by associating *Sadir* with Bharata's *Natyasastra*? Or was it the Sanskrit chanting, the staging of the guru, Arundale's English language commentary, or the new stage light that Devi used to theatricalize the dance that textualized *Bharatanatya*? Did Devi's staging techniques Sanskritize the form of *Sadir*, or was Sankritization resisted by the multilingual form of *Sadir* which remained what it had always been?

The New Beginning

Devi was not interested in any of these questions that concern us today because the three symbolic registers of the *Natyasatra, Nataraja,* and *Guru* were equally important to her. She did not choose from but rather retained her three-pronged consteliation and worked within its conceptual frame for more than fifty years.[19] Perhaps because Devi worked within the structural imperatives of her three-pronged civilizational, anthropological, and historical constellation, she maintained that "even in her most original of innovations, she had not created anything original but

only "adapted the ancient to the new (Ramnarayan 1984: 29). In contrast to American modern dancers, Devi did not claim 'originality' for her innovations, as argued by O'Shea (2003: 24-27), but inscribed her work within the history of received traditions, maintaining that her recreations and innovations were continuous with the structures of received performance traditions, with the spirit of the *Natyasastra*, with the spirit of *Nataraja*, and with the spirit of *gurukul* all at once.

Public Performance/ Private Training

Rukmini Devi also incorporated her three three-pronged symbolic constellation into the institutional goals of her *Kalakshetra* institution. It is well-known that Devi founded Kalakshetra to enable the revival of South Indian theatre arts, including *Bhartanatyam*, drama, music, as well as folk arts, painting, and sculpture. But what is not so well known is that she used the *Nataraja* emblem as her institutional logo. Sketched by Conard Worldring in the 1930s, it was reconfigured by C. T. Nachiappa in 1940s, and used in the promotional materials and journals of the institution, continuing into the present (Nachiappa 2001). She likewise repeated the guru metaphor, reinforced in her public performance, by conceptualising her arts academy not as any ordinary arts centre, but rather as a neo-traditional *guru-shisya* and *gurukul* institution, one in which traditional gurus lived together with students as in a 'kul' or community (Ramani 2003:1-149). She then developed a multilingual curriculum one that emphasised the importance of learning Sanskrit and Tamil languages.

Kalakshetra students studied Sanskrit verses and aesthetic theory not to expound *sastra* but to better understand the aesthetic sensibility and technique of *Sadir-Bharatanatya* that they learned from dance gurus teaching in *Kalakshetra* (Sarada 1985: 21). By encouraging speech act training, including memorizing, and recitation, Rukmini Devi

endeavored to preserve orthogenetic forms like *Sadir* within ontogenetic forms of transmission recreated in the *Kalakshetra gurukul.*

By incorporating the three visual images of *Natyasastra, Nataraja* and *Guru* into the institutional and ideological vision of her *Kalakhshetra* institution, and developing a pedagogy consonant with her aesthetic practice, Devi collapsed the differences between public performance and private training. She created a historical practice and pedagogy for *Bharatanatya* that was congruent with visual images used in the mainstream public domain of performance. By thus linking the public world of performance with private training, Rukmini Devi visualised and made real the textual and anthropological conceptualizations that scholars like V. Raghavan were composing for *Sadir-Bharatanatyam* in the 1930s.

While Devi knew that she had constituted a very broad conceptual frame to enable her own revival of Indian performing arts, she could not grasp the ideological implications of her own aesthetic practice and pedagogy because she used her three-pronged constellation selectively and to emphasize different aspects of her evolving vision. While Devi prioritised the dance guru in the 1930s, she broke off relations with the dance teachers in 1943 when they left her stranded before a performance. But she retained her idea of the *gurukul* by focusing her attention on the music teachers.[20] If she emphasized the solo dance in the 1930, she shifted to dance-drama in the 1940s. If Devi danced songs in praise of Siva/Nataraja in the 1930s, she created dance dramas featuring him as the hero in her dance-dramas of 1944 and 1947.

As for the *Natyasastra,* it operated only metaphorically in her creative imagination, as she herself did not study it as a scholar. Yet she spoke about the importance of using the *Natyasastra* as source text in the 1950s, and built a temple

theatre on the principles laid down in the *Natyasastra* in the 1980s. She thus made her most powerful statement of what the text can mean in practice, while at the same time underscoring the importance of retaining a temple stage conceptualization for Indian classical dance. Devi initiated these shifts in her practice by creatively adapting her three-pronged constellation without at any point in her career giving up on her commitment to the *Guru*, the iconography of *Nataraja*, or to the *Natyasastra*, the three anchoring metaphors and symbols of her revival.

Two Revivals in the 1930s

Two overlapping revivals were conceived in the 1930s: a pedagogical revival realized by scholars in the Madras Music Academy and a performative revival envisioned by Rukmini Devi. Both revivals, one conceptual the other visual conceptual, were in dialogue with each other. They were realized simultaneously in the public domain and enabled the revival of *Sadir* as *Bharatanatyam*, albeit in their own way. Like scholars in the Madras Music Academy, Devi developed a triple reed cultural history for *Sadir-Bharartanatya* and showed urban spectators that the dance belonged to a Sanskrit regional and anthropological history simultaneously. She explained that "all regional dance forms of South India expressed the values of the *Natyasastra* because they accommodated the tenets of the ancient text" (Devi n.d: 22). Like scholars in the Madras Music Academy, Devi envisioned a revival that was premised upon the empirical showing of the dance and its abstraction both at the same time.

Rukmini Devi, in other words, enlarged through repetition, scholarly ideas disseminated in erudite forums of the Madras Music Academy. She endeavoured to realize in the domain of visual cultural practice what Academy officials were proposing theoretically, that is, by reference to textual manuals and by prioritising hereditary practitioners and presenting them in their featured events as bearers of

traditional knowledge. It was Rukmini Devi who showed dancers, teachers, scholars, institution builders, and historians working in the field of the performing arts from the 1930s continuing into the present, how to translate large pedagogical ideas into performative practice, literary histories into performative histories, and literary texts into visual texts. By thus prioritizing practice, Devi shifted the emphasis from theory to practice (*prayoga*), from space (text) to time (performance), from sight (objectification) to sound (music), from authority(*sastra*) to vulnerability, from public performance to private training.

Conclusion:

Rukmini Devi is no more. So why should we worry about her three-pronged *Natyasastra, Nataraja* and *Guru* constellation? I think we need to take this inaugural constellation seriously because the multidisciplinary vision that Devi proposed for *Bharatanatyam* by using the three symbols performatively prevails in contemporary local and global practices of *Bharatnatyam.* The three-pronged constellation informs the theory, history and practice of *Bharatanatyam,* both locally and globally. It manifests itself as the historical paradigm of the revival because urban practitioners outside *Kalakshetra,* and scholars both within and outside Madras Music Academy, affirmed this constellation. Rukmini Devi's inaugural constellation prevailed for more than fifty years because she constituted it by engaging with the totality of what Raymond Williams describes as the 'whole cultural process, including "traditions, institutions and social formations (1977: 121-128).

We can track the large-scale changes in the twentieth-century practice of *Bharatanatyam* only by recognizing that the three visual symbols represent the totality of the conceptual field in which the revival was articulated in the 1930s. Yet the symbolic constellation is also used differently today. While *Natyasastra* and *Nataraja* still manifest

themselves as important symbols and metaphoric ideas in the practice, the traditional *guru* does not enjoy the same prestige that he had in the 1980s. When did the male teacher loose the hold that he had on the field of dance production? What happens when the *guru* falls out of the three-pronged constellation? These are historical questions that we can discuss only by taking Devi's three-pronged constellation seriously.

Scholars like Mathew Allen have argued, mistakenly in my opinion, that it was the willful intention of Rukmini Devi to disinherit *devadasis* and heriditary teachers that deprived them of their rightful place in the revival. (Allen 1997: 63-67). Amrit Srinivasan, on the other hand, has argued that it was the valorization of Sanskrit texts like the *Natyasastra* that marginalized *devadasis* (1985: 1874-5). I want to suggest that it was the reinstatement of the male *nattuvanar* as *guru* in the mainstream aesthetic of *Bharatanatyam*, occupying a place next only to *Nataraja* and to the *Natyasastra* that disempowered *devadasis.* As already mentioned, the male teachers became part of the mainstream aesthetic and desired to teach urban women as opposed to *devadasis* in the 1940s. They dominated and defined the cultural production of the dance from the 1940s until the 1980s.

While Devi's three-pronged constellation enabled male *gurus,* it did not empower *devadasis* as they could neither fit themselves nor their aesthetic into the new theatrical formation. Take as example the case of the legendary T. Balasarawati, who emerged herself from *devadasi* ancestry. It is well known that she tried to adapt her own cultural practice so that it could maintain its own uniqueness and still be part of the mainstream aesthetic. Balasaraswati attempted her double negotiation by selectively using Rukmini Devi's three-pronged constellation to develop her own alternative aesthetic for *Ṣadir-Bharatanatyam.*[21]

T. Balasaraswati used the new name of *Bharatanatyam* to

describe her own iteration of the *Sadir* dance. She engaged with print media technologies by co-authoring a book on *Bharatanatyam* with Dr. V. Raghavan, yet prioritized the oral traditions of *Sadir* and her familial ancestry. Like Devi, T. Balasarawati also used the *Natyasastra* metaphorically and affirmed it as a re-source text for all the classical dance styles of India (Balasaraswati 1988:38). Just like Devi she prioritized the art form developed by the Tanjore Quartet in the nineteenth century as well as the musical traditions of her family. Again like Devi, she spoke eloquently about the devotional, spiritual, and musical aspects of *Sadir-Bharatanatyam*. Yet she refused to place the icon of *Nataraja* on the dance proscenium, even while dancing songs in praise of *Nataraja* that Rukmini Devi introduced into the dance repertoire in the 1930s.

While Rukmini Devi offered instruction to her students within the domain of her *Kalakshetra* institution, Balasaraswati taught dance to aspiring students within the institutional framework of the prestigious Madras Music Academy. She was honoured, like Devi, with numerous national awards, and was respected as "one of the greatest artists to spring out from the southern soil."[22] Despite T.Balasaraswati's incorporation into the mainstream cultural production, her alternative aesthetic remained marginal as she was unable to create a substantial student community or '*parampara*' in India, although she created one in the US.[23]

Why were *devadasi* dancers unable to rebut the mainstream aesthetic? Was it because the *tala* techniques of the dance were held in the exclusive custody of male teachers? What, in fact, was the *devadasi* aesthetic? To interrogate such questions, crucial to understanding the sexual and gender politics underpinning the historical revival of *Bharatanatyam*, we need to focus our attention not on textualization, but on Rukmini Devi's three-pronged constellation. We need to do this because the new, multipronged aesthetic that Rukmini Devi envisioned for

Bharatanatyam, with the help of her three-pronged constellation, emerging itself from mainstream conceptualizations of the dance, became hegemonic and informs the history, theory and practice of *Bharatanatyam*, circulating in the local and global flows of modernity today.

(A version of this paper was presented in the first Rukmini Devi National Seminar, organized by the *Centre for Contemporary Culture*, New Delhi in 2001.)

Notes

1. Most international scholars working on Indian performing arts accept this issue of 'Sanskritization' to be central to the revival. See Coorlawala (1992); Allen (1997) O'Shea (1998, 2001), Chakravorty (1998, 2000).

2. See Coorlawala (1996); Allen (1997); O'Shea (1998, 2001); Chakravorty (1998, 2000).

3. In my doctoral dissertation, I described the importance of textualization in the revival and argued that the renaming of *Sadir* as *Bharatanatyam* must be perceived as a central thematic issue in the twentieth century revival of *Bharatanatyam* and identified it as such (1996:259-276).

4. Also see the essays of Coorlawala and Ramphal in this volume.

5. See Indira Peterson (1998) for a concise description of the complex terms. See also V. Raghavan (1956: 497-505); and Vatsyayan (1980).

6. V. Raghavan's two daughters, Priyamvada Shankar and Nandini Ramani, also studied the Balasaraswati style of dance. They continue to propagate her aesthetic legacy. There are a couple more dancers practicing the Balasaraswati lineage in India, but more research has to be done on the Balasaraswati *parampara* in India.

7. Elsewhere I marked the 1980s as representing a new historical moment in the revival of *Bharatanatyam* and discussed some key political and economic changes announed in the practice. See Meduri (1988: 1-23),(1996: xiii-xlix), 1996: 53-57.

8. Globalization dispersed and regionalized the practice of *Bharatanatyam* in the 1980s. While the India Festivals Abroad, sponsored by the Indian state in the 1980s, transnationalized and dispersed the arts, dance forms were also regionalized in this time. Tanjore was renamed as Thanjavur

in the 1980s, and Madras was renamed as Chennai in the 1990s. For a selective sampling of the new regional histories composed for *Bharatanatyam* in the 1980s, see Amrit Srinivasan (1984, 1985); Lakshmi Viswanathan (1984); Kersenboom Story (1987); and Arudra (1987). Arudra teased open the political question revolving around the linguistic identity of *Sadir* in his essay entitled "The Transfiguration of a Traditional Dance," and concluded that *Bharatanatyam* was really the name for solo dance recitals of Tamil heritage (1986/87a: 31). Arudra's thesis was polemical as it called into question the foundational history that eminent scholars like Vatsyayan had constructed for the dance. According to Vatsyayan, "*Bharatanatyam* is perhaps the oldest among the contemporary classical dance forms of India because of its links to the *Natyasastra* and the overwhelming, literary, sculptural and historical evidence available"(1974: 15).

9. See Srinivasan (1985); Coorlawala (1996); Mathew Allen (1997); O'Shea (2001).

10. Yet Devi, for better or ill, was educated within the liberal, humanist philosophies of the Theosophical Society, and groomed only to enable the cultural and aesthetic revival of Indian culture and the arts, which I discuss in *Translocal Modernities* (forthcoming). As per her training, she could only make comparative, stylistic assessments of Meenakshi Sundram Pillai's style of dance in comparison to Gowri Amma, and was empowered to do this because of her ballet training in the 1920s. Yet even these comments were not strikingly critical because the revival, as it was articulated in the Madras Music Academy (MMA) highlighted these contrasts by privileging male *nattuvanars* who were asked to present papers on the future of *Bharatanatyam* as opposed to *devadasis* presented as dancers. See Meduri (1996: 219-231).

11. While scholars in MMA were aware of the intricate interconnections between drama and other arts as detailed by Bharata in the *Natyasastra*, laypeople, and those who did not know Sanskrit in the 1930s, were only familiar with the more general story of the mythical origins of Indian dance. The mythic story, as outlined by Bharata, describes how God Brahma created the Natyaveda, the science of *natya* (drama) and gifted this system of visual education to sage Bharata and his hundred sons. Sage Bharata is believed to have established a dance troupe and presented his first production in the presiding presence of the cosmic dancer Shiva. Pleased with the dance, Shiva gave his own cosmic dance technique to Bharata, and Parvati his consort gifted the female concept of dance to the production. God Shiva then taught his cosmic dance to Sage Tandu, who passed it on to Bharata and his hundred children (Rao 1967: 11-12).. Urban practitioners of *Bharatanatyam*, then and today, know this origin story of *Bharatanatyam* all too well. They claim,

each in their own way "that Siva in his manifestation as *Nataraja* stands as the very symbol of dance in Indian culture "(Dhananjayan 1984:6).

12. Students of the *Kalakshetra* institution founded by Rukmini Devi in 1936, describe this as the history of the dance (Dhananjayan 1984:6).

13. Meenakshi Sundram Pillai did not conduct the debut but deputed his son-in-law to wield the cymbals. Rukmini Devi explains: I used to work very hard. The dance classes would start very early around seven in the morning and go till seven in the evening with an hour's lunch break. In spite of this Meenakshi Sundram Pillai would grumble that I was not working hard enough. He would call me again for training in the night. ..It was a gruelling routine. But my body was trained and I could take it. But he (Meenakshi Sundram Pillai) did not approve when I wanted to perform on the stage. He said it was too early (Ramani: 2003: 40-41).

14. She also conceptualized what Victor Turner would describe as urban 'liminoid rituals' to enable the historical transition of large symbolic rituals such as the *'Arangetral'* that *devadasis* performed as obligatory debut rituals in pre-colonial India (see Meduri 1990: 107-123; Gaston 1996: 222-257).

15. James Clifford explains that ethnographic texts are 'inescapably allegorical' because they usually denote a practice in which a narrative fiction refers to another pattern of ideas or events...to the stories built into the representational process itself' (1986:99, 100).

16. See (Ramani 2003) for a complete account of the numerous distinguished teachers who taught in *Kalakshetra*.

17. See Sankara Menon's report on *Kalakshetra* (1961) and review in *Swaraj* newspaper (1936, April 11).

18. Other literary texts including Kalidasa's *Kumarasambhavam*, Valmiki *Ramayana*, and numerous other multilingual texts that Rukmini Devi used in her revival, also ceded their literary and pedagogical authority in performance because they were adapted into performance scripts and used to selectively embody poetic values as opposed to prescriptive truths. The texts used in the revival neither restricted nor circumscribed the form of *Sadir-Bharatanatyam*, nor even the creativity of Rukmini Devi for that matter.

19. She revived the traditional repertoire of *Sadir*, created a temple stage for the dance, pioneered the practice of placing the icon of *Nataraja* on the stage, imported new songs from the music concert repertoire into the dance repertories (especially songs like *Natanam Adinar* and *Ananda Natana Prakasam*), revived traditional dance dramas such as the *Kuravanjis*, adapted numerous literary and dramatic texts into

performance scripts and created twenty-five breathtaking ensemble productions during her long and distinguished career between 1930-1980.

20. Elsewhere I have discussed how this moment of 1943, when Rukmini Devi began to teach her students to do *nattuvangam* and when she broke with the male dance teachers, as representing a democratizing moment as *Kalakshetra* students were freed of the gender prescriptions in which the *devadasi* tradition had been restricted. See Meduri (1996: 366-373).

21. In my doctoral thesis (1996), I have described how Balasaraswati created a new aesthetic by seizing the name of *Bharatanatyam* and articulated an aesthetic for *Bharatanatyam* that was both similar to and different from that of Rukmini Devi. But O'Shea extended my critique and carefully marked the differences between T. Balasarawati and Rukmini Devi styles of dance. See O'Shea (1998; 2001).

22. See (Raman and Ramachandran 1984) for a vivid account of T. Balasaraswati's achievements.

23. See Cowdery (1995: 50-57); Meduri (1998, 1996:459-470); O'Shea (2001). The well-known dancers belonging to T. Balasaraswati lineage in India include Nandini Ramani, Priyamvada Shankar, Shyamala, Balasaraswati's daughter Lakshmi Knight, and her son.

References

Allen, M. H. 1997. "Rewriting the Script for South Indian Dance." *The Drama Review* 41: 63-100.

Arundale, George. 1936 "The International Academy of the Arts." Adyar Pamphlet, no 208. Madras: The Theosophical Publishing House.

Arudra. 1986/87a. " The Transfiguration of a Traditional Dance: The Academy and the Dance. Events of the First Decade." *Sruti* 27/28: 17-21.

—.1986/87b. Dancers of the First Decade." *Sruti* 27/28: 17-21.

—.1986/1987c. "The Renaming of an Old Dance: A Whodunit Tale of Mystery." *Sruti* 27/28: 30-31

—.1986/87d. "E. Krishna Iyer (1897-1968): Saviour of a Dance in Distress." *Sruti* 27/28: 32-36.

Balasarawati, T. 1988. "The Art of Bharatanatyam: Reflections of Balasaraswati." *Sruti* 50:37-40.

—. 1991. "Bala on *Bharata Natyam.*" Guhan, S., trans. Madras: the Sruti Foundation.

Clifford, James. 1986. *Writing Culture: The Poetics and Politics of Ethnography.* Berkeley: University of California Press.

Coorlawala, Uttara. 1996. "The Birth of Bharatanatyam and the Sanskritized Body." *The Body in Dance: Modes of Inquiry: Conference Proceedings of the Congress on Research in Dance.*

Cowdery, James R. 1995. The American Students of Balasaraswati." *UCLA Journal of Dance Ethnology* 19: 50-57.

Devi, Rukmini. n.d. Untitled entry. *Kalakshetra Quarterly* IX (3):22.

—.n.d.b. "Bharata Natya Sastra in Practice." *Kalakshetra Quarterly* 11 (3):20-26.

Dhananjayan, V.N. 1992. *A Dancer on Dance.* Madras: Bharata Kalanjali.

Gaston, Anne-Marie. 1996. *Bharatanatyam from Temple to Theatre.* New Delhi. Manohar.

Iyer, E. Krishna. 1957. *Bharata Natya and other Dances of Tamil Nad.* Baroda: The M.S. University of Baroda Press.

Kothari, Sunil. 1979. *Bharata Natyam: Indian Classical Dance Art.* Bombay: Marg Publications.

Meduri Avanthi. 1988. "Bharatanatyam: What are you?" Asian Theatre Journal 5, 1: 1-22.

—1990. "History as Image: Mimesis in *Bharatanatyam.*" Fifth Hong Kong International Dance Conference July 15-28: Conference Papers 11, K-Z: 107-125, Hong Kong: Hong Kong Academy of Performing Arts.

—. 1996a. "Nation, Woman, Representation: The Sutured History of the *Devadasi* and Her Dance." Ph.D. dissertation, New York University.

—. 1996b. "Modern History of *Bharatanatyam*: Vibrant Form or Export Commodity." *Voices,* 1, 3: 53-57.

—. 2005 (forthcoming). *Translocal Modernities: Cultural Identity, Aesthetics and Cosmopolitanism in Bharatanatyam.* Middleton, CT: Wesleyan University Press.

Menon, Sankara. 1961. *Report on Kalakshetra: 1936-1961.* Adyar. Kalakshetra.

Nachiappan, C. 2001. *Rukmini Devi: Bharatanatya.* Chennai: Kalakshetra Publications.

O'Shea, Janet. 1998. "Traditional Indian Dance and the Making of Interpretive Communities." *Asian Theatre Journal* 15, no.1 (Spring): 45-63.

— 2001. "At Home in the World: Bharata Natyam's Transnational Traditions." Ph.D. dissertation, UC Riverside.

Pattabhiraman, N., and Anandhi Ramachandran. 1984a. "The Whole World in Her Hands," Part 1. *Sruti* 4 (January/February): 17-31.

— 1984b. "The Whole World in Her Hands," Part 2. *Sruti* 5 (March): 17-32.

Peterson, Indira Viswanathan. 1998. "The Evolution of the Kuravanji Dance-Drama in Tamil Nadu: Negotiating the Folk and the Classical in the Bharata Natyam Canon." *South Asian Research* 18, 1: 39-72.

Raghavan V. 1956. "Variety and Integration in the Pattern of Indian Culture." *The Far Eastern Quarterly Review*, Vol. XV, 4 (August): 497-505

—. 1974. "*Bharata Natya.*" *Music Academy Journal.* XLV:233-262.

Ramanarayan, Gowri. 1984a. "Rukmini Devi: A Quest for Beauty, a Profile" Part 1, *Sruti* 8 (June): 17-29.

—. 1984b. "Rukmini Devi: Dancer and Reformer, A Profile." *Sruti* 9 (July): 17-29.

—. 1984c. "Rukmini Devi: Restoration and Creation, A Profile." *Sruti* 10 (August): 26-38.

Ramani, Shakuntala. 2003. *Rukmini Devi Birth Centenary Volume.* Chennai: Kalakshetra Foundation.

Ramani, Shakuntala 2003. *Shraddhanjali: Brief Pen Portraits of Great People who laid the Foundation of Kalakshetra.* Chennai: Kalakshetra Foundation.

Sarada. S. 1985. *Kalakshetra Rukmini Devi: Reminiscences.* Madras: Kala Mandir Trust.

Srinivasan, Amrit. 1983. "The Hindu Temple Dancer: Prostitute or Nun?" *Cambridge Anthropology* 8, 1: 73-99.

—1984. "Temple Prostitution and Community Reform: An Examination of the Ethnographic, Historical and Textual Content of the *Devadasis* of Tamil Nadu, South India." Ph.D. dissertation, Cambridge.

—. 1985. "Reform and Revival: The *Devadasi* and Her Dance." *Economic and Political Weekly* 20, no. 44 (November): 1869-1876.

Subrahmanyam, Padma. 1979. *Bharata's Art Then and Now.* Madras: Intermedia.

Vatsyayan, Kapila. 1968. *Classical Indian Dance in Literature and the Arts.* New Delhi: Sangeet Natak Akademi.

—. 1974. *Indian Classical Dance.* New Delhi: Ministry of Information and Broadcasting:

—. 1980. *Traditional Indian Theatre: Multiple Streams.* Delhi

Williams, Raymond. 1977. *Marxism and Literature.* Oxford/New York: Oxford University Press.

CHAPTER 22

RUKMINI DEVI: RETHINKING THE CLASSICAL

Janet O'Shea

Until recently, there were two dominant narratives about Rukmini Devi. One portrayed her as the rescuer of a debased form, while the other charged her, and the other dancer reformers of the revival, with appropriation.[1] In the first version, temple dance, once a pure expression of devotion, became corrupted and the women – devadasis, or servants of god — descended to the level of temple prostitutes. The dance form, like its practitioners, deteriorated. According to this narrative, the repertoire reflected this decline by praising the kings instead of gods and invoking images of erotic encounters and sexual desire. Colonial missionaries identified this social ill but they too were misguided: they condemned the form alongside the women who practised it and began a movement to eradicate it. The dance form almost died out. Luckily, Rukmini Devi saw the beauty in this form, cleaned it up, performed it before a skeptical crowd of Madras elites and won them over. She then went on to teach a 'purified' and 'spiritualized' version to her students. Thus began the *Bharata natyam* revival.

The group of people who play the secondary role in the rescue narrative – the group labeled the devadasi or icai vellala community – tell another story.[2] In this one, Rukmini Devi, sometimes identified by name, more often not, stands for the appropriation claiming of a dance form *Bharata natyam* by elites and of the loss of exclusive control of the form by the icai vellala community. Here, middle-class dancers and promoters lay claim to a disparaged and neglected but

nonetheless luminary form. In this version, these new practitioners reduced the *devadasis* to minor players and replaced a Tamil tradition with a Sanskrit one. In the process they pushed the *devadasis* and their male counterparts, the *nattuvanars*, to the margins of the dance milieu.

A similar, although more subtle, critique of the revival has come through critical studies of this period. Dancers and dance scholars have interrogated the shifts of the revival, querying the politics of change in the hands of practitioners from marginal to elite practitioners.[3] Some of these scholarly accounts, especially those authored in the 1980s and early 1990s, carry with them a feeling of frustration on the part of dancers as to the history of the revival that they received as part of their dance training.[4]

Of course, accounts of the revival do not easily split into binaries. Most of the representations of this period are more nuanced and draw upon a multiplicity of positions.[5] Nonetheless, accounts of the period known as the *bharata natyam* revival show traces of these tendencies. Many *bharata natyam* dancers hear a particular version of the revival story towards the beginning of their training and swallow the whole as the 'real' history of *bharata natyam.*[6]

I am no exception to this trend. I pursued my *bharata natyam* training within the style of the legendary *devadasi* performer Balasaraswati. As a result, when, in my scholarship, I first approached the study of Rukmini Devi's accomplishment, I looked at her work through a critical lens, attending to the classed and gendered overtones of her mission and the influence of the theosophical society's orientalist nationalism on her project. However, delving into the history of the revival has caused me to rethink my initial perception of Rukmini Devi. I reevaluated Rukmini Devi's life work, looking at her position critically but positively. Now I want to see if it is possible to celebrate her achievements without resorting to either of the narratives introduced above.

This is part of a more general concern of mine. I am interested in rethinking the politics of the *bharata natyam* revival and extending the examination of this form into the late twentieth century and the present.[7] I investigate not only the influence of large-scale social factors on dance but also in different ways how performers and choreographers grapple with these concerns. I also query how this affects where we are now and what we can do with this information. In looking at the revival we, dancers, and dance writers,[8] have discussed in detail the ways in which *bharata natyam* became implicated in and subject to large-scale political discourses, especially those of nationalism, orientalism, class concerns, and debates over the status of women. We levelled this critique in order to offset the purely celebratory version of the revival that hinged on the rescue narrative I mentioned earlier.

This critique, however, runs the risk of putting us back in the old position where dance 'reflects' the concerns of its society. In order to acknowledge that dancers contend with but do not necessarily capitulate to the concerns of a given social and political context, I rely upon the idea of choreography as decision-making. I have argued, therefore, that in the 'revival,' *bharata natyam* emerged as 'always already' political.[9] Nonetheless, interpretation of what the form is, what its history is, and what should and should not be done with it diverged almost immediately thereafter. The politicization of *bharata natyam* led to contestation as much as, if not more than, consensus about the dance form's history and origins, its affiliation with the nation and the region, and its rightful community of practitioners.[10] *Bharata natyam*, therefore, provides a platform upon which choreographers and dancers express their own position on debates over regional, national, and local identity. Choreographic decision-making is circumscribed by political concerns but not determined by them. There is room for resistance as well as capitulation and for "reading against the grain."

Thus, in looking at the work of Rukmini Devi, I, first of all, look at her project by investigating choreography as political strategy.[11] Rukmini Devi was a nationalist and a dance reformer; she strove to legitimize a form. Aligning it with the gathering force of nationalism, with nationalist discourse's use of colonial orientalist thought, and with a domestication of women's practices was a very effective way of accomplishing this end. Likewise, the history that she deployed too was creating and attempting to revivify a history for *bharata natyam* in which dance came out of the Sanskrit dramaturgy tradition rather than out of the practices of marginal women, helped to accrue respectability to *bharata natyam.*

But Rukmini Devi also moved beyond the political contests of her time. She approached them differently than she might have if she worked in another medium with a different history. I therefore push my 'reading' of Rukmini Devi's project in order to see how the underlying thematic of her approach prefigures – and perhaps furthers – the choreographic inquiry of the present. Thus, I locate the international and intercultural elements of her project entangled in her nationalism; a nascent (although Victorian) feminism and democratizing agenda underneath her anxiety about gendered respectability;[12] a budding contemporaneity embedded in her reconstruction projects.[13] The attempt to re-read Rukmini Devi's legacy is not just a theoretical manouver. This revisiting is already being done in choreography, in instruction, and in the discussions that dancers are having about the revival and its impact on performance today.[14]

Rukmini Devi and Inter-cultural Inquiry

Rukmini Devi's connection to nationalism predated her involvement with dance. She first entered the Madras public sphere in the 1920s not as a performer but as a nationalist activist and as a representative of Theosophy, an eclectic,

transnational religious movement. As an adolescent, she came under the tutelage of Annie Besant, English theosophist and proponent of Indian nationalism. Devi embraced Besant's nationalist beliefs, promoting the Theosophical Society's social causes and participating in their politically-inflected dramatic productions (Ramnarayan 1984a: 26). She carried this nationalist agenda with her in her attempts to refigure *bharata natyam* so that it would express the unique genius of an ancient Indian culture.[15]

Yet, Rukmini Devi came to *bharata natyam* through resolutely intercultural avenues. In 1928, while touring Australia and Southeast Asia on Theosophical Society business, Rukmini Devi met Anna Pavlova, whose dancing she had seen and admired in India.[16] Pavlova encouraged Devi to learn dance, arranging for her to study with Cleo Nordi until the two women could meet in London. Although the ballerina died before Devi could begin tutelage with her, she left a lasting impact upon the young theosophist and suggested a way for Devi to combine her devotion to dance, theosophy, and nationalism. Pavlova, who had herself installed ballet as a 'high art' and shifted public opinion of the form, encouraged Devi to "revive the art of [her] own country". (Ramnarayan 1984a:29)

Rukmini Devi then enjoyed a brief stint as an interpretive dancer of a similar cross-cultural ilk to Ruth St. Denis, La Meri, and Uday Shankar.[17] Even once she made the switch to *bharata natyam,* ballet continued to inform her approach. For instance, she initially included ballet classes in *kalakshetra* training as she felt that experience in ballet would make the *adavus* "accurate in form" (Sarada 1985: 20-21).

The inter-cultural aspects of Rukmini Devi's career have, in some accounts, been downplayed. Perhaps for later commentators, her reliance on ballet and her experimentation with interpretive dance bear too much of a taint of colonialism. I suspect that this move came out of a

later version of nationalism in which 'authenticity' trumped worldliness. At the present historical moment cultural 'authenticity' is again being queried. Within the field of *bharata natyam,* dancers have acknowledged the form's transnational status and have considered its globality as an opportunity for experimentation. As such, we can now rethink Rukmini Devi's inquiry into classicism, through ballet as well as through *bharata natyam,* can be understood as a product of colonial hybridity but not as an act of assimilation to colonial pressure. Looking at it now, her inquiry prefigured an international awareness within the *bharata natyam* field. It anticipated the move by some present-day choreographers to invoke a dialogue across movement languages without fear of blending in a global homogeneity.[18]

The Dancer-Choreographer

Rukmini Devi was able to experiment with training and form because of another innovation that she brought to the *bharata natyam* field: the invention of the dancer-choreographer category.[19] Prior to the 1930s, dancers achieved renown as performers but they generally did not take up choreography or instruction. Dancers remained under the authority of a male guru. The latter trained the dancer, composed the dance phrases of repertory items, and acted as *nattuvanar,* or conductor of the musical ensemble. These *nattuvanars,* in turn, trained in dance techniques and developed and maintained repertoire but they did not usually perform publically.

Devi, by contrast, took up the role of choreographer and teacher herself while training her students in music conducting.[20] She therefore eroded a gendered division of labour in which an individual could either be a dancer or a choreographer but not both. This shift has offered twentieth-century dancers a unique opportunity: to create new work based on their own experience as a performer.[21]

This transformation can be interpreted in two different ways: as appropriative or democratizing. The shift from the 'traditional teacher' to the dancer-choreography was predicated on Rukmini Devi's aim to transfer the dance to "women of good families." As such, she brought the biases of her time to this endeavour: she believed it would 'improve' the form when respectable, upper-caste women performed it. In addition, she prompted the entry of female, upper middle-class performers into the field of instruction and choreography, thereby marginalizing some traditional *nattuvanars.*

Nonetheless, this move was also democratizing. When Devi created the category of dancer-choreography, she posited that one didn't have to be born into the 'right' community to learn, perform, or teach *bharata natyam.* In practice, this has resulted largely in the entry of upper and middle class dancers into the field. Despite that trend, however, lower class and lower caste dancers and dance students now have access to the form. This initiated, for instance, a fuller democratizing that has happened in diasporic Sri Lankan Tamil communities where girls of a wide range of class backgrounds study *bharata natyam.*

While the class implications of this move are debatable, gender clearly remained at issue. Devi was concerned with feminine respectability and her innovations were inflected by a Victorian morality. So, for instance, she claimed a resolutely public role for herself while choreographing dances that celebrated conventional domesticity. This symbolic domesticity, in turn, supported her nationalist agenda because of the role women had been given by nationalists in the propagation of national culture.[22] So, middle-class women, through their ostensible domestic respectability and their allegiance to tradition and spirituality, imbued the dance form with a sense of increased classicism and legitimacy thereby rendering a more valid representation of national identity.

However, Devi also revolutionized the gender aspects of the dance form. She offered women new positions of authority – teaching and choreographing as well as performing – within the dance field. As such, she provided her students with opportunities for self-representation and for the representation of the form. These options had been previously closed to the *devadasi* dancer. It also offered them an informed, educated, and authoritative position vis a vis any choreography they performed.[23] Devi also democratized dance by providing roles to male dancers in her choreography and in training boys in dance. She created the possibility for men to take up roles in performance as well as in choreography and instruction.

The Contemporary Classical

Despite Devi's experience as a performer, her most significant contribution to *bharata natyam* came through her composition of new works. She choreographed her own versions of traditional dance repertory items and also used older compositions, previously used only for concert music, as the basis for choreography.[24] She was most renowned, however, for creating evening-length, ensemble productions, or 'dance dramas' that used a *bharata natyam* movement vocabulary as its basis and that centered on mythological and literary themes. I am calling this approach, in which new work draws on the principles but not the form of past practice, contemporary classicism. This method, in turn, set the stage for the choreographic productivity of the late twentieth century and of the present moment.

On the one hand, Rukmini Devi's project was one of reconstruction. She set out to recapture, through *bharata natyam,* the features of the Sanskrit 'total theatre' as described in the Sanskrit aesthetic theory text, the *Natyasastra* (Peterson 1998: 58). She maintained that her revisions found sanction in the aesthetic values of ancient Sanskrit drama as she understood them from dramaturgical texts.[25] As such, she

referenced Sanskrit dramaturgical texts as foundational and inspirational. She had one of her senior students, S. Sarada, reconstruct movements from the *Abhinaya Darpana* for use in the *kalakshetra* movement vocabulary and she trained her students in Sanskrit dramaturgical theory, including the recitation of verses from the *Abhinaya Darpana.* As she saw it, she less reinvented *Bharata Natyam* than reclassicized it. She legitimized the innovations by arguing that the changes she made aligned *bharata natyam* more closely with its original, historical form.

On the other hand, this was a reconstruction based on the values, not the content, of ancient practice. She did not reconstruct movement from the *Natyasastra* or *Abhinaya Darpana* herself. The movement vocabulary that she used in class derived largely from the traditional dance form of *devadasi* practitioners. Nonetheless, she maintained that the *Natyasastra* gave her the opportunity for expressing new ideas: "the technique in this play [her Ramayana series] may appear new ... but every movement is according to the *sastra* though not presented in stereotyped form (in Ramnarayan 1984c: 32)." She also claimed that her ventures accessed "the spirit of the traditional methods" (in Ramnarayan 1984c: 29) while not necessarily mimicking their form. Such a strategy caused S. Sarada to make the claim that the *kalakshetra* dance style as a whole was "new" but also "concurring with the descriptions contained in the ancient treatises of dance" (1985: 21).

Within Rukmini Devi's rhetoric 'tradition,' the '*sastras,*' and sometimes even *bharata natyam* become conceptual entities, or "guiding spirits." This kind of recourse to the metaphysical comes, most likely, out of her experience with theosophy as well as out of her struggle to reconcile invention and allegiance to tradition. However, I think that there is a more interesting way of looking at her project: as a contemporary classicist project that looks to the practices of the past for inspiration and that values continuity without demanding the continual replication of form. As such, within Rukmini Devi's

choreography, the classical emerges as a set of choreographic principles that a dancer can work with and within.

In the process, Rukmini Devi began to tease apart the previously intertwined notions of the 'classical' and the 'traditional.' "Classical," in general terms, denotes an adherence to a specific set of defined principles while "traditional" connotes an unbroken, handed-down heritage. The distinction made in English between the two terms has a parallel. It has a long history in Indian aesthetic thought as in, for example, the distinction between *sastra* and *parampara* or classical text and oral tradition.

Nonetheless, through her emphasis on the values of the past Rukmini Devi introduced innovations to *bharata natyam* in both pedagogy and performance which, she maintained, neither broke from tradition nor replicated it. Rather, she infused *bharata natyam* with choreographic structures and themes, which, for her, expressed the values of traditional practice while not necessarily mimicking its form.[26] The attention she gave was to the spirit, rather than the form, of older forms , separated, in practice, classical aesthetics from specific items of traditional repertoire.[27]

This notion of the classical, as distinct from the traditional, allowed Rukmini Devi room to experiment without compromising an aesthetic that she saw as fundamental to an Indian heritage. This re-activation and re-definition of the classical, in turn, opened avenues for the kinds of inquiry that we see today's choreographic inquiries that are based in *bharata natyam*'s movement vocabulary. Interestingly, Devi's recourse to the distant past also paradoxically legitimized change[28] by establishing a history for *bharata natyam* long and encompassing enough that the dance could not have avoided transforming.[29]

Rukmini Devi, in her teaching, in her choreography, and in her verbal representations of her work, attended to the relationship between the past and the present. She also set

the stage for the future. The kind of critical inquiry into classical aesthetics, as separate from tradition, enabled the proliferation of new choreography in the late twentieth century and in the present. The elements that I emphasize here–an international awareness, the category of the dancer-choreographer, and an attention to choreographic principles–produced a contemporaneity in Rukmini Devi's project. As a result, if we extract the theoretical principles from her project the way she extracted them from classical practices, I believe that we can find, in her endeavours, the predecessor of contemporary and even experimental new work in the Indian dance field. Her inquiries offered the *bharata natyam* field both an outlook and a set of specific devices for looking forward.

(A version of this paper was presented in London, at the Rukmini Devi Week Seminar, organized by the Nehru Centre, London and the *Centre for Contemporary Culture*, New Delhi in collaboration with the Society of Dance Research Scholars, and the AHRB Cross-Cultural Centre for Music and Dance, University of Surrey in 2003.)

Notes

1. Here, I use the term 'revival' to refer to the recontextualization of *bharata natyam* that occurred in the 1930s and 1940s. I use the term 'revival' recognizing that its use has been problematized (Srinivasan 1983, 1985; Meduri 1996; Allen 1997). This term is also separate from the nineteenth-century reformist and revivalist movements that emphasized the modification and reconstruction of Indian society respectively. As Srinivasan (1983, 1985) and Ramnarayan (this volume) have indicated, both imperatives informed the recontextualization of *bharata natyam* in the 1930s.

2. As represented most clearly by Balasaraswati but also by other icai vellala practitioners. See Pattabhiraman and Ramachandran (1984), O'Shea (1998, 2001, forthcoming) for a further discussion of Balasaraswati's resistance to dominant representations of the revival. I also noted this counter-narrative as appearing in the accounts of other

icai vellala practitioners such as T. S. Ulaganathan.and T. R. Navaneetam (personal correspondence 1996).

3. These interrogations of the revival include Srinivasan (1983, 1985), Meduri (1988, 1996), Jeyasingh (1990, 1995), Coorlawala (1996), Gaston (1996), Allen (1997), as well as my own (1998, 2001, 2003, forthcoming).

4. Joan Erdman (1996) also links dancers' frustration with revivalist rescue narratives with scholarly inquiry.

   Avanthi Meduri (1988) invokes this narrative in order to critique it. Amrit Srinivasan (1983, 1985) researched the devadasi system as a corrective to this narrative. My 1998 essay on the competing agendas of Rukmini Devi and Balasaraswati represents my own attempt, as someone whose first access to *bharata natyam* came through Balasaraswati's instructional lineage, to come to terms with these different divergent versions of history. I believe that Matthew Allen's (1997) comes from a similar perspective. Shobana Jeyasingh articulates a different kind of frustration, with an unproblematized notion of tradition being used to confine *bharata natyam*-based choreography to the 'ethnic dance' margins of the global performance milieu (1990, 1993, 1995).

5. In addition to the texts mentioned above, I would also point out that Kapila Vatsyayan's (1977, 1992) groundbreaking studies address the complexities of *bharata natyam* practitioner's engagement with the past. In addition, a number of essays by dance critics, including Arudra (1986/87), Pattabhiraman and Ramachandran (1984), and Gowri Ramnarayan (1984) demonstrate the divergent points of view at work in the revival.

6. I do not mean to suggest, of course, that the historical narratives of the revival have not changed over time. I base my understanding of these two versions of history on my own experience with *bharata natyam* which began in 1988, on critical studies of that period, also largely authored in the 1980s (Arudra 1986/87, Pattabhiraman and Ramachandran 1984, Ramnarayan (1984), Sarada (1985), Dhananjayan, V. N. and Shanta (1986), Dhananjayan (1986), and Balasaraswati (1975, 1984, 1988,) and Rukmini Devi's (n.d.) own accounts.

7. I use the term "politics" in several senses here. First, I mean to suggest that art forms, as social practices, engage with concerns of power. Second, I mean to highlight that the revival was driven by individuals, including Rukmini Devi and E. Krishna Iyer, concerned with the fate of the as-yet putative nation-state. Likewise, institutions such as the Music Academy supported classical art forms in the interest of bolstering

national pride. Third, I use the idea of politics to draw attention to the strategies that dancers shared with political activisits of their time. Dance practitioners of the revival frequently put forth their own understanding of the dance form's history which, in turn, affiliated the dance form with particular communities. For a further articulation of this idea, see O'Shea (2001) and for a discussion of the divergent versions of national and regional identities articulated in choreographic and discursive representations see O'Shea (forthcoming).

8. As identified in note 3.

9. I draw the idea of applying the Derridean concept to *bharata natyam* from Meduri (1996).

10. My concern with contestation also emerges out of my own experience with the dance style of Balasaraswati and the marginal status that this style and its accompanying version of history held in the late twentieth century dance milieu.

11. I define choreography as the planned and intentional selection of movement for use in performance or instruction. Choreography, in this sense, refers less to a specific end product (as in "a work of choreography") than to a thought process. It does not, then, only refer to the invention of a new movement vocabulary or of the development of an original item of repertoire. I draw this idea of choreography as decision-making from Susan Foster. I base this idea on her theorization of the semiotics of choreography (1986) and her notion of bodily practice as thought process (1995).

    Bharata natyam practitioners differ as to the correct usage of the designation 'choreography.' Nandini Ramani, for instance, argues that choreography is a 'Western' term and that therefore it should only apply to a modern approach to dance production in which a single choreographer takes responsibility for the creation of an entire piece, including its thematic content, its movement vocabulary, and its structure (personal correspondence 1999).

    Menaka Thakkar, by contrast, argues that the distinction between performance, composition, and instruction does not apply to *bharata natyam*. She argues that nearly all advanced work in the field of *bharata natyam* involves composition. To her mind, traditional teaching methods allow for a transition from performance to composition. Because a teacher incurs responsibility for repertoire, including the compilation of phrases, taking on instruction gives a dancer the opportunity to create movement sequences as part of the transmission of conventional

items of repertoire. As such, in characterizing her own career, Menaka Thakkar does not identify a moment at which she began choreographing new work, citing instead, a gradual shift into composition as her teacher's assistant, as a teacher herself, and then as a creator of evening-length pieces with new structural formats (personal correspondence 1998, 1999).

Lata Pada similarly maintains that her move from performance to choreography was a transition between discipleship, teaching, and the creation of new work. She describes her own career trajectory in terms of a move from an immersion in tradition, within a modified gurukula system (in which she stayed with her guru for an extended period of time as an adult) followed by the exploration of new movement and thematic content (personal correspondence 1999).

12. For a further discussion of the gendered implications of Rukmini Devi's inquiries, see Srinivasa (1983), Meduri (1996: 331-336; 350-353) and O'Shea (2001: 228-235).

13. See Meduri in this volume.

14. To signal just a few of the ways in which bharata natyam practitioners are rethinking the impact of the revival, I refer to Menaka Thakkar who identifies Rukmini Devi as a contemporary figure for her time and, as such, as inspirational for Thakkar's own inquiries (personal correspondence 1999). Likewise, choreographer Mavin Khoo has used a rethinking of the revival, and specifically of Rukmini Devi's investigation into ballet and bharata natyam, to further his choreographic inquiry into the two classical forms (personal correspondence 2002, 2003).

15. I refer to Rukmini Devi as a nationalist because she entered the dance field as an activist but, more importantly, because she developed a cultural revivalism that shared strategies with the approach of activists that Sumathi Ramaswamy (1997) describes as metropolitan nationalists. As I argue elsewhere (1998, 2001, forthcoming), she articulated this perspective through choreographic and discursive means. Her recourse to a pan-Indian community (articulated, for example, in her appeal to Sanskrit texts for legitimacy, her interest in pan-Indian mythologies as sources for inquiries, her aim of spiritualizing the form, as well as her concern with gendered respectability) is also complicated by her deployment of local and regional elements of practices, including the movement vocabulary and items of repertoire from the *devadasi* tradition (see also Srinivasan 1983, 1985). She also rendered the form 'national' on a practical level through standardized and institutionalized

dance training (O'Shea 2201: 111-112) and specifically, through the use of Sanskrit and English in instruction (Coorlawala 1996: 67). For more discussion of the intersections between Rukmini Devi's project and nationalist discourse of the time, see also Srinivasan (1983), Meduri (1996, 2003)Allen (1997), and Peterson (1998).

16. Ramnarayan discusses Rukmini Devi and Pavlova's first encounter in Bombay, their chance meeting at sea, and their subsequent friendship in some detail (1984a: 29). Likewise, Sarada mentions that Pavlova inspired Devi (1985: 40).

17. For instance, a review in the Hindustan Times (December 14, 1944) described her initial performances as "if anything, too eclectic. To the mechanized music of gramophone records, she used to give easy renderings of Egyptian, Hungarian, and South American dances, relieved somewhat by a thoughtful presentation of Hiawatha or a somewhat Pavlova-like reproduction of the swan dance" (in Ramnarayan 1984b: 17).

18. I identify Rukmini Devi's inquiries as being transnational without capitulating to European norms through her own description of her work. For example, she rigorously separated 'international' from an association with 'Western' aesthetics:

> It is surprising that some people ... actually think that we [Kalakshetra] can be international only if we teach Western music, dance, etc...True internationalism in arts is the effort to study and understand all art forms everywhere. The visits and meetings between great scholars, artists, and worthwhile people of the East and the West automatically create the understanding of the harmony of the human family (Rukmini Devi in Ramnarayan 1984b: 23).

19. See my discussion of the term 'choreography' above.

Although Rukmini Devi did not describe herself as a choreographer, she has been identified as such in retrospect as in, for example, the Note on choreography

V.N. Dhananjayan's article, "Rukmini Devi, the Choreographer." Sruti article on RD (Ramnarayan)

20. She initiated the latter shift of nattuvangam into female, brahman middle-class, female hands in order to minimize *Kalakshetra's* dependence upon "traditional teachers" (Sarada 1985: 50). This was largely a virtue made of necessity initiated by the sudden departure of nattuvanar Chokkalingam Pillai (Meenakshi Sundram Pillai's son) from

Kalakshetra (Ibid: 49). That Rukmini Devi was left without a conductor for impending concerts called her attention to this dependence and encouraged her, under duress, to rectify it.

See Meduri 1996: 366-372, 386 for a further discussion of this shift.

Allen (1997) also uses the nattuvanar issue as a point of departure for his inquiry.

In theorizing the intersection of class and gender in the negation of a sex-based division of labor, I do not mean to suggest that all female nattuvanars are brahman. Icai vellala women, like Indira Rajan and K. J. Sarasa, have also taken to nattuvangam. These women, usually dancers or former dancers, carve out a place for themselves in a changing dance milieu through their accomplishment in rhythmic conducting. As such, they resist the alliance between icai vellala men and brahman middle-class women that constituted twentieth-century *Bharata Natyam* and , simultaneously refuting assumptions within their own community that only men can achieve the level of rhythmic sophistication required to be a dance conductor.

21. Meduri (1996: 376) calls this approach 'experimental work.'

22. Partha Chatterjee, the Home and the World. Chatterjee (1993). See also Roy (1998) for a similar argument about poet Sarojini Naidu.

23. Srinivasan gives the following quote from a leading dancer of the 1980s in which the dancer conflates gendered subjectivity, theoretical knowledge, and the representation of an inferior 'Other':

    The *devadasis* only danced. They knew nothing of the theory of music which underlies dance and therefore they could not win the respect of their accompanist musicians ... You must let them [the musicians] know who is supreme and they will automatically leave you alone as a woman. The Brahmin girl is better in the dance than the *devadasi* because she is better looking and more intelligent (1983: 94).

    In the eyes of viewers and critics, Rukmini Devi exemplified subjectivity expressed through theoretical knowledge. For example, Gowri Ramnarayan quotes Sankara Menon, Vice-President of *Kalakshetra* as saying that Rukmini Devi was not alone as a luminary performer of the 1930s but that the decade's *devadasis,* although brilliant dancers, "danced without understanding what they were doing. They were dancing to a set of rules given to them, which were flogged into them through severe training" (Ramnarayan 1984a: 22).

24. See Allen (1997) for a discussion of Rukmini Devi's choreography of Nataraja pieces.

25. Rukmini Devi used Sanskrit aesthetic theory texts as a guiding principle. For example, Ramnarayan quotes her as saying:

    It is wonderful to see how the *Natyasastra* can give the opportunity for expressing new ideas ... The technique in this play [her Ramayana series] may appear new ... but every movement is according to the sastra though not presented in stereotyped form (1984c: 32).

    Ramnarayan corrects the misconception that Rukmini Devi developed the *Kalakshetra* style of *Bharata Natyam* by reconstructing movements from the *Natyasastra* stating that "[I]t is clear that Rukmini Devi did not study the ancient texts with the intent of translating theory into practice" (1984c: 30). She moreover quotes Sankara Menon as arguing that "[t]here is really no direct connection between Rukmini Devi's choreography and the *Natyasastra* ... Rukmini Devi did not study the *Natyasastra*" (quoted in Ramnarayan 1984c: 30). Senior *Kalakshetra* disciple and Sanskritist S. Sarada refers to the *Kalakshetra* style as "new" and as "concurring with the descriptions contained in the ancient treatises of dance" (1985: 21).

    Although she did not undertake projects of reconstructing dance vocabulary from texts, Devi did permit the introduction of reconstructed movements to her technique. S. Sarada reports that she "prepar[ed] of practical lessons for the *Mandalas*, turns, jumps, etc. as described in the *Abhinaya Darpana* correlating and approximating with traditional usage of postures etc. in the practical dancing of *Bharata Natya*" (1985: 21).

    Both Sarada (1985: 21) and Coorlawala (1996: 66) comment on the introduction of verses from the *Abhinaya Darpana* to *Kalakshetra* dance theory sessions.

26. That Rukmini Devi negotiated invention through recourse to the values, not the form, of the past, is apparent in critical writings on her work:

    Through her intuitive vision, Rukmini Devi succeeded in making innovations buttressed by the framework of what was essential in tradition (Ramnarayan 1984c: 27).

    Likewise Ramnarayan quotes Sarada Hoffman, senior *Kalakshetra* disciple, as describing Rukmini Devi's dance dramas as "traditional in that they carry the traditional spirit" (1984c: 28).

27. The implicit contrast I am drawing is with Balasaraswati for whom,

classicism aligned with the maintenance of items of repertoire inherited from the *devadasi* dance tradition.

28. Rukmini Devi likewise legitimized her innovations by claiming to bolster the dance form's religiosity. She therefore initiated such changes in stage practice as placing iconographic representations of gods onstage and offering an obeisance to the stage itself and to the nattuvanar that, as Gaston suggests, "reritualized" *Bharata Natyam*. According to Gaston, Rukmini Devi was the first dancer to place an icon of the god Siva in his form as Nataraja, or the cosmic dancer onstage (1992: 156-157). Matthew Allen suggests that this focus on Siva Nataraja, rather than on the more heroic, human, and sensual deities like Murugan and Krishna, itself played a key role in inscribing respectability into *Bharata Natyam* practice (1997: 64, 82, 94).

    Gaston (1992) understands the re-ritualizing of Bharata Natyam to include the reconstruction and reintroduction of devadasi rituals into late twentieth-century *Bharata Natyam* training as well as the invention of new rituals intended to further sanctify the dance form.

29. *Kalakshetra* exponent Narasimhachari, for instance, expresses a similar view to Rukmini Devi when he legitimizes change through a recourse to ancient origins: "*Bharata Natyam* is two thousand years old, how could it not have changed?" (personal correspondence 1999).

References

Allen, Matthew Harp. 1997. "Rewriting the Script for South Indian Dance." The Drama Review 41 (3): 63-100.

Arudra. 1986/87a. "The Transfiguration of a Traditional Dance: The Academy and the Dance, Events of the First Decade." *Sruti* 27/28: 17-21.

—. 1986/87b. "Dancers of the First Decade." *Sruti* 27/28: 23-28.

—. 1986/87c. "The Renaming of an Old Dance: A Whodunit Tale of Mystery." *Sruti* 27/28: 30-31.

—. 1986/87d. "E. Krishna Iyer (1897-1968): Saviour of a Dance in Distress." *Sruti* 27/28: 32-36.

Balasaraswati, T. 1975. "Bharata Natyam." Guhan, S., trans. Presidential Address for the 33rd Annual Conference of the Tamil Isai Sangam, Madras, 21 December.

—. 1984. "Bala on Bharata Natyam." Sruti 5: 11-15.

—. 1988. "The Art of Bharatanatyam: Reflections of Balasaraswati." Sruti 50: 37-40.

—. 1991. Bala on Bharatanatyam. Guhan, S., trans. Madras: the Sruti Foundation.

Chatterjee, Partha. 1993. "The Nation and Its Women." in The Nation and Its Fragments: Colonial and Postcolonial Histories. Princeton, New Jersey: Princeton University Press.

Coorlawala, Uttara Asha. 1996. "The Birth of Bharatanatyam and the Sanskritized Body." The Body in Dance: Modes of Inquiry; Conference Proceedings of the Congress on Research in Dance.

Devi, Rukmini. n.d. Untitled entry. Kaḷakshetra Quarterly IX (3): 22.

—. n.d. b. "Bharata Natya Sastra in Practice." Kalakshetra Quarterly II (3): 20-26.

Dhananjayan, V. N. 1992. A Dancer on Dance. Madras: Bharata Kalanjali.

Dhananjayan, V. N. and Shanta Dhananjayan. 1986. "Rukmini Devi the Choreographer." Kalakshetra Quarterly 8 (3-4): 30-34.

Erdman, Joan L. 1996. in ed. Gay Morris, *Moving Words: Re-Writing Dance.* London and New York: Routledge.

Foster, Susan Leigh. 1986. Reading Dancing: Bodies and Subjects in Contemporary American Dance. Berkeley, Los Angeles, London: University of California Press.

—. 1995. "Choreographing History" in Foster, ed. Choreographing History. Bloomington and Indianapolis: Indiana University Press.

Gaston, Anne-Marie. 1996. "Bharata Natyam: from Temple to Theatre." New Delhi: Manohar.

Jeyasingh, Shobana. 1990. "Getting Off the Orient Express." Dance Theatre Journal 8 (2): 34-37.

—. 1993. In Academy of Indian Dance, "Traditions on the Move" Open Forum. Transcript of Presentation. pp. 6-9. (Appendix, compiled and produced by Tina Cockett.)

—. 1995. "Imaginary Homelands: Creating a New Dance Language." Border Tensions. Guildford: Department of Dance Studies, University of Surrey.

Meduri, Avanthi. 1988. "Bharatha Natyam: What Are You?" Asian Theatre Journal 5(1): 1-22.

—. 1996. Nation, Woman, Representation: The Sutured History of the Devadasi and Her Dance. Ph.D. dissertation. New York University.

O'Shea, Janet. 1998. "Traditional Indian Dance and the Making of Interpretative Communities." Asian Theatre Journal 15(1): 45-63.

—. 2001. At Home in the World: Bharata Natyam's Transnational Traditions. Ph.D. dissertation. University of California, Riverside.

—. 2003. "At Home in the World? The Bharata Natyam Dancer as Transnational Interpreter." The Drama Review. 47 (1) (T177): 176-186.

—. Forthcoming. "Serving Two Masters? Bharata Natyam and Tamil Cultural Production." in Soneji, Devesh and Peterson, Indira Viswanathan, ed. Transformation in South Indian Art. Middletown, CT: Wesleyan University Press.

Pattabhiraman, N. and Anandhi Ramachandra. 1984a. "Balasaraswati: The Whole World in Her Hands" (Part One). Sruti 4: 17-30.

—. 1984b. "Balasaraswati: The Whole World in Her Hands" (Part Two). Sruti 5: 17-31.

Peterson, Indira Viswanathan. 1998. "The Evolution of the Kuravanji Dance Drama in Tamil Nadu: Negotiating the 'Folk' and the 'Classical' in the Bharata Natyam Canon." South Asia Research 18(1): 39-72.

Ramaswamy, Sumathi. 1997. Passions of the Tongue: Language Devotion in Tamil India 1891-1970. Berkeley and Los Angeles: University of California Press.

Rammarayan, Gowri. 1984a. "Rukmini Devi: A Quest for Beauty." Sruti 8: 17-29.

—. 1984b. "Rukmini Devi: Dancer and Reformer." Sruti 9: 17-29.

—. 1984c. "Rukmini Devi: Restoration and Creation." Sruti 10: 26-38.

Roy, Parama. 1998. Indian Traffic: Identities in Question in Colonial and Postcolonial India. Berkeley and Los Angeles: University of California Press.

Sarada, S. 1985. Kalakshetra Rukmini Devi. Madras: Kala Mandir Trust.

Savigliano, Marta E. 1995. Tango and the Political Economy of Passion. Boulder: Westview Press.

Srinivasan, Amrit. 1983. "The Hindu Temple-Dancer: Prostitute or Nun?" Cambridge Anthropology 8(1): 73-99.

—. 1985. "Reform and Revival: The Devadasi and Her Dance." Economic and Political Weekly XX(44): 1869-1876.

Vatsyayan, Kapila. 1977. Classical Indian Dance in Literature and the Arts. New Delhi: Sangeet Natak Akademi.

—. 1992. Indian Classical Dance. New Delhi: Publications Division, Ministry of Information and Broadcasting, Government of India.

CHAPTER 23

RE-INVOKING RUKMINI DEVI: QUESTIONS FROM A DANCE MAKER IN BRITAIN

Vena Ramphal

Classical South Asian dance has lived in Britain for about seventy years with the first noted performances given in London by Uday Shankar in the 1930's. Today, *Bharatanatyam* in particular and South Asian dance in general is becoming prominent amidst the diverse types of artistry that have a voice in Britain. During this time the dance world of Britain has seen a shift in orientation towards classical South Asian dance styles, which might best be described as a move away from perceiving these forms as immigrant art forms to seeing them as British South Asian dance. In terms of training this shift means that there is a growing infrastructure on a national level for the teaching of South Asian dance. In 1999 a South Asian Dance faculty teaching *Bharatanatyam* and *Kathak* was established within the Imperial Society for Teachers of Dancing.[1] There are approximately sixty schools of classical South Asian dance in the London area.

The twentieth century saw remarkable changes in the classical South Asian dance form we know as *Bharatanatyam.* The first half of the century saw it being renamed, brought to the urban concert stage and attaining national renown. The second half saw its prolific spread as an internationally practised art form. Several people and institutions were involved in the first phase of this history; among them Rukmini Devi is a key figure. Her family's intellectual leanings and involvement with the Theosophical Society had a lasting

impact on her.[2] The latter played an important role in her life and with her marriage to Theosophist George Arundale she became increasingly central to the Society's activities.[3] Importantly, the Theosophical Society became the context for Rukmini Devi's work with *Bharatanatyam.*

This period in the history of *Bharatanatyam,* the 1920's to the 1940's, is most often described in terms of 're-s': revival or restoration are particularly common terms. Matthew Harp Allen points out that it was also a re-population, re-construction, re-naming, re-situation.[4] He also notes re-storation in Richard Schechner's sense of 'a splicing together of selected strips of performative behaviour in a manner that simultaneously creates a new practice and invents an historical one.'[5] The time in which we live is often described in terms of 'posts-': post-modernity, post-structuralism, post-colonialism, post-feminism.

I wondered how looking back at this revivel might inform our thinking and questioning in and of our contemporary moment of 'posts'. As a young *Bharatanatyam* student the image of Rukmini Devi that I received was nothing short of a veneration. I received my *Bharatanatyam* training in London and my experience of being taught about Rukmini Devi is, I think, fairly representative of the kind of information imparted to *Bharatanatyam* students in Britain, and I suspect in India too. That can be summed up as follows:

'Rukmini Devi was a brave, brahmin woman who rescued *Bharatanatyam* from the degradation of being performed by *devadasis.* She made the dance respectable(!) and it is only because of her that you are able to learn this great cultural heritage of yours. She was a very great lady.'

And that's about it. This very partial image of her was my starting point for preparing this paper. I was interested in looking at this representation of her - however partial - to ask anew what we can learn from it. What we can learn, not so much about Rukmini Devi, but what we can learn for ourselves.

Given the tools of post-structuralism, which are most useful if their 'restless and revisionary energy... transform the present into an expanded and ex-centric site of experience and empowerment',[6] it seems particularly apt to allow ourselves to re-search for new meanings in the representations of Rukmini Devi. There are, of course, a number of questions that such research might ask. I shall focus on a few acknowledging that this endeavour, like the image of Rukmini Devi painted by my dance teachers, is also partial. Granted that partiality, I acknowledge that I ask my questions and present this article as a Britain based artist, born and educated in London. My ancestors were Indian and my parents are Guyanese. My relationship with *Bharatanatyam* in India is refracted through the lenses of both geographical and cultural distance and my interests - in both senses of the word - are informed by my positioning in time and space.

I want to start by looking at *Bharatanatyam* as created in Rukmini Devi's image. I was taught as a child that *Bharatanatyam* was a 2,000 years old dance form originating in the temples of South India. It came from and stood for a golden era in the history of India and epitomised the best of Indian culture. This view of *Bharatanatyam* posits a single, unified history of the art and indeed of Indian 'culture'. This type of approach makes a burden of centuries of tradition. With regard to its twentieth century history alone *Bharatanatyam* is hetrogeneous, the 'revival/reform' period amply demonstrating this. It is worth touching on some of the changes experienced by the dance form during this time.

Many dance forms in India had a history of being patronised by royal courts and temples. In South India *sadir* was one such form. During the early years of the twentieth century *sadir* was performed and taught within hereditary families of a particular caste - the *isai vellala* community. The *devadasis*, temple officials whose duties included dance, were from this community. By the late nineteenth century social reformers had started an anti-nautch movement which aimed to end

the *devadasi* institution, primarily on the grounds that the devadasis were morally lax women - prostitutes, even. By 1947 the anti-nautch movement had brought about the demise of the institution of *devadasis* in Madras State. Janaki Nair insightfully places the abolition of the *devadasi* institution in the context of the rise of a nationalist patriarchy in India in the late nineteenth and early twentieth centuries. The economic responsibility of women in the *devadasi* system (they were the main breadwinners for their families) and their unconventional family structure (they conducted extended sexual liaisons with male members of elite society, but did not marry them) did not sit well with the onset of nationalist patriarchy which advocated a male headed, monogamous family. The *devadasi* had to go.[7] Their dance - *sadir* - became disenfranchised and was looking for a new home. This was where many such as Rukmini Devi transformed, or reformed *sadir* into a performance form for the urban stage.

One of the conceptual underpinnings of this transformation was the promotion of the dance as an expression of authentic Indian culture. *Sadir* was consequently renamed as *Bharatanatyam.* The name is a reference to Bharata – the ascribed author of the *Natya Sastra* - India's oldest extant text on dramaturgy, including dance.[8] Proponents and promoters of *Bharatanatyam* strategically claimed close allegiance to the *Natya Sastra.* This is reflected in numerous writings on *Bharatanatyam* such as those of Rukmini Devi and V. Raghavan.[9] A relationship was set up whereby *Bharatanatyam* is validated as upholding the classical aesthetics of the *Natya Sastra* but also the *Natya Sastra* has been validated by *Bharatanatyam* as a fount of those classical aesthetics. In presenting the history of the *Natya Sastra* in this manner I am not saying that the claim of a relationship between *Natya Sastra* and contemporary practice is false; on the contrary, it is very clear that there is extraordinary continuity with the text in some aspects of dance practice (hand gestures, certain body

postures, the segmentation of the dancing body and the classifications of expressive dance. But it is also clear that this is not the case in all aspects (movement vocabulary and important technical terms, for example differ significantly). I am saying that the complexity of the relationship between the *Natya Sastra* and twentieth century *Bharatanatyam* is obscured by this strategy. Dancer and scholar Padma Subrahmanyam discusses this complexity as well as the obfuscating effect of the naming strategy.[10] Given the political context of the time– the end of colonial rule and the period immediately following independence – it is hardly surprising that there was a deeply felt concern to validate Indian culture. The claim of antiquity was a particularly useful tool in this project. In this case, the answer to the question, 'What's in a name?' was, 'The authority of tradition, the validation of the Sanskrit literary canon, high aesthetic and spiritual principles - the hallmark of a great civilisation; in short, national pride.' All this echoed in the appellation 'Bharata'.

Simultaneously, intellectual influences from outside South Asia were brought to bear upon several people involved in the revival of *Bharatanatyam*. For Rukmini Devi, the Theosophical Society's international community and her travels abroad on Society work influenced her outlook. This is overlooked in the type of unitary presentation of *Bharatanatyam* discussed above. I want to view the inherent hybridity in *Bharatanatyam*'s history positively and ask what possibilities it opens up. By acknowledging this miscegenation we can let go of the claim to a pure, unitary, originary Indian (read Hindu) past and the burden this imposes.

In Britain today this claim plays itself out in a perceived split between traditional/classical *Bharatanatyam* and innovative/contemporary *Bharatanatyam* work. This exclusive dichotomy is one of the major constitutive elements in discourses on *Bharatanatyam* in Britain. The former carries the weight of its unitary Indian tradition and is supposedly 'authentic' but locked in its heritage, while the latter

supposedly breaks free from tradition allowing the dancer creativity and individual freedom. The latter is also more fundable. I would want to question the basis of this perceived split. The exclusive opposition between tradition and creativity relies on the view of authentic *Bharatanatyam* as static, a mere repetition of repertoire learnt from the guru. The implication here must be that the 'traditional' dancer is a mere repository of learnt material, a passive Oriental.[11] This view of *Bharatanatyam* is increasingly challenged in the discourse and practice of a number of artists in Britain. However the claims about contemporary *Bharatanatyam* work which make the tradition/innovation dichotomy possible remain largely unquestioned. While this is a separate task I would say here that for me, access to the traditions of *Bharatanatyam* do not lock me out of creativity, contemporaneity or artistic choice. I have refused to choose between the two, not opting for both but rather seeing the split as a false one. In dance, I would like to have my cake and... have my cake.

One of the words Matthew Allen uses to describe the revival period was 're-population' referring to the conscious appropriation of the practice of *Bharatanatyam* by one social group from another. *Sadir* had climbed the social ladder when it became *Bharatanatyam.* Rukmini Devi was very conscious that she was learning, and later teaching a dance form that had been taken from the *devadasi* community into a brahminised, middle class, a community of 'good families', as she euphemised. The adjective 'brahmin' stands out in my memory in the description of Rukmini Devi I heard as a student. Whenever I was told about her this word was always there clear, significant and troubling. At this point I must say that I am very aware of the debt that I owe Rukmini Devi—it is true that her efforts contributed to the conditions in which it was possible for me, and others to learn *Bharatanatyam.* But those efforts also allow me to ask: who is allowed to dance? What is at stake in linking the art form to a specific community? At her time this played out in a

conscious division between the *devadasi* community and the 'good families'—a hierarchy of social groups. In the current context of dance training in Britain the stakes are different. Much *Bharatanatyam* dance training takes place under the umbrella of *cultural* activity, with families of South Asian extraction enrolling their children into a class for them to learn about their cultural roots.

In this scenario learning *Bharatanatyam* is about reaffirming a particular identity, cultural and perhaps national.[12] The 'cultural' trappings are visible in, for example, insistence on the student wearing particular attire (sari and bindi) to class. What concerns me here is that by making these the context for *Bharatanatyam* training it makes the dance the property of a particular cultural group. Clearly, I would not want to deny the specificity of any dance form—cultural or otherwise. I am saying that in this set-up we create insiders and outsiders—those who belong to culture of the dance and those who do not. We need to ask to whom does the dance belong? What communities are we creating? Who are we excluding?

The Rukmini Devi I was taught about was very much a brave woman. I don't know whether my teachers intended her gender to be significant, but it was for me. The feminist in me was fascinated and delighted that this woman had challenged one aspect of the patriarchal society in which she lived. This is, of course a very, very partial take on the situation and needs to be heavily qualified, not the least because the *devadasi* community from which she took *Bharatanatyam* was matrilocal, matrilineal and matrifocal. Along with Janaki Nair we could argue that in fact *Bharatanatyam*'s new context was more patriarchal than its devadasi setting. However, I want to hold on to the partially true image of the brave, determined woman who rescued *Bharatanatyam*. I want to hold on to it purely as a starting point from which to think about what part *Bharatanatyam*

plays in the lives of today's students in Britain. I think it is significant that several dance teachers bemoan the number of promising dancers they lose to the institution of marriage. While we have this image of rebellion against patriarchy in Rukmini Devi, *Bharatanatyam* still suffers from being, in the eyes of many, a premarital activity.

The charge is often brought against *Bharatanatyam* training is that it is a sort of preparation for marriage, a type of finishing school. I would like to disagree with this and suggest that the problem is more subtle. It seems to me that the reason so many good women dancers are lost to marriage is that far from being a preparation for it, the practice of dance stands precisely in opposition to the expectations of wedlock among the 'good families' of South Asian extraction who send their daughters to learn about their own culture through *Bharatanatyam.* It seems to me that within the discourses that create this community of good families, wifehood does not sit well with the displayed physicality of dance. There is a conflict between the cultivation of a cultural identity and the cultivation of gendered female identity. It is as if the studentship of dance is about acquiring a cultural and cultured identity but then this process trips up when it bumps into the marital identity. While *Bharatanatyam* is so fond of Rukmini Devi's rebellion it would do well to take more direct inspiration from it.

This brings me to the presentation of gender within the *Bharatanatyam* repertoire, specifically within the representation of *sringara* (erotic love). It is well known that one of the issues which vexed Rukmini Devi about the *devadasi* dance was its erotic content. While I feel very ambivalent about the 'cleaning up' of eroticism, (does it deny the body, is it somewhat prurient? On the other hand does it 'save' the performer from taking on an objectification in the gaze of the onlooker?) I do think that at this point we need to ask, 'What do we want to say with dance? What do I want to say with British *Bharatanatyam*?' However while we view Rukmini

Devi's attitude to *sringara*, we need to continue to critique our own. In the professional arena this has, of course, been taken up with a number of dancers consciously challenging normative representations of womanhood. This needs to filter through to the training establishments on a number of levels. Another front on which we can move this forward is to go from an examination of representing women to an analysis of gender. We still often forget that men have a gender too. This would require a deconstruction of masculinities as well as femininities. I emphasise that I'm suggesting this level of analysis in the training of *Bharatanatyam* students.

I would like to revisit the well known anecdote that Anna Pavlova was instrumental in getting Rukmini Devi to learn *Bharatanatyam*, instead of studying ballet. In Rukmini Devi's own words, '...Pavlova once said to me you can learn ballet but I think that everyone must try to revive the art of his own country.'[13] This was particularly an apt advice given the political situation of India at that time. Following Rukmini Devi's efforts for *Bharatanatyam* the dance form became very much a national symbol. As discussed above, in some circles it continues to be a means of affirming a national/cultural identity. However, at this point, I want to turn to the words 'diaspora' and 'post-coloniality'. In the British context I think that the term diaspora now holds out more than the possibility of transnational communities for people who have dispersed from a particular geographic region, such as South Asians. There is a sense in which we all live in diaspora, increasingly so, as we become more aware of the multicultural composition of British society, particularly in the cities. We have the opportunity to move beyond the concepts of 'your country' and 'my country' which Pavlova voiced and with which Rukmini Devi had to deal. In terms of dance this frees us from the current assumption that we automatically 'represent': whether its representing South Asian culture, Indian art, Hinduism, spirituality or any of those other essences with

which the East has been burdened. This suggestion is of course open to the critique that it is positing dance as being extractable from discourse and representation. Hence my invocation of post-coloniality. I would not suggest that art stands outside representation, only that we need to consider what we are representing. The resistance offered by post-colonial theory is a possible means through which *Bharatanatyam* can begin to engage rigorously with its pre-colonial history, come to terms with its colonial past and dance forward from its 'multi-cultural' present.

The problem of the multicultural present can be summed up by saying that *Bharatanatyam* in Britain, along with other dance forms remain the 'multi' in multicultural. The centre around which these other dance forms pivot is Western contemporary dance, which calls itself simply Contemporary dance. This itself is an act of violence - it obliterates the fact that there are other contemporary dance forms in the world. We are in a situation where Western contemporary dance is Dance, and every thing else is a specific type of dance. Western contemporary dance needs to be mired with the specificity present in Asian, African and other other dance forms so that it can no longer attain to the status of Universal. By speaking back in a post-colonial voice we can start to shift the relationship among the various dance forms that live in our diaspora, acknowledging their complex pasts while refusing to be locked into them. This, I think, is the most fitting way to honour Rukmini Devi in the present moment.

(A version of this paper was presented in London, at the Rukmini Devi Week Seminar, organized by the Nehru Centre, London and the *Centre for Contemporary Culture*, New Delhi in collaboration with the Society of Dance Research Scholars, and the AHRB Cross-Cultural Centre for Music and Dance, University of Surrey in 2003. An earlier version of this article was published in Dance Theatre Journal Vol. 19 no. 3)

Notes

1. Established in 1904, the ISTD is a registered educational charity and offers training courses and examinations covering a wide spectrum of dance styles from across the world.

2. The Theosophical Society was founded in New York in 1875 by the clairvoyant Helena Blavatsky and Henry Olcott. Aiming to promote universal brotherhood the Society undertook comparative study of religion. It draws particularly on Hinduism and Buddhism although all religions are viewed as versions of Theosophy, meaning 'wisdom of God'. The interest in Asian religions led to the headquarters being moved to Madras in 1877. The social reformer Annie Besant became Olcott's successor in India. The Society caught the interest of several Indian politicians and intellectuals such as Rukmini Devi's father, Nilakantha Shastri.

3. For details see Matthew Harp Allen, 1997, p.70-74 and Avanthi Meduri, 1996, p: 140-148; 277-294.

4. For a discussion of developments within the form between 1920-1960 see Meduri 1996.

5. Allen, p.63-4.

6. Homi Bhabha, 1994, p.4.

7. Janaki Nair, 1996.

8. For a discussion of this point see Avanthi Meduri, 1996, p. 269-273.

9. Rukmini Devi, in Sunil Kothari ed., 1979, p.13. Also V. Raghavan, in *The Journal of the Madras Music Academy*, Vol. XLV.

10. See Padma Subrahmanyam 1997, p.175-6.

11. The underlying dynamic of this discourse remains highly orientalising, in the Saidian sense, of 'traditional' work.

12. While *Bharatanatyam* has claimed a place as a national treasure, an embodiment of classical Indian art, its affiliations are often more parochial, linked to Tamil identity for example. Janet O'shea discusses this at length in her doctoral thesis *At Home in the World: Bharata Natyam's Transnational Traditions.*

13. Ramnarayan quoted in Allen, 1997, p.94.

References

Allen, Matthew Harp. (1997) 'Rewriting the Script for South Indian Dance' *The Drama Review* (41, 3).

Bhabha, Homi K. (1994) *The Location of Culture.* London: Routledge.

Kothari, Sunil. Ed. (1979) *Bharata Natyam: Indian Classical Dance Art.* Bombay: Marg Publications.

Meduri, Avanthi. 1996. 'Nation, Woman, Representation: The Sutured History of the Devadasi and Her Dance.' Tisch School of Arts/NYU (Ph.D. dissertation).

Nair, Janaki. 1996. *Women and Law in Colonial India.* New Delhi: Kali for Women.

O'Shea, Janet. 2001. 'At Home in the World: Bharata Natyam's Transnational Traditions.' UC Riverside, (Ph.D. dissertation).

Raghavan, V. 'Bharata Natya' in *The Journal of the Madras Music Academy,* Vol. XLV.

Rukmini Devi. 'Spiritual Background' in Kothari, 1979, pp13-16.

Subrahmanyam, Padma. (1997). *Natya Sastra and National Unity.* Kerala: Sri Ramavarma Government Sanskrit College, Tripunithura.